(Continued)

THE TESTING TRAP

How State Writing Assessments Control Learning

Georege Hillocks, Jr.

Foreword by Miles Myers

TEACHERS COLLEGE PRESS

Teachers College, Columbia University
New York and London

Published by Teachers College Press, 1234 Amsterdam Avenue, New York, NY 10027

Library of Congress Cataloging-in-Publication Data

Hillocks, George.
    The testing trap : how state writing assessments control learning / George Hillocks, Jr.
      p. cm. — (Language and literacy series)
    Includes bibliographical references (p.) and index.
    ISBN 0-8077-4230-9 (cloth : alk. paper) — ISBN 0-8077-4229-5 (pbk. : alk. paper)
    1. Educational tests and measurements—United States—States. 2. English language—Composition and exercises—Evaluation. I. Title. II. Language and literacy series (New York, N.Y.)
    LB3051 .H534 2002
    371.26'0973—dc21   2001055688

ISBN 0-8077-4229-5 (paper)
ISBN 0-8077-4230-9 (cloth)

Printed on acid-free paper
Manufactured in the United States of America

09 08 07 06 05 04 03 02   8 7 6 5 4 3 2 1

Contents

Foreword

If you have been wondering what has gone wrong in school reform since *A Nation at Risk* (National Commission on Excellence in Education, 1983), you have in your hand a book that will help you understand at least one of the big problems—the administration and structure of state tests of written composition. For over 40 years, George Hillocks, first a secondary teacher of English and later a professor at the University of Chicago, has been helping us understand some of the critical problems of teaching English, and in this book he once again helps us in an area where we need it most. Let me review the journey-with-Hillocks that has brought me to this book. Fifteen years ago, 3 years after *A Nation at Risk* triggered a national debate about how to improve our K–12 schools, Hillocks in his *Research on Written Composition* (1986a) put his focus on classroom instruction, and he has kept his focus on the classroom ever since. At a time when generic models of teaching—long lists of teacher behaviors encompassing many subjects—dominated much of the contemporary thinking about teaching, Hillocks insisted on the importance of larger pedagogical structures, for example, mode of instruction (the role of the teacher in the classroom) and the focus of instruction (sentence combining, model essays, and so forth).

But where did these pedagogical structures originate? In the teacher's conception of subject matter, answered Hillocks, and in his 1999 study *Ways of Thinking, Ways of Teaching*, Hillocks took an up-close look at the epistemological beliefs of teachers (what is important knowledge in composition?) and at the teacher's stance toward students (are my students able to learn what I teach?). Through the lenses of interviews and observations of teaching episodes, Hillocks found not only different models of subject knowledge (knowledge-is-constructed and knowledge-is-delivered, for example) but also different stances toward student learning (optimistic and pessimistic, for example). He argued that because the subject matter of composition is by its very nature constructivist, teachers who attempt to teach composition with a lecture-recitation approach are not as effective as they could be. However, he asked, how does one change teachers who are pessimistic about their students and who think knowledge is delivered? He concludes, "the findings here suggest that teacher change will come with far more difficulty than anyone may have expected. . . . Change will be a matter of far more than learning new methods of teaching or instituting a new curriculum for teachers to follow. . . . it is unlikely that teachers will change as a result of outside efforts to change methods or curriculum" (1999. pp. 134–135). For an age looking for the quick fix through state policy, Hillocks recommends a much more complicated approach: "Reformers will have to find ways and means of helping teachers reconstruct their knowledge and stance" (1999, p. 135). Although he points to a few examples of professional networks as a promising direction, Hillocks leaves us asking what impact, if any, state curriculum mandates might have.

In the book you have in your hand, Hillocks answers our question. He makes clear that at least one state mandate, assessment, does have a significant impact on what is taught about composition in the K–12 classroom. This impact goes well beyond that commonly known fact that if writing is assessed, writing is taught. The impact extends to the teaching of the specific features of writing highlighted in a given state assessment. In addition, Hillocks points out that the recent national hullabaloo about adopting new standards of significant knowledge in the K–12 English curriculum has generally ignored the kind of knowledge promoted by state-adopted tests. Hillocks suggests that it is the assessments, not the standards, that are having the most direct influence on what is taught, and he points to examples of a state's writing standards that are not implemented in the state's writing assessment. In fact, the book raises the question of whether the inconsistency between state assessments and state standards might be one of the best-kept secrets in the current trends of school reform.

However, Hillocks reminds us that there is an even deeper inconsistency: Assessments, despite their influence on what is taught, do not teach teachers how to teach effectively, and in fact, assessments may work against helping teachers learn to teach effectively. Yes, assessments change some parts of teaching, but, says Hillocks, "If states want teaching to improve, they will have to intervene at the level of teaching." At this point, Hillocks confronts us with the bedrock of change in teaching: first, teaching conditions (class size, for instance) and, second, professional development (planning for instruction, for instance). It appears that state assessments may be an unfortunate result of a state's unwillingness to fund public education at a satisfactory level, and the structure of state assessments may actually prevent teachers from learning to teach composition. At a recent Asilomar conference in California, several composition teachers suggested that many of the contextual features of California assessments undermine the professional development of K–12 teachers: (1) security provisions that prevent teachers from examining test items and student responses; (2) scoring procedures in which teachers do not do the scoring and do not develop the rubrics and scoring guides; and (3) the absence of procedures for challenging a score (Asilomar Report on Assessment from the California Association of Teachers of English and the Curriculum Commission of the Central California Council of Teachers of English, 2001).

In this book, Hillocks points to several important professional development networks as places where teachers learn to teach—in Kentucky and Oregon, for instance—and I've wanted to know more about how those networks and others like them worked. For many years, Hillocks himself nurtured an outstanding professional development network for K–12 teachers at the University of Chicago, and I hope that in his next work Hillocks will return to the details of that experience. In the meantime, treasure the helpful insights from this book. Hillocks will open your eyes about the impact of K–12 testing on the teaching of composition.

—Miles Myers

Acknowledgments

This study would not have been possible without funding by the Spencer Foundation that made the interviews in Illinois, Kentucky, New York, Oregon, and Texas possible. I am grateful to the over 400 teachers, administrators, and university personnel who assisted by speaking to me and my assistants about the testing programs in their states and their own practices in relationship to those programs.

As the research progressed, many people helped with various dimensions of the work. Kendra Sisserson, project coordinator, scheduled nearly all of the interviews, kept track of the transcription process, conducted many of the interviews, worked on planning the coding system, gathered state documents, and generally kept the project on track for 4 years. Vera L. Wallace, my research associate, expertly conducted many interviews, typed some transcriptions, and coauthored Chapter 6 of the present volume. Her assistance and encouragement throughout have been invaluable.

Many others were engaged in parts of the research. I am grateful to Ramona Hartweg for her expert typing of most of the transcripts. Coding the interviews was an important but tedious process; I am grateful to Sarah Spachman, Rachel Samlan, and Kendra Sisserson for their work on the first round of coding, and to Carolyn Novy, Julianna Cucci, Karen Furlong, and Bruce Novak, who worked under pressure to recode all of the teacher interviews with highly reliable results. Thanks also go to Kristin Wittman and Lori Huebner who worked on the analysis of state assessments outside the five case study states and on preparing the final manuscript.

At various points as the research progressed, Vera, Kendra and I submitted our plans and statements of our progress to panels of experts on writing, education, and assessment. The panel members contributed valuable suggestions and critiques of our work-in-progress, for example, the coding system used. I am grateful for the advice of all the panels, whose members included teachers, state assessment officials, researchers, and people knowledgeable about writing: Sarah W. Freedman, Lolita Green, Ken Hermens (OR), Larry Johannessen, Starr Lewis (KY), Miles Meyers, Martin Nystrand, Susan Sawers (IL), and Michael W. Smith.

Michael W. Smith also provided valuable advice on the organization and approach of several first draft chapters. When the first draft was complete, I sent relevant chapters to officials in Illinois, Kentucky, New York, Oregon, and Texas, with a request for comments, corrections, and feedback in general. Michael L. Dunn, Chief Education Officer of the Illinois State Board of Education; Starr Lewis, Associate Commissioner of Education at the Kentucky Department of Education; and Karen Kolanowski of New York's Education Department responded with useful commentary. I have taken advantage of their advice wherever possible. In addition, I received careful and helpful commentary on the entire first draft from Miles Meyers and Peter Smagorinsky. Their combined expertise has been very helpful in my revisions. Commentary from Michael Greer and Carol C. Collins of Teachers College Press have also been most helpful.

Finally, much of the first draft of the book was prepared while I was a Fellow at the Center for Advanced Study in the Behavioral Sciences in Stanford, California. I thank the Spencer Foundation for the financial support that permitted my stay at the Center.

CHAPTER 1

The Politics of Mandatory Assessment

The second half of the twentieth century saw repeated panic about the ineffectiveness of American education. By then, we had come to equate test scores with education, and when SAT, ACT, and other test scores began a steady decline in the sixties, we assumed that the entire educational system was in jeopardy. One after another international study of educational achievement showed American students at the bottom of the ladder in mathematics and science. At the same time businesses and colleges were lamenting the poor writing skills of the students who entered their ranks. In 1983 the National Commission on Excellence in Education [NCEE], a panel appointed by the Reagan administration, published *A Nation at Risk*, a report that blasts American education:

Our Nation is at risk. Our once unchallenged preeminence in commerce, industry, science, and technological innovation is being overtaken by competitors throughout the world. . . . We report to the American people that while we can take justifiable pride in what our schools and colleges have historically accomplished and contributed to the United States and the well-being of its people, the educational foundations of our society are presently being eroded by a rising tide of mediocrity that threatens our very future as a Nation and a people. . . .

If an unfriendly foreign power had attempted to impose on America the mediocre educational performance that exists today, we might well have viewed it as an act of war. As it stands, we have allowed this to happen to ourselves. We have even squandered the gains in student achievement made in the wake of the Sputnik challenge. Moreover, we have dismantled essential support systems which helped make those gains possible. We have, in effect, been committing an act of unthinking, unilateral educational disarmament.

These are strong claims. To support them, the report lists several "indicators of the risk." Here is a sample:

International comparisons of student achievement, completed a decade ago, reveal that on 19 academic tests American students were never first or second and, in comparison with other industrialized nations, were last seven times.

Some 23 million American adults are functionally illiterate by the simplest tests of everyday reading, writing, and comprehension.

About 13 percent of all 17-year-olds in the United States can be considered functionally illiterate. Functional illiteracy among minority youth may run as high as 40 percent.

Average achievement of high school students on most standardized tests is now lower than 26 years ago when Sputnik was launched. . . .

The College Board's Scholastic Aptitude Tests (SAT) demonstrate a virtually unbroken decline from 1963 to 1980. Average verbal scores fell over 50 points and average mathematics scores dropped nearly 40 points. . . .

Many 17–year-olds do not possess the "higher order" intellectual skills we should expect of them. Nearly 40 percent cannot draw inferences from written material; only one-fifth can write a persuasive essay; and only one-third can solve a mathematics problem requiring several steps. . . .

The report claims that these "deficiencies" come at a time when the "demand for highly skilled workers in new fields is accelerating rapidly." However, in a time of increasing diversity, they are even more important for thinking through the ethical, moral, and political issues if our society is to become equitable and just.

A Nation at Risk makes a series of five major recommendations about content, standards, time, teaching, and leadership and fiscal support. In each of these five areas, the report makes several "implementing recommendations." Some of these are more easily implemented than others. Under time, for example, the recommendation suggests making more effective "use of the existing school day," a recommendation that entails little or no cost. The major recommendation about content in high schools is also an easy one: that all high school students take 4 years of English, 3 of math, science, and social studies, and a half year of computer studies. However, the more specific recommendations under content, about what should be going on in classrooms, are not easy to implement at all. Consider these examples:

1. The teaching of English in high school should equip graduates to: (a) comprehend, interpret, evaluate, and use what they read; (b) write well-organized, effective papers; (c) listen effectively and discuss ideas intelligently; and (d) know our literary heritage and how it enhances imagination and ethical understanding, and how it relates to the customs, ideas, and values of today's life and culture.

8. The curriculum in the crucial eight grades leading to the high school years should be specifically designed to provide a sound base for study in those and later years in such areas as English language development and writing, computational and problem-solving skills, science, social studies, foreign language, and the arts. These years should foster an enthusiasm for learning and the development of the individual's gifts and talents.

Placing English first in the list and focusing on comprehension, interpretation, evaluation, and ethical understanding is significant, especially with the emphasis on how they relate "to the customs, ideas, and values of today's life and culture." Pretty clearly, members of the Commission had in mind the development of individuals who are capable of thinking deeply and critically about the problems and issues facing a society of increasing diversity, bringing ethical standards to bear, and acting on these ideas and values. Add to that the emphasis in other goals on fostering "an enthusiasm for learning and the development of the individual's gifts and talents."

Such recommendations are crucial but also probably the most difficult to implement because they demand changing the character of teaching that has gone on in American classrooms for over a century. In every curricular area and at every level, the need for teacher change is enormous. Throughout the twentieth century, studies documented the persistence of lecture and recitation in American classrooms. In 1984, the year after the publication of *A Nation at Risk*, J. Goodlad reported on a study of American schools in all regions of the country that led him to this conclusion: "The data from our observation in more than a thousand classrooms support the popular image of a teacher standing or sitting in front of a class imparting knowledge to a group of students. Explaining and lecturing constituted the most frequent teaching activities, according to teachers, students, and our observations" (1984, p. 105). More recently, a team of researchers headed by Martin Nystrand (1997) observed 451 lessons (class periods) in 58 eighth-grade language arts classes and 54 ninth-grade English classes. Nystrand writes of the findings:

When teachers were not lecturing, students were mainly answering questions or engaged in seatwork. Indeed, on average 85% of each class day in both eighth- and ninth-grade classes was devoted to a combination of lecture, question-and-answer recitation, and seatwork. Discussion and small-group work were rare. On average, discussion took 50 seconds per class in eighth grade and less than 15 seconds in grade 9; small-group work, which occupied about half a minute a day in eighth grade, took a bit more than two minutes a day in grade 9. (p. 42)

Back in 1964, Paul Olson of the University of Nebraska described American classrooms as a "desert of ennui." Things have not changed.

Research shows that students reach the kinds of goals recommended by the Commission best when they are engaged in discussion with their peers and the teacher about complex materials and problems (Nystrand, 1997; Hillocks, 1986a). To implement a recommendation that calls for the intelligent discussion of ideas demands that teaching change. However, in the category of teaching, the Commission makes no recommendations

about changing the teaching in schools. It speaks only of teachers in preparation, not those already in schools, and calls for them only to "meet high
educational standards, to demonstrate an aptitude for teaching, and to
demonstrate competence in an academic discipline." Unfortunately, meeting high educational standards, having an aptitude for teaching, and developing competence in an academic area do not entail knowing how to
help students learn to "(a) comprehend, interpret, evaluate, and use what
they read; (b) write well-organized, effective papers; (c) listen effectively
and discuss ideas intelligently; and (d) know our literary heritage and how
it enhances imagination and ethical understanding, and how it relates to
the customs, ideas, and values of today's life and culture" (NCEE, 1983).
Nor does it mean that teachers will be able to "foster an enthusiasm for
learning and the development of the individual's gifts and talents." It is
unfortunate that the Commission would overlook the disparity between
its goals for content and its goals for teaching. But the oversight may well
have been intentional. To change teaching in schools would require massive infusions of tax dollars for educating teachers about methods that
research has shown to be highly effective in helping students do the higher
level thinking that the Commission's goals call for.

The easiest goal of all to implement is that of standards. *A Nation at
Risk* recommends "that schools, colleges, and universities adopt more rigorous and measurable standards, and higher expectations, for academic
performance and student conduct, and that 4–year colleges and universities raise their requirements for admission." The report claims, "This will
help students do their best educationally with challenging materials in an
environment that supports learning and authentic accomplishment." The
implementing recommendations include using grades as "indicators of
academic achievement so they can be relied on as evidence of a student's
readiness for further study," raising college admission standards, making
learning materials and textbooks more rigorous, more up-to-date, and
more reliable. But the chief of these simply called for "standardized tests
of achievement" to

be administered at major transition points from one level of schooling to another
and particularly from high school to college or work. The purposes of these tests
would be to: (a) certify the student's credentials; (b) identify the need for remedial
intervention; and (c) identify the opportunity for advanced or accelerated work.
The tests should be administered as part of a nationwide (but not Federal) system
of State and local standardized tests. This system should include other diagnostic
procedures that assist teachers and students to evaluate student progress.

Of all the recommendations in the report, this is the one that has been
most widely adopted. Shortly after the publication of *A Nation at Risk* many

states that had never had systematic standardized testing began to implement them. Over two thirds of the states now require some sort of state testing at several grade levels in a variety of subject matters from reading and writing to math, science, and social studies.

THE PROBLEM

The central problem of testing is knowing whether a test does what its proponents claim it does or not. Does a test of reading indicate how well a student can read and use real material in an everyday learning situation? Does a test of writing indicate how well a student may be able to write in any given situation? In other words, can the tests provide meaningful measures of achievement for individuals? Can they provide useful measures of how well schools are doing in educating our young people? States with assessment programs believe they can.

Most states use multiple-choice tests to measure achievement in most subject matter areas, the kind of test in which the respondent fills in the bubble representing what he or she thinks is the right answer. The tests recommended in *A Nation at Risk,* are not supposed to be aptitude tests; rather, they should attempt to examine students' knowledge of the content studied and the thinking skills and strategies developed. However, multiple-choice tests cannot test the higher level strategies, such as bringing together a variety of disparate information and making sense of it, or compiling evidence in support of a proposition and demonstrating that the evidence actually supports the proposition. Multiple-choice tests present the correct answer with three or more distractors or foils intended to draw test takers' attention from the correct answer. (In test making, distractors that do not draw responses are eliminated and replaced with others that do.) Therefore, the test taker cannot create an answer. Moreover, many studies indicate that the multiple-choice tests of achievement in pressure-filled environments drive teachers to drill on the content most likely to appear on the tests (Sacks, 1999). The more class time devoted to such drill, the less class time can be devoted to higher-level thinking. The problem, then, is whether or not the tests instituted for assessing achievement can actually test the knowledge most worth having or only some appearance of knowledge.

Ostensibly, writing presents a different case. Once tested in multiple-choice format, writing is now tested almost exclusively by requiring the production of real writing samples. In most states, students are given prompts of various kinds and asked to write in response to them. A major purpose of this book is to determine what such tests actually test.

When schools are truly interested in higher level thinking, they demand a good deal of writing on complex topics, even when they do not have strong writing programs. Teachers have always known that writing is the means of assessing high levels of conceptualizing, analysis, application, synthesis, and argument. Good essay exams do not call for simple regurgitation of material memorized from a text or the teacher's lectures, but require the synthesis of material drawn from many sources in ways that may not have been dealt with directly in class, in ways that reveal true understanding.

In the past 30 years, researchers and theorists have come to know that teaching writing entails teaching thinking. Further, they would argue that people learn through writing. Putting the ideas on the word processor or on paper clarifies them and enables us to think through what we really mean. Many years ago, psychologists found that there is a limit to what we can hold in short-term memory and the number of criteria we can use in making absolute judgments. George A. Miller (1956) called it "the magic number 7, plus or minus 2." To oversimplify a bit, this is the limit on the number of chunks of information (words) we can hold in mind at any given time without benefit of some mnemonic device. That is, the majority of us can remember only five to nine such items. Each of these, if they are not arbitrarily chosen, is likely to have several chunks associated with it, but these must be recalled from long-term memory.

This limit to short-term memory has been demonstrated in many different experiments. Obviously, writing increases this capacity enormously. If I am examining a policy with nine reasons to support it, I am already at or near the limit of what I can keep in short-term memory, and I have not begun to include the evidence supporting each of the reasons or the qualifications or the warrants involved. How difficult will it be then to examine the other side of the issue and to compare and evaluate both! Writing can make this complexity present to the eye and aid in thinking through it. Writing is more than a mnemonic device. Its presence makes it an aid in thinking through highly complex processes and problems. But if writing is an aid to thinking, it is also obvious that thinking is requisite for most writing. The serious teaching of writing and thinking must go hand in hand.

Some people may think that school students ought not to be engaged in the kinds of thinking that I refer to. But the careful analysis, testing, and evaluation of the assumptions underlying our personal actions and public policies, particularly as they affect others, is essential to the survival of a society that is equitable and just (see Nussbaum, 1997). If children do not begin thinking seriously in school, where and when will they begin? Part of the problem in this country is that systematic thinking about difficult problems appears to be confined to an elite group. Most Americans are not willing to think much beyond their own desires and perspectives, which often determines what they think is right and appropriate. Perhaps most people cannot think carefully about complex problems. But we know that children and young people can and do think systematically and persistently about highly ambiguous, intractable, and frustrating problems with energy and a kind of joy (see, for example, the high school class in Chapter 1 of my book *Ways of Thinking, Ways of Teaching*, 1999).

In my over 40 years in education, I have spent thousands of hours visiting in classrooms, as a colleague of teachers, as a secondary school English department chair, as a director of freshman English, and as a researcher in secondary, community college, and university classrooms. The vast majority of the classes I have observed in these capacities have been as Goodlad and Nystrand describe them. They have consisted mostly of teacher talk. When students do talk, it is most often to answer questions that may be answered in a single word or short phrase that bears little or no relationship to the preceding answer. That is to say, the classroom discourse is largely disconnected and serves mainly to let teachers know if students know bits and pieces of isolated information about whatever is being studied.

But on many occasions I have witnessed not only the intelligent discussion of ideas but the impassioned discussion of issues that the students clearly felt were important to examine in detail even though they were often quite complex and sometimes intractable. Recently, I observed a remarkable discussion in a Chicago high school classroom, taught by Ms. Sarah Levine. Ms. Levine was teaching students how to develop different kinds of arguments. Her sequence of activities related to argument had been in progress over most of the school year. Toward the end of the sequence, Ms. Levine set up a role-playing activity to engage students in deliberating over a very complex issue: what to do about the possible revival of Chicago's gang loitering ordinance. The ordinance had been rejected by the courts, but the city council wanted to reintroduce it in revised form. In brief, the ordinance permitted Chicago police to scatter known gang members found to be loitering on the streets or in other public places and to arrest them if they did not move on. The roles that students were to play were those taking different perspectives on the ordinance: adults frightened by gang members loitering on their streets; police who thought the ordinance necessary for them to control gang activities on their beats; police who thought the ordinance was impossible to enforce; gang members; representatives of persons who had been falsely arrested under the old version of the ordinance; and so forth.

The teacher supplied copies of the ordinance, several news stories, opinions from the American Civil Liberties Union, and other relevant documents. Students in each role were also assigned to find other information in the library or on the Internet that would support their position or give them insight into the positions of other groups. Since many had had encounters with loitering gang members or police, Ms. Levine encouraged them to write up those experiences and use them in their own arguments. Students spent class time developing these arguments and testing them on their peers.

At the beginning, as students worked within their own groups, their effort was to develop a consistent and coherent position supported by specific evidence that they could pull from various documents and from their own experience. When students had prepared their positions, they were to present them to an adult panel composed of a university professor, an experienced lawyer (one of whom worked for ACLU), a school administrator, a school security officer, and a student who served as chair of the panel.

The first phase of the 3-hour panel presentation (students were released from other classes for the session) involved presenting the arguments from each group. This round of presentations was followed by small-group discussion for students to plan rebuttals and then the presentation of rebuttals, persuasive arguments in which students questioned seriously the positions of the other groups. After these rounds, the floor was opened to questioning and reconsideration and compromise so that students found themselves engaged in negotiation about what policy would best serve community interests. No solution was reached by the panel.

Although I do not have transcripts of the classes, I attended two such sets of presentations by two different classes as the panel's university professor. Students operated the entire 3-hour sessions. Teacher interventions were practically nonexistent. Student thinking was at a very high level. Following the 3-hour sessions, students were to write a paper in which they presented a case from a point of view that synthesized more than one perspective and suggested an acceptable solution.

In both sessions, the focus was on thinking through very complex problems, using evidence to support a position, and showing how that evidence did indeed support the position. Students did most of the talking, but the talk was focused and structured by the teacher demands for relevant evidence and careful thought. I have observed many other classrooms whose characteristics may be summarized as follows:

• Teacher talk is minimized, but student discussion is maximized.
• Discussion focuses on structured problems that are complex and not subject to simple solutions.

- Discussions are intended to serve as preparation for writing but also serve to help students learn strategies for critical thinking that are applicable to other problems.
- Discussions take the form of deliberative thinking about alternatives through examining the arguments, contesting their relevance, and so forth.

Clearly, these differences result in classrooms that are far different from what Goodlad and Nystrand and many other researchers find. At the same time, research indicates that such teaching makes a difference in the quality of student writing and comprehension of literature (Hillocks, 1986a; Nystrand, 1997). In other words, it makes for higher level thinking. It is also clear that it makes a difference in the lived curriculum. Time after time I have witnessed students who are eager to participate in and reluctant to end such sessions. In short, the kind of teaching going on in classrooms makes a huge difference in what students learn. A major question for this book concerns the kinds of teaching encouraged by the different state assessments. Do they encourage the kind of thinking we see in Ms. Levine's classes, or something else?

THE POLITICIZATION OF ASSESSMENT

In the presidential campaign of 2000, George W. Bush managed to politicize school reform and to valorize assessment as never before in national politics. In October of 1999, he delivered a talk before the Manhattan Institute Forum titled *The Future of Educational Reform*, claiming that "the diminished hopes of our current system are sad and serious—the soft bigotry of low expectations." This phrase stayed with him throughout the campaign as he relied upon it to make him appear a liberal defender of the underclasses and downtrodden. At the same time, he proposed cutting off federal funds to schools that did not achieve desired goals and establishing charter schools and a voucher system:

I set out a simple principle: Federal funds will no longer flow to failure. Schools that do not teach and will not change must have some final point of accountability. A moment of truth, when their Title 1 funds are divided up and given to parents, for tutoring or a charter school or some other hopeful option. In the best case, schools that are failing will rise to the challenge and regain the confidence of parents. In the worst case, we will offer scholarships to America's neediest children. In any case, the federal government will no longer pay schools to cheat poor children (Bush, 1999, n.p.)

Bush explains that the "final object of education reform is not just to shun mediocrity; it is to seek excellence. It is not just to avoid failure; it is to encourage achievement." And here he slips in his most common refrain: "Our nation has a moral duty to ensure that no child is left behind." But he wastes no time in inserting another of his key themes, that of high standards. "At this moment," he says, we "have a great national opportunity— to ensure that every child, in every public school, is challenged by high standards that meet the high hopes of parents. To build a culture of achievement that matches the optimism and aspirations of our country."

Bush goes on to bewail the loss of standards in the schools:

Schools where spelling bees are canceled for being too competitive and selecting a single valedictorian is considered too exclusive. Where advancing from one grade to the next is unconnected to advancing skills. Schools where, as in Alice in Wonderland, "Everyone has won, and all must have prizes."

He ties this loss of standards to deficiency of character. "Most parents know that the self-esteem of children is not built by low standards, it is built by real accomplishments. Most parents know that good character is tied to an ethic of study and hard work and merit—and that setbacks are as much a part of learning as awards." In short, the low standards of schools can now be associated with poor character.

Bush claims that "until a few years ago . . . Democrats and Republicans argued mainly about funding and procedures. . . . Few talked of standards or accountability or of excellence for all our children." He says that this is beginning to change:

In state after state, we are seeing a profound shift of priorities. An "age of accountability" is starting to replace an era of low expectations. And there is a growing conviction and confidence that the problems of public education are not an endless road or a hopeless maze. . . . Raise the bar of standards. Give schools the flexibility to meet them. Measure progress. Insist on results. Blow the whistle on failure.

These so-called principles become his mantra, repeated time after time in almost exactly the same way.

He claims to have evidence of the appropriateness of such an educational program. In Texas, he says,

We are witnessing the promise of high standards and accountability. We require that every child read by the third grade, without exception or excuse. [In actual fact, there is provision for many students to skip the tests.] Every year, we test students on the academic basics. We disclose those results by school. . . . In 1994, there were 67 schools in Texas rated "exemplary" according to our tests. This year, there are 1,120. We are proud, but we are not content. Now that we are meeting our current standards, I am insisting that we elevate those standards.

The standards, of course, are the Texas standards.

In this talk, Bush outlines what he will do as president. The cornerstone of his reform is that every state have its own "real accountability system—meaning that they test every child, every year, in grades three through eight, on the basics of reading and math; broadly disclose those results by school, including on the Internet; and have clear consequences for success and failure. States will pick their own tests, and the federal government will share the costs of administering them." He promises federal monetary rewards to states that are successful in raising scores. But "if scores are stagnant or dropping, the administrative portion of their federal funding—about 5 percent—will be diverted to a fund for charter schools. We will praise and reward success—and shine a spotlight of shame on failure." Bush calls this program a "fresh start for the federal role in education. A pact of principle."

"Without testing," he says, "reform is a journey without a compass. Without testing, teachers and administrators cannot adjust their methods to meet high goals. Without testing, standards are little more than scraps of paper. Without testing, true competition is impossible. Without testing, parents are left in the dark."

Throughout the campaign, Bush continued to emphasize the importance of testing and he consistently used the Texas assessment as his grounds for making the claims about the importance of testing. In the first of the presidential debates of 2000, he states, "Testing is the cornerstone of reform. You know how I know? Because it's the cornerstone of reform in the state of Texas." In the second and third debates, Bush reiterated these points.

At this writing, President Bush has a plan for improving education (available at www.ed.gov/inits/nclb/part2.html) which includes the proposals we might expect. It also includes some that no one would toss out: decreasing "the academic achievement gap between rich and poor, between Anglo and minority," improving literacy, and "boosting teacher quality." However, everything hinges on accountability. States must develop plans for testing in every grade level, every year from third to eighth grade. They must participate in National Assessment of Educational Progress for math and reading at the fourth and eighth grade levels. (That means testing a stratified random sample of students throughout the state.) Further, the states must develop a "system of sanctions and rewards" for holding local schools "accountable for meeting performance objectives." As for "boosting teacher quality," states that "develop teacher assessment

systems that measure teacher performance using gains in student achievement" will receive "grants for excellence in teaching." Note that this language says nothing about actual excellence as part of the criteria for rewards, only developing the system of assessment. States that develop
accountability systems within two years of the enactment of the President's
plan will receive rewards. And testing policies are reinforced with rewards
and sanctions that reach down from the federal level, through the state
bureaucracies, to local schools and individual classrooms. Everything
hinges on testing. And the stakes are high.

We have to ask, however, whether Bush's "principles" of annual testing and "blowing the whistle on failure" really constitute reform. The turn-
around described by Bush, with little or no expense, is a reformer's dream.
If there are real, substantive academic gains, then we could say that this
reform truly worked. In fact, we know that testing programs tend to re-
strict the curriculum to the kinds of knowledge and skills tested. They are
likely to generate drill and memorization in classrooms. Teachers are likely
to feel considerable stress because they are held accountable for the level
reached by their students even though there is no measure of the same
students at the beginning of the school year.

Finally, should we expect tests, in and of themselves, to bring about
higher achievement in schools? Do we believe that testing will bring about
change in what happens in classrooms, change that will in turn bring
about different and perhaps higher levels of student achievement? Do we
believe that simply the threat of sanctions will encourage students and
teachers to work harder? Why should we believe that?

INTERPRETIVE FRAMEWORKS AND REFORM

Most people realize that many reforms represent little or no change. School
administrators and government officials often announce reform and put
changes into effect, but nothing happens, and a few years later the reform
positions are reversed with little or no fanfare. Why do we accept these
claims for reform uncritically?

Cognitive psychologists say that all of us approach the world with sets
of schemata, scripts, and so forth that help us make sense of new situations.
We have a schema that tells us how to act and what to expect in a restau-
rant. As every parent knows, children have to learn that schema so that they
know "how to behave," not to use the napkin as a handkerchief, not to stand
up in the chair and sing loudly, and so forth. Some sociologists approach
policy issues by examining what they call the underlying cognitive structures, myths, and stock explanations. They are concerned with why people

accept contradictory explanations of social and political realities. Edelman (1977) argues that the "availability of both views makes possible a wide spectrum of ambivalent postures for each individual and a similarly large set of contradictions in political rhetoric and public policy" (p. 7).

I want to deal with school testing in a similar way, but I prefer the term *interpretive framework*. An interpretive framework is a network of related ideas involving a set of examined or unexamined assumptions and explanations that we use to interpret situations that we encounter in the world. Philosophical concepts are interpretive frameworks. Aristotle's ideas about moral virtue in the *Nichomachean Ethics* become a set of tools for judging some person's virtue or for thinking about the nature of a virtue or virtue in general. The assumptions underlying philosophical concepts are usually examined, and some last a long time and become important in how we interpret phenomena in the culture. In the case of the *Nichomachean Ethics*, Aristotle argues that the ideas of virtue he examines were already existent in the culture, that he simply conducts an inquiry to make them explicit. However that may be, the ideas remain a powerful interpretive framework in western culture.

I suspect that most of the interpretive frameworks that we carry around in our heads remain unexamined. I have interviewed many teachers at the high school and community college levels (Hillocks, 1999) who state and appear to believe that their students do not have adequate backgrounds for learning what is supposed to be taught in a particular course. One teacher says, "No matter what I do, they never improve." Here is how the argument breaks down.

1. When a teacher covers everything to be learned, any students with appropriate background should be able to learn what is required.
2. I have covered everything to be learned. Yet these students fail.
3. Therefore, the students must have inadequate backgrounds.

The conclusion in this argument precludes the necessity for examining the assumptions underlying the conceptions of students and the nature and effects of the teaching. Further, the conclusion becomes the premise for new arguments about how to teach the course, what material to include, how to organize it, how to make assignments, and so forth. If students lack the necessary background, then it appears necessary to supply some version of it. In most cases, the courses involved become regressive, supplying students with background that does not help them become successful.

Another example comes from the reform efforts in the Chicago public schools. Anagnostopoulos (2000) examined the effects of a specific policy designed to implement the more general policy of "no more social promotion." This specific policy has to do with ninth grade students who do not pass enough courses to gain the status of 10th graders. They are retained in ninth grade homerooms, attend assemblies with ninth graders, and become known as "demotes." However, they take 10th grade courses either in classes made up of demotes or in mixed classes with students who did pass the ninth grade courses. In the schools studied, there were too few teachers to offer enough classes for hundreds of students to retake the ninth grade classes they had failed. Anagnostopolous shows that there is no change in the way in which the students are taught. In effect, there is no change in policy at all. There is a change only in the homeroom assignment, but social promotion remains. The pseudopolicy manages to avoid the appearance of social promotion. Eventually, of course, this will have the effect of driving students out of high school without diplomas as it becomes more and more apparent that they will not have enough credits to graduate on schedule.

It appears that the media, administrators, and teachers accept this pseudopolicy as real because it conforms to the assumptions in one of our interpretive frameworks that explain how schools work. That is, we assume that schools work by moving students from one grade level to the next, that this movement is tantamount to achievement, and that failure to achieve brings about failure to move to the next grade. The policy in the Chicago public schools plays on our assumptions by playing with the labels. We assume that if students are placed in ninth grade homerooms and attend ninth grade assemblies, they will be working in classes at the ninth grade level or at least at whatever level the school system and teacher sets in the ninth grade.

Testing pervades our culture: our schools, television, newspapers. We can go to bookstores and buy books that are filled with tests, sometimes along with advice about how to pass them. We play games that involve tests in our leisure: twenty questions, games with nothing but quizzes about trivia, charades. We believe that tests indicate achievement, intelligence, or aptitude, or all of these. Further, we believe that tests are a legitimate means of making distinctions among people on the basis of who passes, who fails, who wins a million dollars, and who does not. Test scores become the basis of predictions about people and their futures. We believe that if test scores go up, students must be learning more, moving closer to excellence, as Mr. Bush would have it. We assume further that if the scores go up, the schools are doing a better job of educating the students because we believe that test scores reflect education. We assume that schools and states and test makers know what high standards are and how to test them. At the same time, many of us have a deep distrust and even hostility toward tests. We hear parents complain that their children suffer because of all the tests in schools. Many teachers and administrators interviewed for this study complain about the frequency and the quality of tests. We also believe that tests are not a good indicator of what we can do. How many times have we heard people complain about tests that did not test what they knew but only what they did not know? Such beliefs exist side by side with the positive attitudes. While we deny the validity of tests, we are delighted with high scores on the same tests. While I complain about the necessity of my children's taking the SAT, I am pleased when their scores are high. One of the school principals interviewed for this study complained at length about the testing policies put in place by the state of Illinois and his district. At the same time, he was very proud that his eighth graders had raised scores on the Illinois writing test by 30%. While a clear ambivalence exists, it seems to me that the balance is tipped in favor of tests, particularly those that have single word answers, because of popular TV quiz shows.

The ambivalence appears to leave most people open to the influence of politicians who make clear and unambiguous statements, or at least statements including no qualifications. Let me turn to Bush's interpretive frameworks. In the first presidential debate, Bush claimed that "testing is the cornerstone of reform." He also claimed that "you need to test every year, because that's where you determine whether or not children are progressing to excellence." He has said that we need to "raise the bar of standards" and "blow the whistle on failure." These ideas are stated as rules or absolutes. There are no qualifiers and no conditions stated in which they might be open to rebuttal. People appear to accept these ideas uncritically. In the 2000 election campaign, even Al Gore appeared to agree with them. We do not think to question these "principles" because they are a part of our interpretive framework, our set of assumptions and explanations about how schools work. In the campaign no one questioned them. We simply accepted them because, while we may be ambivalent about testing, the Bush statements are built into the assumptions that we make uncritically about schooling and education.

But all of Bush's self-styled principles are open to question.

1. What are the standards underlying the testing program and in what ways do they represent excellence?
2. To what extent are the tests capable of detecting excellence?
3. What counts for meeting standards or for improvement? What does it mean to "raise the bar of standards"?
4. What impact does "blowing the whistle" on failure have on classroom instruction? Does it really lead to excellence?

These are some of the major questions with which this book will be concerned. Let me provide a quick example of how important the answers to these questions are. During the presidential campaign of 2000, Bush frequently used the word *excellence* in regard to education, claiming that his goal for education would be excellence, but he never defined the term. Undefined, it remains what I used to teach ninth graders was a "glittering generality," a word that had no concrete referent but carried with it a lot of affective baggage. For most of us, when applied to education, excellence for an individual student means consistently outstanding performance in one or more fields of endeavor. When we think of excellent performance for a whole school, we assume that, on average, students in the school demonstrate very high academic performance.

In his remarks on education, Bush appears to use the term in the same way as the rest of us. The interpretive frameworks about schools that most of us use encourage us in this belief. To be certain, however, we need to inspect the Bush standards, or any standards, by which performances of individuals and schools are judged excellent. When we examine them, what Bush calls excellent turns out to be poor, at best mediocre. Therefore, we need to examine the tests themselves and their standards to see what counts as excellent for both individuals and schools. But we will also have to find what teachers do in classrooms and what supervisors and administrators do in schools to implement the reforms.

CHAPTER 2

The Study of State Writing Assessments

Chapter 1 raised several questions about tests, their uses, and effects that are relevant to writing assessments everywhere. When I began research on the impact of state mandatory testing, I chose to study writing assessments for three reasons. First, writing involves a range of high-level thinking processes, and it seems to me very important to discover how state assessments affect those processes. Second, because writing is not tested through multiple-choice items, it seemed at least possible that writing instruction could resist the pressures and results attributed to multiple-choice testing. Finally, if states are concerned about encouraging high-level thinking in schools, that interest is more likely to be reflected in writing assessments than in assessments for other subject matter areas. When the research began, 37 of the 50 states had some kind of assessment of student progress in writing. These assessments were developed more or less independently so that underlying conceptions of writing, standards, prompts, testing conditions, criteria, and scoring procedures differed from state to state.

The obvious questions are how these differences affect the kind and level of thinking going on in classrooms and the extent to which the varying conditions have negative or positive effects on student learning. Most state assessments had been instituted partly as a means of insuring that writing was being taught effectively. At the same time, one might predict that an assessment and its conditions dictate to some extent what effective teaching is. States are investing millions of dollars, thousands of teacher hours, and hundreds of thousands of student classroom hours in mandatory writing assessments. If the investment of all this money and time is having a positive effect on student achievement, it may be worthwhile. If assessments limit the kinds of writing taught or the ways they are taught, or the thinking that good writing requires, then the assessments may be of questionable value.

THE SAMPLE

To answer these questions, I undertook in-depth studies of writing assessments in five states: Illinois, Kentucky, New York, Oregon, and Texas. The states were chosen for geographical distribution as well as for differences in the types of assessments. Texas, Illinois, and New York have writing-on-demand assessments. Kentucky has both a writing-on-demand assessment and a portfolio assessment. At the time we began our research Oregon was in the early stages of developing a portfolio assessment. The portfolio assessment requires each student to develop a collection of writings over some period of time, in Kentucky, over the course of a school year or more. In Oregon, the portfolio is a collection of writing done in the classroom and used in addition to the writing-on-demand assessment. New York's assessment includes three essays in response to passages presented in the test and one about literature read outside the testing situation. None of the other states in our sample provide those kinds of writing prompts. Oregon's on-demand assessment once involved a criterion (voice) that set it apart from many other writing-on-demand assessments. It takes place over 3 days, also setting it apart from many other writing-on-demand assessments.

In selecting the states for study, I was also concerned to select states in which the assessment stakes differed. Some states are said to have "high-stakes" assessments because the fortunes of individual students, schools, and school districts rise or fall on the results. In Texas, for example, students who do not pass the 10th-grade writing assessment, despite several attempts, may not graduate from high school. Further, the schools and even districts may be dismantled if test scores do not improve in a certain length of time. In these states, officials process assessment results in formulas for evaluating the achievement level of schools and school districts from one year to the next. If schools do not achieve satisfactory progress ratings, their faculties may be disbanded or the students may be assigned to a new school district.

Other state assessments are considered "low-stakes" because no one is ostensibly at risk. When I began this research, I believed that Illinois had what was regarded as a low-stakes testing program. Passing the writing assessment in Illinois is not, at the moment, requisite for graduation from high school. State officials cannot take over a failing school or system. The state simply places schools with scores below a certain level on a watch list. The sample of five states presents a representative range of practices in assessment.

Within each of the states, we interviewed state department officials responsible for the writing assessments and teachers and administrators in each of six school districts: two large urban districts, two suburban districts (one middle-class and one blue-collar), one small town, and one rural district. On average we conducted interviews with nine teachers and three to five administrators in each district for an average of 78 interviews in each state and a total of over 390.

RESEARCH QUESTIONS

Prior to beginning the major research project, I conducted several interviews in Texas (six) and Illinois (four). These and a general familiarity with assessments, common practices in the teaching of writing, and research in the teaching of writing allowed for developing a set of questions that I thought would help reveal how each assessment is conducive to various practices in the teaching of writing. It would be important to examine the theories of writing underlying the assessments, the kinds of writing tested, the scoring criteria, scoring procedures, materials for teachers, and a variety of dimensions of teacher-reported practices.

Theory of Writing and Kinds of Writing

When a state mandates a statewide writing assessment, it necessarily focuses on certain kinds of writing tasks to be tested and prescribes the criteria to be used in judging the students' efforts, thereby privileging whatever curricular content appears to be closely related to the assessment and necessarily ignoring other possible content. Sometimes states present an explicit rationale for the kinds of writing to be tested, sometimes not. Even without the explicit statement, the kinds of writing selected indicate what the state regards as important and what it sees as the nature of writing. Rationales in combination with the kinds of writing selected and the criteria brought to bear on the written products indicate a theory of writing: what is important, how the types relate to each other, what the process of writing is, and so forth.

Even without an explicit theory, the kinds of writing tested may influence the kinds of writing taught in schools. The Illinois Goals Assessment Program (IGAP) tested personal narrative, persuasion, and exposition. There are many other kinds of writing that do not fall in these categories: drama, poetry, fiction, for example. Would Illinois teachers deal much with the others? If an assessment severely restricts the kinds of writing with which students work, it also restricts students' development as writers.

Scoring

Each state has created a scoring rubric (scale) that indicates what the state regards as important in good writing. It would seem natural for teachers who are concerned that their students do well on the tests to become familiar with the criteria and to teach them directly or to adapt them for use with students. On the other hand, it might be that teachers would have their own criteria, which they believe might amount to a better measure of effective writing and still accomplish the state goals and result in good scores.

Different scoring rubrics have different characteristics and emphasize different criteria. For example, the IGAP criteria are quite specific in some regards and not so specific in others. Until 1999, for a top score on a persuasive or expository piece of writing in Illinois, the writer needed to stipulate the major points of the essay in the first paragraph as a preview of what is to come in the following paragraphs. Such a preview is not required in any of our other states. Another variation in judging the quality of writing is what counts as support for ideas from state to state. New York calls for evidence in the support of claims in writing. Most other states call only for elaboration of ideas, which may simply mean the restatement of the same idea in nearly the same language. As this book will demonstrate, such variations make a difference in what students learn about thinking and writing. What difference do these variations make in teaching? These and related problems will be addressed through interviews and through the analysis of the criteria themselves and the compositions that the states present as fulfilling and not fulfilling their criteria.

Scoring Procedures

Scoring procedures differ widely among the states. In Illinois and Texas, student writings are sent to a scoring agency out of state. In Oregon, the State Department of Education hires Oregon teachers from around the state to score papers at regional centers. In Kentucky and New York, teachers in each school score the writing produced by students in that school, with the state department monitoring the results. It is reasonable to expect that these differences will have some effect on both the teachers' and the students' thinking about writing. What will those be?

Materials for Teachers and Students

All of the state departments of education in our study have developed materials to help teachers prepare their students for the assessment. These materials inevitably focus on the types of writing to be assessed while ignoring other types. Usually, they are scoring guides that include rubrics and sample compositions at each level. Sometimes states and local districts provide guides to teaching as well. Assessments appear to provide a gold mine for little publishers, some of which appear to have sprung up in response to the assessments. In Texas, for example, there are several publications by a few publishers that promise to help teachers prepare students for the assessments. Schools and teachers use these with some regularity. Some schools purchase copies of student guides and workbooks for all students in the tested grade levels. The question is how well do these adhere to what research shows are the best practices in teaching writing? To what extent do they support the goals of the state writing assessments?

Rhetorical Stance and Teaching

What influence do assessments have on the way teachers think about the nature of writing and learning and the kind of learning environment they create? Combinations of these make up what I will call a rhetorical stance. James A. Berlin (1982), a well known rhetorician, argued that there are four different theories of rhetoric, each based on a different epistemology, defined generally as conceptions of truth and how we arrive at it. Berlin clearly explicates the epistemological dimensions of the four rhetorics, and suggests that these have implications for teaching. Recent empirical research and theory delineate the pedagogical dimensions of these rhetorics (Hillocks, 1999). The research and theory suggest that when teachers adopt a rhetorical stance, they also commit to a theory of knowledge and to the theory of teaching implied in its assumptions. This study will be concerned with three of the rhetorics.

The first of the three is very common in schools and colleges today and is commonly called current traditional rhetoric (CTR). The underlying assumption about knowledge in this rhetoric is that truth is objective and may be apprehended directly through observation of the world and our experience of it. Eighteenth-century versions of this rhetoric focused on the modes of writing (description, narration, exposition, and persuasion), but after the beginning of the twentieth century, college composition began to focus on exposition (Connors, 1981), a trend that appears to be no less true in high school curricula. Textbooks that focus on exposition deal with different types: definition, classification, comparison-contrast, cause and effect, evaluation, and so forth. Many contemporary theorists argue that these types are not simple expositions. They do not simply set out what is known to be true. Rather, they make a case for something. Thus an evaluation of a movie is not an exposition but an argument about why the movie is good or poor.

The two rhetorics that we have yet to examine, may both be referred to as constructivist. A constructivist epistemology recognizes that knowledge is not apprehended directly through the senses. Rather, knowledge is necessarily constructed through the filters of our existing knowledge. When any of us perceive something, we interpret it through our existing knowledge. The interpretation appears to be the perception.

For example, I have had several opportunities to observe the Easter processions in Antigua, Guatemala. I was very impressed with the hundreds of people—all costumed, some carrying flowers and banners—platforms with statues of saints, the massive platform with Christ and the cross in some stage of the crucifixion story, and finally a smaller platform with a statue of the Virgin Mary. Because I had some knowledge of Christian beliefs I could interpret the processions generally, but I could not make interpretations of some of the details at all. I did not have the knowledge of the Guatemalans who saw the processions in quite different ways than I could.

More fundamentally, scientists tell us that humans perceive phenomena as undifferentiated fields until they learn how to distinguish what they see. If you examine the old cartoon in Figure 2.1, you are likely to see an old grouchy-looking woman or a beautiful, fashionable young woman, but not both. You will have to interpret the lines that you see until you can perceive the other. Scientists argue that each of us must learn to interpret what we see so as to identify certain items by differentiating them from their environments (Attneave, 1971).

Contemporary educational theory and research argue that effective learning must be constructivist in nature, that students learn best and perhaps only when they can construct knowledge for themselves within the framework of their existing knowledge (e.g., Dewey, 1938; Hillocks, 1999; Nystrand, 1997; Vygotsky, 1978). This means that students must have interactions with others and materials in order to learn. The traditional models of teaching through lecture and recitation do not work efficiently. One eighteenth-century grammarian, Lindley Murray (1849), talked about "transfusing" sentiments into the minds of others. If that were possible, teaching would be easy. But every teacher knows it is difficult. Students tend to grasp new concepts by assimilating them to concepts they already have. Constructivist teachers recognize this and do not proceed through lecture and recitation. CTR, however, nearly always allows lecture and recitation to dominate classrooms in writing (Hillocks, 1999) because it assumes that students need simply to learn the forms and that the forms can be explained. CTR teachers assume that once students see

FIGURE 2.1. Two Women (W.E. Hill in *Puck* as "My Wife and My Mother-in-Law")

what a comparison-contrast composition should contain, they will be able to write one. Therefore, they teach only the form and neglect teaching the strategies appropriate for making effective comparisons and contrasts.

The first of the constructivist rhetorics I will call expressivist. In expressivist textbooks, according to Berlin (1982), "truth is conceived as the result of a private vision that must be constantly consulted in writing." The books "emphasize writing as a 'personal' activity, as an expression of one's unique voice" (p. 772). Here, there is little of logic, the senses, or types of writing. Far more important is personal insight and the ability to allow writing to grow organically from the writer's own ideas. In this rhetoric, teachers proceed by allowing and encouraging students to develop their existing ideas through the writing process and through sharing those ideas with others (for a detailed example, see Hillocks, 1999, pp. 79–91).

The third or "new" rhetoric Berlin (1982) calls "epistemic" because it functions "as a means of arriving at the truth" (p. 773). In this rhetoric,

Truth is dynamic and dialectical, the result of a process involving the interaction of opposing elements. It is a relation that is created, not preexistent and waiting to be discovered. . . . The New Rhetoric denies that truth is discoverable in sense impression since this data must always be interpreted—structured and organized—in order to have meaning. (p. 774)

That is, truth must be argued through dialectical processes. Teachers who adopt this rhetorical stance will engage their students in small-group discussions in which students bring their various experiences and knowledge to bear on problem solving. Because the problems are substantive, they involve various levels of probability rather than absolutes. Thus students will concentrate on supporting claims with evidence and often arguing the rules that show how evidence is related to claims. To arrive at any reliable, though probabilistic, conclusion requires an effort to ameliorate our personal subjectivity through dialectical processes, allowing others to scrutinize and criticize our ideas.

Each of the distinctions above is a matter of emphasis. Sensory perception is not restricted to current traditional rhetoric. We will necessarily find it in each of the other types. However, in expressivist rhetoric it is subjected to the operation of personal insight; and in epistemic or new rhetoric to dialectic.

What do the distinctions among these rhetorics entail for teaching? Current traditional rhetoric assumes that truth is somewhere waiting to be discovered, that it exists independently of the investigator. The language that we use to talk about investigation commonly reflects emphasis on the senses. Words such as *research, discover, observation, findings, analysis,* and *insight* all suggest that the investigator may look and, with some manipulation of data, discover the "objective" truth existing independently of the observer. This assumed simplicity in finding truth, I suspect, helps to explain the emphasis on exposition. If truth is directly apprehensible, it is necessary for a writer merely to explain it. Argument is unnecessary. Further, if truth is unproblematic, except for the use of technical tools that assist observations, then instruction may focus on the form of the writing. Once students know the appropriate structures, finding the necessary content is a matter of individual effort but is largely unproblematic.

Thus, the focus in classrooms that adopt current traditional rhetoric is on teaching form while largely ignoring content. In one recent study most of the teachers involved were essentially tied to current traditional rhetoric. Their practice was to lecture on the requirements of the form, for example, what should be in an introduction, what should be in the body and conclusion, how to go about developing an evaluation, a comparison, or a definition (Hillocks, 1999). Very little time was devoted to student talk. The teachers adopting this rhetorical stance did not take students through the investigation of content in order for them to learn appropriate strategies for thinking about the kinds of data or problems involved. They did not involve students in small-group discussions. When teachers are committed to this rhetoric, one can expect that they will focus on explaining the structure of the writing. This kind of rhetoric typifies what Meyers (1996) calls decoding/analytic literacy.

In expressivist rhetoric, findings are personal insights about experience, backed by details and perhaps arguments about the phenomena in question. The development of ideas is viewed as dependent on the person's beliefs, insight, and experience. Thus, in one classroom, the professor encouraged students to respond one at a time by telling what he or she saw in the mind's eye after the professor had read a piece of writing. What he wanted was a recreation of the written texts but with the detail that any respondent sees as he pictures the written scene in the mind's eye, a personal reconstruction of the story. From such personal reconstructions of writing by others, he moved to coaching students as they recreated personal experiences of their own as the remainder of the students listened.

Although the professor suggested the "universals" from which students should choose the experience to detail, it was clear that students could choose what they wished. We might expect to find this in any class whose teacher has adopted the stance of expressivist rhetoric. We might also expect to find sharing the written or oral products. Here, the focus is on the content generated by students, not on form except as the models chosen by teachers exemplify some form upon which the teachers hope to focus. But lectures on the details of the form or genre are minimized.

If a classroom is committed to epistemic rhetoric, discussions of various issues dominate classroom time. A major difference between this rhetoric and the others is that the agency for learning is not simply the individual but the individual's interactions with a group. It assumes that learning is socially situated (Leont'ev, 1981; Luria, 1976; Vygotsky, 1978) and that individuals learn procedures for idea development and for thinking through problems in the give-and-take of discussion, especially when problems have been structured for that purpose.

Attention to outward form in epistemic rhetoric is minimized. As explained above, attention is focused on substantive arguments, sometimes about facts, what happened or happens in the real world of experience; sometimes about judgments of events, people, and ideas; and sometimes about policies, what should be done in a given situation considering all the factors involved. As a result, when such a rhetoric is in place, we will see students engaged in talk about problems as a means of learning how to think about them and thereby write about them.

These are likely to be collaborative discussions in which students develop arguments of inquiry, the purpose of which is to arrive at agreed-upon, sound interpretations of texts or other sets of data (Walton, 1999). For example, Ms. Levine's teaching in Chapter 1 is epistemic in this way. In one secondary classroom that I observed, the teacher, Mr. Gow, led the students through an examination of an engraving by Gilray which is a satire of the Prince of Wales. Mr. Gow, through the discussion, helped students see how to use contrasting features of the drawing along with their existing knowledge (their expectations) to interpret the picture. Then he moved his students into groups and presented a new problem for them to deal with: interpreting Hogarth's *Beer Street* and *Gin Lane*. Working in small groups, at first they simply examined and reported what they saw. Shortly, they began to interpret and explain what the drawings meant and what Hogarth's purpose was. Their discussions included disagreements, but ordinarily even the disagreements contributed to more complete understandings of the works.

After about 20 minutes, Mr. Gow called upon the groups to present their ideas to the class. These presentations tended to focus on different ideas about the engravings. As students dealt with the questions that arose, they incorporated more of the contrasting details of the two pictures into their own understanding of them. With very little teacher input, the class arrived at highly sophisticated interpretations. (See Hillocks, 1999, pp. 10–17, for details of the transcript.)

Because epistemic classrooms remain very unusual in American schools, it will be useful to summarize their characteristics:

- Student discussion is maximized.
- Discussion focuses on structured problems that are complex and not subject to simple solutions.
- Discussions often serve as preparation for writing but may also serve to help students learn strategies for critical thinking that they will later use in writing, although not necessarily about a given topic of discussion.
- Discussion takes the form of deliberative thinking about alternatives.
- Ideas and their development are central, with form emerging from them.

Clearly, these differences in the rhetorical stance could make a difference not only in the lived curriculum that students experience, but also in the quality of student writing. Research shows that when composition is taught from the stance of CTR, results tend to be very weak. Classroom teaching that makes use of expressivist rhetoric, on the other hand, has positive effects on the writing of students about eight to nine times as great. In teaching that takes an epistemic stance, the effects are 22 times as great (Hillocks, 1986). The question is which rhetorics are encouraged by the different state assessments. We can expect those that encourage CTR to have far weaker effects than either of the other two.

Mode of Instruction

A fourth set of questions has to do with the mode of instruction that teachers adopt as they prepare students for the assessments. Previous research and theory has delineated three modes of instruction in the teaching of writing (Applebee, 1986; Hillocks, 1986b). Basically, these are differentiated by the extent to which classrooms are teacher or student centered and by the level and kind of structure among the student-centered modes of teaching. In the first, which I will call presentational, the teacher is the main conveyor of information that students are to take in and learn. Most classroom talk moves from teacher to student and back to the teacher. It tends to follow a pattern in which the teacher initiates the talk with a question or comment to which students respond, and then the teacher evaluates the student response before initiating the next triad. This is often called the IRE pattern for initiation, response, evaluation (Nystrand, 1997).

A second mode, what I will call the workshop mode, is student centered and minimally structured. The teacher organizes classrooms into workshops in which students work on projects of their own choosing and develop them independently and largely as they see fit. Teachers who develop such learning environments develop what they call minilessons, short lessons that students may be able to use in their writing (Atwell, 1987). In the workshop setting student talk is encouraged in response groups as students read their writing to others, receive feedback from peers, and discuss ideas. Argument as described above does not seem to play a part in this workshop mode. Teachers typically avoid or minimize the IRE pattern.

The third learning environment is student centered but much more highly structured in that the teacher sets up problems that all students work on prior to independent work. These problems are usually designed to help students learn sets of fairly specific strategies as in Mr. Gow's class and Ms. Levine's classes above. Learning tasks are scaffolded so that students have support as they encounter new tasks. The teachers also make use of specific criteria for judging student work, criteria that students come to learn through work on the project. The activities of the class are usually aimed at helping students learn strategies that they will be able to use in many other situations. Teachers maximize collaborative work and minimize both IRE and lecture. Independent work is also common, but it usually is a culmination of other work and, in my experience, always follows intensive work on learning the required strategies first. I will refer to this mode of teaching as environmental to reflect that learning is the result of the interaction of all aspects of the classroom: teachers, peers, materials, and ideas.

The question here is the extent to which assessments encourage these various modes of instruction. Will some assessments be more conducive to workshop teaching, some to presentational teaching, and some to environmental? Will some occur more often in some districts or states than others?

Writing Process

It seemed reasonable to assume, with all the emphasis on writing processes in the past 25 years, that teachers would be using it as an important part of their work on writing. In 1981, a study by Applebee indicated that the teaching of writing in American high schools took very little time. The vast majority of teachers in all subject areas focused on more or less mechanical uses of writing as in taking notes. "On average, only 3 percent of lesson time was devoted to longer writing requiring the student to produce a paragraph of coherent text. Personal and creative uses of writing had little place in the high school curriculum, occupying less than one half of one percent of lesson time" (p. 30). Often the writing encountered by students was writing for the teacher intended to tell what the students knew about some topic assigned by the teacher, as in tests. When the writing was more extensive, the teacher most often assigned the topic and thus the purpose, and provided directions to follow. For the most part, students wrote so that teachers might evaluate specific learnings about some subject matter. Teachers expected students to write a composition and do well on a single draft. They did not provide preplanning, revising, and other parts of what many teachers now refer to as the composing process.

The writing process movement has been very influential in professional organizations over the past 3 decades through a host of books and journal articles and through the National Writing Project. Proponents of teaching writing as process generally argue that the theories of current traditional rhetoric are ineffective because they tend to present knowledge about written forms rather than helping students learn the strategies and processes for writing. Many teachers now know the necessity of students' learning the whole process of writing, from various kinds of prewriting, such as brainstorming, through final editing and publishing. Figure 2.2 provides an outline of the writing process and definitions.

Research has shown that this process is not linear, but recursive, meaning essentially that the writer does not move forward in a straight line in which she collects data, makes an outline, develops a first draft from the outline, revises, edits, and publishes. Rather, she is more likely to collect data, make an analysis, begin a first draft, return to the data for further collection or analysis, revise the draft while it is still in process, move forward again only to return once more to the data, and revise ideas again. In writing this chapter, I have returned to the interviews and the quantitative analysis four times so far to confirm and disconfirm ideas that I thought I had worked out. In 2 days I am planning to conduct six interviews to confirm or disconfirm different ideas. Writing is simply not a linear process. But traditionally schools have treated it as though it were. Advocates of the writing process usually believe that the process should be the basis for the development of most school writing.

Do assessments have any impact on the use of the writing process in classrooms? Do they encourage or discourage the writing process? These are very important questions. The less emphasis on learning writing process, the less able students will be to deal with writing situations outside the classroom.

Attitudes Toward the Assessments

Another question has to do with teacher and teacher-perceived student attitudes toward the assessments. As I began the research, it was obvious that many teachers resented the assessments, were angry or fearful about being

FIGURE 2.2. Writing Process Elements

Prewriting is preparation for writing including such techniques as brainstorming, clustering, and mapping.

> **Brainstorming**: the rapid suggestion of ideas related to and prompted by some stimulus. This is not an analytic activity. Rather its function is to produce initial ideas from participants' existing knowledge. These ideas may then be **clustered** (associating related ideas) and/or **mapped** (showing the relationships among ideas in some graphic way). (See Atwell, 1987; Graves, 1983; Hillocks, 1986a)
>
> **Selecting a Genre or Means of Presentation:** the selection of a form or genre from the writer's repertoire for writing (Hillocks, 1995).

Drafting: developing the first draft using a recursive process. This may be carried out by students acting independently or in consultation with the teacher or other students as they discuss problems they are having.

Feedback: the process of learning how an audience responds to one's writing. Feedback may come from teacher or peers after a draft is complete but before it is published or receives a final grade. Feedback can be provided in a variety of different processes, including small-group discussions, written comments on the paper, and individual conferences. Teachers may aim feedback at the development of content, formal features, or at finding and correcting errors in spelling, punctuation, sentence structure, and so forth.

Revising: the process of making changes in a manuscript at many different levels from cosmetic concerns to whole-text revisions (Bridwell, 1980). Largely in traditional writing curricula, students have learned to make predominantly cosmetic revisions at the word and sentence level. Teachers engaged in teaching the writing process urge students to review what they think about the content of their writing and other high-level problems.

Editing: the process of cleaning up a manuscript that focuses on lower level features of writing but which often gives rise to higher level revisions.

Publishing: any of the processes by which students share their writing with others, including reading aloud to others, displaying the writing on bulletin boards, making small books of their writing, and developing classroom collections of writing.

held responsible for the work of their students, and felt that too much pressure was being brought to bear on them. The questions in this area have three major dimensions: (1) How do teachers and administrators feel about the assessments in terms of their effects on student learning? (2) How do they feel about the pressures brought to bear on them as the people responsible? (3) What is their perception of students' responses to the tests?

Impact of the Assessments on Other Parts of the Curriculum

Because some teachers indicated in the early interviews that certain parts of the curriculum were pushed aside in order to prepare for the tests, the question of the impact on other parts of the curriculum became important. I thought that perhaps in the middle and secondary schools, the language arts curriculum would not be affected, but it seemed wise to try to investigate that issue. In elementary school, I thought the impact might be more widespread, possibly affecting other subject matter areas such as science or social studies.

Teacher Education About Writing and Writing Pedagogy

It is widely known that teachers of English in the secondary schools have little or no training in the teaching of writing. They are, after all, graduates of English departments concentrating on literature. Elementary and middle school language arts teachers tend to have even less background in writing. They have tended to concentrate on reading. In the past 20 years, the National Writing Project and its many sites in nearly every state has been helping to educate more and more teachers in the teaching of writing. As it turns out, a small but significant number of our interviewees had some work with the Writing Project. An obvious question is whether that added education makes any difference in the teachers' interpretations of the assessment, how they respond to it as teachers, their views of writing, rhetorical stance, and preferred classroom environments.

METHODS OF THE STUDY

Interview protocols for teachers varied from state to state because of differences in assessments. However, all interviews were designed to prompt talk about how teachers prepared their students for the assessment, the nature of writing taught, beliefs about important methods of teaching writing, the extent to which the writing assessment supported the writing curriculum that teachers would like to see in place, attitudes toward the assessments, pressure on students and on teachers themselves, and the kinds and extent of the teachers' own training in writing. While interviewers used the protocol, we thought it best to engage teachers in talk in such a way that many items would arise in the course of the conversation. That is, we hoped that the interviews would be ethnographic interviews (Spradley, 1979). The disadvantage was that when teachers were loquacious about certain issues or when interviews were cut short for one reason or another, we sometimes were unable to cover all the issues that we had hoped to cover. The interviews averaged 45 minutes, with a range of 20 minutes to over 2 hours. Fortunately, very few were only 20 minutes.

Coding Interviews

Once interviews had been collected across all states, it was necessary to determine what commonalities and differences existed among the teachers in the various states. We set out to code the interviews for 69 separate items having to do with the questions indicated above. Most of the items involve low-inference coding, such as teachers' use of the state scoring rubric, a local rubric, or some adaptation of one of those; teachers' positive or negative attitudes toward the assessment; their focus on the five-paragraph theme; their uses of the elements of the writing process; and so forth.

Other codings involved higher inference. For example, we coded dominant rhetorical stance as one of the following unless we had insufficient information: current traditional, expressivist, or epistemic. This item also allowed for coding grammar or writing about literature as a major focus of instruction in place of a rhetorical stance. Another item allowed for coding evidence of any one of these. Teachers, of course, would not mention our terms or claim to have a rhetorical stance, although some did say that they focused on writing about literature. Coders had to infer the rhetorical stance from statements by the teacher. The interviewers were to ask teachers what they did to prepare their students for writing, and their descriptions of what they did usually permitted these inferences. For example, teachers who described activities such as those in Ms. Levine's classroom would have been coded as epistemic.

Another high-inference coding involved categorizing apparent mode of instruction as presentational (teacher centered), workshop (student centered, low structure), or environmental (student centered, high structure). Again, teachers' descriptions of what they do provided the basis for making inferences about their usual practices. Examples of each of these high-inference categories will appear in the following chapters.

Early attempts at coding resulted in 83% exact agreement between two coders. However, as we proceeded we realized that many codings had very low exact agreement, as low as 60 percent. Therefore, the procedure was changed, and we started over. We recoded all interviews so that each teacher's interview was coded by two trained researchers. When they disagreed on any item, a third coder resolved disagreements in consultation with at least one of the original coders. This procedure proved to be very time consuming but worth the effort. Ironically, on this second round of coding, the exact agreement rarely fell below 85%. In the second round of coding, however, all disagreements were negotiated with a third reader.

Analysis of Materials

We collected documents describing the writing assessments from all states that have them. In the target states where interviews were conducted, we collected related documents from commercial publishers, state and district offices, and documents used by teachers in the classroom. These materials were subjected to careful analysis to get at their underlying assumptions, their consistency with state goals, their relationships to broader theories of writing and the teaching of writing, and their consistency with what is known about the teaching of writing through research.

Panels of Consultants

In keeping with the ideas of epistemic rhetoric, we believed that it would be useful to have knowledgeable outsiders review our work and consult with us about the best directions on how to proceed. One of the most useful of these several meetings was the discussion of our coding system. Consultants made outstanding suggestions about our categories and our system for using them. Some have also reviewed the final report as it has been produced. The members of the panels have kept us more levelheaded and objective.

WHAT THIS RESEARCH DOES NOT DO

The original proposal requested funds to support observation of classrooms in each target state. However, such funds were not made available. Despite this impediment, we believe that, taken together, the qualitative analysis of the interviews with teachers and administrators, the quantifiable codings of the teacher interviews, and analysis of the documents provide a useful picture of what happens as a result of the state assessments. Teachers and administrators were very forthcoming about their methods of preparing students for the assessments, and we detected no attempts to misinform or mislead.

CHAPTER 3

Foundations of Testing

Tests of writing do not grow on trees. But if they did, they would come from several kinds of tress. In two 3-hour sessions in June, August, or January, New York's 11th graders receive passages to read or listen to and write about and a prompt that asks them to write about literature that they have read prior to the exam. In March, Texas 10th graders have a day to write a persuasive essay on an issue briefly described in a few sentences. Also in March, Illinois 10th graders, from 1990 through 1999, wrote in two 40-minute sessions. In one, they received a single prompt designed to generate narrative, expository, or persuasive writing. In the second session, they received two prompts, one for each kind of writing not represented in the other session; they wrote about one. In Kentucky, 12th graders receive two prompts of which they choose one for writing and have 90 minutes to write. However, Kentucky, unlike most other states, uses a portfolio assessment as the major writing assessment. These differences in high school assessments reflect comparable differences at other grade levels. Clearly, tests are constructed by people with different knowledge and sets of beliefs about what writing is and what counts as a test of writing.

THE ROLE OF LEGISLATION

Most state assessment programs originate in a piece of legislation. Usually the legislation sets out several academic areas to be tested and the grade levels at which tests are to be given. It may indicate the kinds of tests to be used. The Texas legislation, like that in most other states, requires "criterion referenced tests," tests for which standards of performance are set in advance and students are judged in terms of how closely they approach those standards. It further directs the Texas Education Agency (TEA) to develop "appropriate . . . assessment instruments designed to assess essential knowledge and skills in reading, writing, mathematics, social studies, and science." The same section states a bit later that "the instruments shall be designed to include assessment of a student's problem-solving ability and complex thinking skills using a method of assessing those abilities and skills that is demonstrated to be highly reliable" (Public School System Accountability, 1995–1997, 39.023). The legislation leaves decisions about what the essential knowledge and skills are and what counts as "a student's problem-solving ability and complex thinking skills" to the Texas Education Agency.

Sometimes legislation presents only a very general outline of the standards upon which the criteria are to be based. The Illinois legislation, for example, indicates that "as a result of their schooling, students will be able to write standard English in a grammatical, well organized and coherent manner for a variety of purposes" (Illinois State Board of Education [ISBE], 1994, p. 178). However, a piece of writing may be grammatical, well-organized, and coherent without being well-reasoned, thoughtfully developed, or effective in any way.

Sometimes the legislation is more fully developed, calling for specific kinds of tests and certain standards. In Oregon, for example, legislation calls for "a series of performance-based assessments and content assessments benchmarked to mastery levels at approximately grades 3, 5, 8, and 10. The assessment methods shall include work samples and tests and may include portfolios" (Oregon Educational Act for the Twenty-First Century, 1995, 329.465; based on earlier legislation 329.025 and 329.035). More specifically than most states, the Oregon legislation also indicates the kinds of thinking to be tested. For what is called the Certificate of Initial Mastery, the assessment is to

   (a) Ensure that students have the necessary knowledge and demonstrate the skills to read, write, problem solve, reason and communicate;
   (b) Ensure that students have the opportunity to demonstrate the ability to learn, think, retrieve information and use technology;
   (c) Ensure that students have the opportunity to demonstrate that they can work effectively as individuals and as an individual in group settings; and
   (d) Ensure that student assessment is based on academic content standards in mathematics, science, history, geography, economics, civics, English, second languages, the arts and physical education. (329.465)

Most notable in this call is the emphasis on thinking, problem solving, and reasoning, and on working as an individual in group settings, neither of which we see in Texas or Illinois.

In New York the legislature long ago (1784) invested the control of education in a Board of Regents that has jurisdiction over all public educational institutions in the state including elementary and secondary schools, universities, museums, and other educational enterprises. The Board of

Regents stipulates academic areas to be tested, the nature of the exams, and the testing schedule in the state.

In most states the legislation is no more specific than to indicate the academic areas for testing, a very general set of standards, and the grade levels to be tested. In most of the legislation, statewide assessment is assumed to be the only necessary reform. Ordinarily the legislation does not call for changes in curriculum or the reeducation of teachers, even though education officials know that teachers may not have expertise in the areas to be tested, such as writing. They appear to assume that ineffective teaching and learning is a problem of moral deficiency and that testing will prompt both teachers and students to greater effort.

Kentucky, in a number of ways, is a notable exception to this national trend. Kentucky's assessment began as a result of a lawsuit brought by the Council for Better Education, composed of 66 school districts, 7 boards of education, and 22 individual students representing the districts served by the boards of education. Defendants included the Governor, the Superintendent of Public Instruction, the President Pro Tem of the Senate, the Speaker of the House of Representatives, and the State Board of Education and its members. The suit challenged the "equity and adequacy of funds provided for the education of young Kentuckians" (Legislative Research Commission [LRC], 1994, p. 6). The Kentucky State Constitution requires that the state provide for "an efficient system of common schools throughout the state" (LRC, p. 5). A judge of the Franklin Circuit Court agreed and declared that the General Assembly had failed to provide for such an efficient system. On appeal, the Supreme Court of Kentucky found that the system of common schools in Kentucky was unconstitutional.

The Kentucky Supreme Court declared that an efficient system must be maintained and funded by the legislature, be free, available, substantially uniform, equal, adequate for all Kentucky children, and monitored by the General Assembly to insure that there is "no waste, no duplication, no mismanagement, and no political influence" (LRC, p. 7). Further, the Court made clear that schools are operated on the premise that an adequate education is a constitutional right and that funding must be sufficient to provide an adequate education. It went on to define an adequate education as developing seven "capacities":

(i) sufficient oral and written communication skills to enable students to function in a complex and rapidly changing civilization; (ii) sufficient knowledge of economic, social, and political systems to enable the student to make informed choices; (iii) sufficient understanding of governmental processes to enable the student to understand the issues that affect his or her community, state, and nation; (iv) sufficient self-knowledge and knowledge of his or her mental and physical wellness; (v) sufficient grounding in the arts to enable each student to appreciate his or her cultural and historical heritage; (vi) sufficient training or preparation for advanced training in either academic or vocational fields so as to enable each child to choose and pursue life work intelligently; and (vii) sufficient levels of academic or vocational skills to enable public school students to compete favorably with their counterparts in surrounding states, in academics or in the job market. (Rose v. Council for Better Education, 1989, p. 37)

The Court explains in a footnote that "these seven characteristics should be considered as *minimum* goals in providing an adequate education. Certainly, there is no prohibition against higher goals."

It is important to note how much more elaborate Kentucky's statements of standards are than in other states. Nevertheless, the key word in these statements is *sufficient*. The Kentucky Supreme Court does not explain what sufficiency is or what communication skills are necessary to function in a complex, changing civilization. It left that for others. It does not explain why it believes that "sufficient knowledge of economic, social, and political systems" will enable students "to make informed choices." And it does not explain how "sufficient understanding of governmental processes" will "enable the student to understand the issues that affect his or her community, state, and nation."

I agree with Nussbaum's (1997) cogent arguments that the most troublesome issues facing all Americans now and in the foreseeable future are those of human dignity, equity, and justice. Making informed choices and understanding the issues in this area require far more than a knowledge of "economic, social, and political systems" and "governmental processes." For citizens to make informed choices and understand the issues in this arena, they must have a profound understanding of the human condition and the principles by which our systems affect it. That profound understanding entails empathy and compassion, but more than that it entails the ability to identify, explicate, evaluate, and to reject or modify the assumptions underlying the issues (see Nussbaum, 1997). The Kentucky decision does not make these dimensions of "understanding" and "informed choice" explicit, but it provides a framework within which others can make them explicit.

These events and decisions have given the Kentucky assessment what appears to be an advantage over those in other states. They have provided a broader framework for the assessment, and they have made the assessment part of systemic reform instead of an added feature that is expected to change the whole in positive ways with the least effort. While Kentucky redesigned the carriage of education in the state, most other states simply give the drivers bigger whips. The Kentucky Court decision makes that very clear:

This decision applies to the entire sweep of the system—all its parts and parcels. This decision applies to all the statutes creating, implementing and financing the *system* and to all regulations, etc., pertaining thereto. This decision covers the creation of local school districts, school boards, and the Kentucky Department of Education to the Foundation Program and to the Power Equalization Program. It covers school construction and maintenance, teacher certification—the whole gamut of the common school system in Kentucky. (Rose v. Council for Better Education, 1989, p. 42)

The Court also make its idealism clear.

We view this decision as an opportunity for the General Assembly to launch the Commonwealth into a new era of educational opportunity which will ensure a strong economic, cultural and political future. (p. 43)

A second difference is tied to the Court's use of the term *capacity*, a term that implies that knowledge alone is not enough. Knowledge must be coupled with the ability to do. If the General Assembly is to monitor the efficiency of the system, it will have to determine what students know and are actually "able to do" in real situations (LRC, p. 13), rather than only in test situations. The portfolio system is designed to assess what students are able to do in independent writing situations.

The General Assembly passed the Kentucky Education Reform Act (KERA) which called not only for high educational goals, an assessment to monitor and measure the extent to which schools meet the goals, and an "accountability system to reward schools improving their success with students and to intervene in schools failing to make progress," but also increased funding for teacher development. It authorized 5 days per school year for professional development and made a major commitment to funding the new education initiatives (LRC, p. 13). According to Starr Lewis, the director of the writing assessment for several years, the state legislature initially voted $2 million per year for funding six Writing Projects at universities around the state, each affiliated with the National Writing Project for teacher education in writing. In contrast, while the Texas assessment program includes sanctions for students and school systems, it makes only minor provisions for furthering teacher development.

Kentucky's initial legislation called specifically for portfolios as the means of assessment in all academic areas, a particularly important development for writing. Subsequently, a writing-on-demand provision was added. Further, the legislation calls for schools to develop "their students' ability to . . . use basic communication and mathematics skills for purposes and situations they will encounter throughout their lives" and to "connect and integrate experiences and new knowledge from all subject matter fields with what they have previously learned" (KRS, 158.6451). Combined with the requirement that "schools shall expect a high level of achievement of all students" (KRS 158.6453), these statutory requirements suggest that the kinds of writing tests that appear in other states will not be acceptable in Kentucky, at least not on their own.

Kentucky began with very high goals and a sophisticated view of assessment in writing, because, according to Starr Lewis, "a professional development program [in writing] . . . had been in place before the reform. The Kentucky Writing Project has been offering a variety of professional development [activities] for Kentucky teachers since 1986." She believes that it "contributed to having a foundation in place for the portfolio. For many Kentucky teachers, the idea of writing for different audiences and purposes and in many forms was not a new idea." Clearly, it also provided a core leadership group sophisticated about writing.

THEORETICAL BASES FOR TESTING WRITING

When the demand for testing is made law, someone has to decide what the tests will examine, what the content of the subject matter is, and what part of that subject is legitimate for testing. What is the knowledge that schools are responsible for teaching to our students? That may seem obvious. But it is quite complex and certainly less than obvious. States usually publish academic standards, but those are stated in such general terms that they cannot be used to produce test items. The knowledge and skills to be tested must first be defined. Take the case of writing. What kinds of writing are there? There are lists, legal briefs, poems, fiction, plays, notes to friends, business letters, diaries, arguments about policies, statutes, definitions, editorials, advertisements, jokes, interviews, human interest stories, and the list goes on. Which of these should students know? Which are worth testing? How may those be defined so that a test can be developed? Further, what will count for quality for each of the kinds of writing? When state departments of education set out to carry out their legislative mandates, they have to answer questions for every subject matter to be tested. Often, they set up a panel of people with the presumed expertise to answer these questions. The quality of the answers depends to some degree on the quality of the panel and their level of knowledge.

In Illinois

An Illinois document, *Write On, Illinois!*, lists 45 teachers from around the state who served on "IGAP Writing Advisory, Standard Setting, and Validation Committees." Most of the 45 members were from Illinois school districts, along with two from private postsecondary institutions, neither of whom are known specialists in writing (ISBE, 1994, p. 208). People on this list developed a theory of writing, claiming that the categories of persuasive, expository, and narrative represent "all three domains of writing." The rationale claims the test to be comprehensive, to cover the whole of writing. However, the typography excludes advertising, poetry, drama, jokes, and many other kinds of writing.

The definitions of the kinds of writing to be included on the tests are general, at best. *Write On, Illinois!* (1994) sets out the writing tasks as follows:

Persuasive: The assignments are of two types: the position paper in which students take a position and develop one side of an argument OR the problem/solution paper in which students develop both a problem and a solution. (p. 15)

Expository: Students are asked to explain, interpret, or describe something based upon background experiences or information provided in the prompt. These assignments differ from the narrative in that the writer does not include personal reactions or feelings in describing or presenting information. (p. 65)

Narrative: The assignments are of two types: the paper in which students recount and reflect upon a personally significant experience OR the paper in which students report and record reactions to an observed event. For assignments in which students share or recount personal experiences, they are expected to describe the action and their reactions. In reports of observed events, students narrate an event and describe the reactions of participants. (p. 119)

In 1999, Illinois revised their testing and scoring guides slightly. The persuasive and expository prompts are listed as a single category (persuasive/expository), presumably because they used the same criteria. The 1999 version removes the problem/solution essay and the stricture against including personal feelings in the expository. Otherwise, the definitions remain virtually the same. These three types of writing have been tested in Illinois since 1989.

In addition to claiming comprehensiveness, *Write On, Illinois!* claims that the Illinois test itself is exemplary:

Now, we the teachers in this state, are in control of a state writing test that is considered to be state-of-the-art. . . . The test is more intricate and useful in the information it gives us than any other writing test we have seen. (ISBE, 1994, p. 1)

If the test is state-of-the-art and if it focuses on skills that are truly comprehensive and fundamental, then it appears sensible to teach those skills and to track student progress on them over several grade levels. Once the student has mastered these fundamentals, he or she can then advance to the other skills that are important if he or she is to grow. However, the rationale does not identify the fundamental features of writing, what is fundamental about them, how they foster growth, nor what the other skills are that the test does not test.

The division of writing into three domains and the criteria used to evaluate writing identify the underlying theory as a version of current traditional rhetoric. Teachers who used this rhetoric in American schools and colleges from the nineteenth century on, focused on teaching the forms of writing and their parts. Typically, textbooks and teachers taking this approach to writing ask students to study models of the kinds of writing to be learned, conduct reviews of the parts of the models in class, then assign a piece of writing of that kind. As late as the 1990s, we find this approach to teaching writing prominently featured in secondary textbooks such as Warriner's famous *Grammar and Composition* series published by Harcourt Brace Jovanovich (Kinneavy & Warriner, 1993).

In Texas

The Texas Education Agency also put together a panel of teachers from schools, colleges, and universities around the state to develop a framework for curriculum in the English language arts including a theory of writing upon which their tests would be based. Essentially, the panel adopted a theory of writing developed by James Kinneavy (1971). A booklet entitled *The English Language Arts Framework, Kindergarten–Grade 12* [TEA *Framework*] (Texas Education Agency, n.d.) says that

Underlying the approach to language study is the view that the purpose of language is communication, the process of conveying meaning from a sender to a receiver. Any communication event has at least four variables. These variables— sender, receiver, situation, and signal—change from one communication event to another and thereby affect the nature of the communication event. (p. 7)

In addition, the theory claims that there are four purposes possible for discourse: informative, persuasive, literary, and expressive.

1. When the writer's or speaker's purpose is informative, the emphasis is on the situation or subject matter, and the "language primarily explores questions, provides information, and produces verifiable evidence for given questions."

2. When persuasive, emphasis is on the receiver (listener or reader), and the "language generally attempts to change the thinking of individuals or groups."
3. When literary, emphasis is on the signal, and the language is "intended to provide aesthetic pleasure to both sender and receiver."
4. When expressive, emphasis is on the sender, and the language reflects "an attempt by the sender to clarify what he or she thinks or feels as well as to provide an outlet for those thoughts and feelings." (TEA, n.d., pp. 7–9)

Examples of kinds of writing that exhibit each of the four purposes appear in Figure 3.1.

In addition, the TEA *Framework* sets out four forms of language:

1. "Description recreates an image or situation as the sender perceives it existing at a given time."
2. "Narration, in contrast to description, focuses on the dynamic nature of its subject and generally employs the logic of chronology to relate activity or change in the subject."
3. "Classification, which like description is static in nature, gives order to images and situations through comparison of their characteristics."
4. "Evaluation measures an object, process or idea against a standard or norm to arrive at a judgment about it." (pp. 9–10)

Contemporary composition theorists see many of these categories as problematic at best. For example, "proving a point by generalizing from particulars," which appears in the TEA *Framework* as an example of informative writing, virtually calls itself persuasive. For example, if we are trying to persuade people of something, we are clearly trying to persuade them that our ideas are correct, trying to prove a point by generalizing from particulars. Again while satire is usually classified as literary, the satirist is clearly trying to do more than evoke simply aesthetic pleasure. Think of Orwell's *1984*.

On the other hand, whether we agree with these distinctions or not, the categories of form (mode) combine with those of purpose to provide a far richer analysis of writing and a more sophisticated theory of writing than we find in Illinois. Any one of the forms might take on any one of the purposes. Thus, narrative may have an informative, persuasive, literary, or expressive purpose. At the same time, any of the purposes might take any of the forms. For example, evaluations might be informative, persuasive, literary, or expressive.

FIGURE 3.1. Purposes of Writing and Examples

Informative Focus on subject matter	**Persuasive** Focus on receiver	**Literary** Focus on signal	**Expressive** Focus on sender
1. Diagnosis	1. Advertising	1. Short story	*Individual*
2. Proving a point by generalizing from particulars	2. Political speech	2. Lyric	1. Journal
	3. Legal oratory	3. Narrative	2. Diary
3. News article	4. Editorial	4. Limerick	*Group*
4. Report		5. Drama	1. Manifesto
		6. Joke	2. Contract

These combinations provide a matrix of 16 cells, each with a generic writing task and each with many possibilities. Figure 3.2 attempts to lay out the intersections of these categories. In some of the categories, I have used real works (those with named authors or sources). Titles in quotation marks but with no source are simply hypothetical examples of the type. But I found it difficult to fill out this chart. The ambiguities are such that what qualifies in one slot often seems to qualify in another. While Chaucer's "Nun's Priest's Tale" of Chaunticleer and Pertelote is a literary narrative, it is also a cautionary tale, complete with a few morals. It appears to be aimed at changing the listener, like any fable of Aesop, and must be considered persuasive in that sense. When I first made the chart, I put Upton Sinclair's *The Jungle* under persuasive narrative. It certainly was persuasive in establishing the first of the pure food and drug acts. But it is a novel, and therefore, literary. When it comes to that, is there any piece of writing intended for a real audience that is not persuasive in some way? The newspaper reporter who talks about catching the reader in the first few sentences is clearly interested in persuading and has her eye on the reader even though the piece of writing might be considered informative.

While these and other ambiguities exist in the theory and are particularly noticeable in practice, they need not concern us any further here. The informative and persuasive purposes are parallel to the expository and persuasive writing in the Illinois theory. However, the literary and expressive purposes are quite different from anything in Illinois. Kinneavy (1971) explains that expressive writing may not be written to affect an audience in any particular way. It is often personal writing that is for the satisfaction of the writer. It may display very informal properties, but it may be

FIGURE 3.2. Texas Theory of Discourse

Mode	Purpose			
	Expressive	Literary	Informative	Persuasive
Narrative	Journal entry about event	Chaucer's "Nun's Priest's Tale"	*"How to Make a Bird House"	"How Big Tobacco Has Hurt the Public"
Descriptive	Diary entry about a place	Byron's "She Walks in Beauty"	World Book entry: sharks	*Edwards' "Sinners in the Hands of an Angry God"
Classificatory	"What I Love and Hate about School"	Stevens' "Thirteen Ways of Looking at a Blackbird"	"Kinds of Desert Animals"	*"Good and Bad Things about TV Ads" (Texas 8th-grade prompt)
Evaluative	Personal evaluation of a movie	Keats' "Ode on a Grecian Urn"	"The Best Homes for Gerbils"	*"Who should win the best relative of the year award?" (Illinois prompt)

*These types are tested in Texas. Literary descriptive was tested until 1993, after which it was eliminated from the pantheon of prompts.

more formal. The closest that Illinois comes to expressive writing is the personal narrative.

In Kentucky

The assessment program in Kentucky, according to Starr Lewis, did not have an explicit theory of writing at the beginning as did Texas. At the same time, those engaged in thinking about it had adopted James Britton's categories of transactive, literary, and expressive writing (Britton, Burgess, Martin, McLeod, & Rose, 1975). In addition, the assessment adds a category of reflective writing, which is highly specified as a letter to the portfolio reviewer that deals with the writer's own development as a writer and reflects on the pieces in the portfolio.

Britton's theory, like Kinneavy's, is based on communication theory that posits differences in the attention of a speaker or writer. That is, the communicator's attention may be focused on her own thoughts, the audience, the message, or the arrangement of words that make up the message. Britton calls these emphases, respectively, expressive, conative, informative or referential, and poetic. After examining writing done in British schools, he and his colleagues developed an analysis of three functions of writing that places conative and referential together in the same superordinate category of transactional.

Britton and his colleagues define *expressive writing* as "writing done close to the self . . . and revealing as much about the writer as his matter" (1975, p. 141). The types or genres of writing included here are much the same as in the Texas category of expressive. They define *transactional writing* as writing to achieve ends in the real world; as such, it includes writing to persuade and to inform. In persuasive writing, "action, behavior, attitude, or belief are influenced by reason, argument, and strategy; potential resistance is acknowledged, and an attempt is made to overcome it" (p. 146). They do not define informative writing as such, but rather its subcategories including eyewitness accounts, reports of events that are completed, generalized narrative, and more abstract kinds of writing, like writing about ideas and theoretical writing. In all of these, the assumption is that the writer's attention is focused primarily on the subject matter rather than on the audience.

Britton's final category is comparable to Kinneavy's literary writing in which the writer's attention is focused primarily on the code or the language used and its arrangement. Unlike the Texas assessment, Kentucky's includes this kind of writing.

Kentucky's *Writing Portfolio Development, Teacher's Handbook* [*Portfolio Development*] (Kentucky Department of Education [KDE], 1999b) provides examples of the kinds of writing that may be included in these three categories. Expressive writing includes personal narrative, memoir, and personal essay. *Portfolio Development* defines *personal narrative* as focusing on "a *single* significant incident from the writer's life . . . supported by details that emphasize the significance of the experience" (p. 13), a memoir as "focused on the significance of the relationship between the writer and another individual . . . supported by memories of specific experiences" (p. 13), and personal essay as "focused on a central idea about the writer or the writer's life . . . supported by a variety of incidents from the writer's life" (p. 14).

Literary writing explicitly includes poetry, short stories, and plays or scripts, with the latter including scripts for films, radio or television broadcasts, commercials, and videos.

Portfolio Development defines transactive writing as produced to get something done in the real world (e.g., to provide ideas and information for a variety of purposes, to persuade readers to support a point of view). These pieces are written for purposes and audiences beyond completing an assignment to demonstrate learning for the teacher. The idea of authentic purposes and audiences implies that students will actually use forms like those encountered in the real world. (p. 14)

Portfolio Development presents a long list of those forms: "business letters (to solve problems, respond to complaints, analyze situations, request action, etc.); reviews of books, films, videos, television programs, restaurants, cultural events, works of art, and so forth; commentary; handbook; editorial/letter to editor; pamphlet; interview; fitness plan, . . . lab reports for inquiry labs; cost analysis; academic journal article; feature article (newspaper, magazine)" and so forth (p. 15). Each of these can be regarded as a genre with its own conventions and variations.

As the description of these categories suggests, the architects of the assessment believed that writing should be for a real audience, rather than simply for a teacher, and for a real purpose, rather than simply for a grade or to show what had been learned. These ideas are in tune with the legislation's call for students to develop skills in communication "for purposes and situations they will encounter throughout their lives." Although both Texas and Illinois talk about audience and purpose, that emphasis is not apparent in the kinds of writing selected for testing in those states.

Writing for a real audience and a real purpose means that conventional assignments to write about a poem, short story, novel, or play that has been thoroughly discussed in class will not suffice for use in a portfolio, though they may have other instructional uses. It further means that conventional research papers, in which students take on some topic, find sources, and incorporate what they read into the resulting research paper, will not suffice. In fact, *Portfolio Development* explicitly warns against portfolio entries "for which the teacher is the audience and the writer's purpose is to complete an assignment." Particular "problematic entries" include the "'3.5' essays [five paragraphs explaining three points], 'canned' lab reports, research papers, book reports, and other reports *written to demonstrate learning to the teacher only*" (p. 14, emphasis in original). Since none of these represent writing for the real world, they do not meet the Kentucky Supreme Court requirements.

In short, the Kentucky theory has a bit in common with the theories in Illinois and Texas. All three emphasize narrative, exposition, and persuasion. However, the similarity ends there. Both Texas and Kentucky include literary and expressive writing in the underlying theories, at least. But in the Texas assessment such writing is dismissed for testing. Kentucky makes both forms a portfolio requirement. Kentucky is more concerned with real-world purposes and audiences than either Texas or Illinois.

In New York

New York appears to have no theory of writing associated with its old or new assessments. There is no concern with types of writing. Rather, the concern is with the theory of language arts: that becoming skilled in language arts requires work in reading, writing, listening, and speaking and that these should be integrated. New York's *Preliminary Draft Framework for English Language Arts* [NY *Framework*] (New York State Education Department [NYSED], 1994) states that it does the following:

- highlights purposeful language use as the basis for learning about language forms and conventions . . .
- focuses on what learners should be able ro do as the result of instruction and experience . . .
- describes skillful language use in learners at different stages of development . . .
- respects the integration of the language arts, for proficient achievement in reading or listening can only be revealed through writing or talk, and proficient writing or talk is measured by the responses of readers or listeners (p. 3)

Establishing language use as the basis of the reforms, the NY *Framework* outlines four areas of language use to be emphasized: language for information and understanding, for literary response and expression, for critical analysis and evaluation, and for social interaction. In each of these areas, the NY *Framework* outlines standards in combinations of "speaking and writing" and "listening and reading" for elementary, intermediate, and commencement levels. The individual statements about writing under each of these areas at the "commencement level" provide a picture of the kinds of writing that we might expect to see in the assessments. Under language for information and understanding, the following statements about writing appear:

- writing expository reports, including extended research reports that acknowledge the complexity of issues or subject matter, that document sources of information, and that are well organized to convey overarching ideas and supporting evidence and details
- using a wide range of forms, including those available through word processing and desktop publishing, to present information on a wide range of subjects clearly, coherently, and effectively, taking into account the nature of the audience and using various organizational patterns for developing the text (such as particular to universal, abstract to concrete, comparison and contrasts)
- in writing and oral presentation, supporting decisions about interpretations and relative significance of information with explicit statement, evidence, and appropriate argument (pp. 20–21)

Under literary response and expression, the NY *Framework* lists these standards:

- discussing in an interpretive essay how themes, events, characters, and setting contribute to the meaning and effect of a literary text
- discussing reasons for particular stylistic techniques and rhetorical devices (such as analogies, imagery, repetition, and rhythm) and their effects on audience interest and engagement in spoken and oral texts
- using in their own writing such literary structures and devices as stanzas, chapters [sic], metaphors, foreshadowing, characterization, description, symbolism, and different forms of dialogue and narration in a purposeful way to capture feelings, attitudes, and ideas
- explaining, orally and in writing, their responses to literature with reference to prior literary and life experiences, forming generalizations and distinctions as a result of hearing multiple viewpoints and recognizing multiple levels of meaning (p. 25)

Additional standards are listed in the NY *Framework* under language for critical analysis and evaluation:

- presenting conclusions orally and in writing from synthesizing material read and viewed, making generalizations based on patterns, trends, and themes
- responding to a text imaginatively based on an analysis or perspective about the text (for example, composing a letter from Ophelia to Hamlet written just before her "mad scene")
- explaining the impact of an author's own views and intentions on a text [sic]
- critiquing the completeness, clarity, and validity of technical reports by peers and others (e.g., reports of science experiments, social science research) through careful reading and knowledge of related subject matter and method (pp. 29–30)

Here it would be interesting to know what counts for a critique and for knowledge of method in social science research. Note that this area of language use, unlike the others, includes standards for revising and editing.

The final area is outlined by the NY *Framework* language for social interaction. It deals with "writing effectively in a variety of print and electronic forms on subjects related to school, work, social occasions, and community affairs, making effective connections among message, audience, and context." The forms that this writing might take include "letters to friends, relatives, or literary authors: group invitations to school or community events; introductions for an exchange student to the school community; and e-mail exchanges on topics of mutual interest with students in other schools" (p. 33).

Of the twelve standards that relate to kinds of writing to be done, only two have anything to do with literary writing: one of these is for response to a text while the other requires that students use literary techniques in their writing, not that they produce stories, poems, plays, or other literary forms. None deals with persuasion or expressive writing as kinds of writing or as goals for writing. Only two use terms such as *evidence, support,* and *argument.* These details suggest that New York is primarily concerned with expository writing, writing that treats subject matter, the truth about which is largely a foregone conclusion. The allusion to patterns of organization in one standard reinforces this idea. Further, six of the standards have to do with responding to other texts, strongly suggesting that a major purpose of writing in school will be to reveal the extent to which students understand and analyze other texts. More than any other state examined, then, New York's assessment can be expected to focus on what most states would call expository writing about texts.

While this focus on exposition appears to be a quite limited view of writing, it does have certain strengths. It recognizes the importance of content in writing and in the testing of writing. The foci on the functions of language for information and understanding, for critical analysis and evaluation, and for literary response and expression, all imply a concern for content that many states do not share in their rationales and that will have implications for classrooms.

In Oregon

In the absence of a theory of writing, Oregon made a choice to test narrative, imaginative, expository, and persuasive writing. This choice stems from current traditional rhetoric, the same tradition from which Illinois draws, but Oregon has included imaginative writing. Originally, when this typology of writing arose, George Campbell included imaginative writing as one of the major types, subsuming narration, description, and poetry (Berlin, 1984, p. 7).

Since Oregon presents no explicit theory of writing—though the state intends to produce one—the best one can do is to infer the underlying theory from their definitions of the kinds of writing. According to the *Oregon Statewide Writing Assessment: Test Specifications* in four booklets for Grades 3, 5, 8, and 10 (Oregon Department of Education, 1997) narrative writing "recounts a personal experience based on something that really happened." Narrative is different from imaginative writing in that the former is based on the real, "whereas imaginative is meant to be fiction," telling "about a situation or story based upon the writer's imagination" (p. 1). Expository writing "provides information, explains, clarifies, or defines. The writing informs or amplifies the reader's understanding." On the other hand, persuasive writing "attempts to convince the reader to agree with a particular point of view and/or to persuade the reader to take specific action. The topic must be debatable: there are clearly reasons for more than one point of view. Persuasive writing differs from expository in that it does more than explain; the writer also takes a stand and endeavors to persuade the reader to take the same stand" (p. ii).

Oregon requires these four kinds of writing probably because they appear to represent the major or most important kinds of writing or the fundamental skills of writing. The notion is common that if students are able to write these successfully, they will be able to write any more specialized types in the work world outside school.

LEGISLATION AND THEORY

Clearly, legislation sets the initial parameters for testing: what should be tested, the kinds of tests to be administered, and the grade levels to be tested. In addition, legislatures make the decisions about what the stakes in testing will be. In Texas, students must pass the writing assessment in order to graduate from high school. In New York, as of 2004, students will have to pass several Regents Exams in order to graduate, including the language arts exam that includes several writing samples. In Kentucky, some school districts tie portfolio scores to graduation, but the policy is not statewide. In Oregon, passing the writing test is tied to receiving a Certificate of Initial Mastery. If students do not pass the writing test, they must continue to take the test until they receive a passing score, or until they drop out of school, but the test is not tied to graduation. In both Kentucky and Texas, test results are used as one set of variables in a formula designed to rate school effectiveness, and the state may take action to remediate or eliminate poorly performing schools. In Illinois, while test results are published by school and grade level, the state has no power to intervene in the operations of the school. In addition, Kentucky and Texas have reward systems that allow for bonuses to teachers and administrators whose schools show a certain degree of progress.

As suggested at the beginning of the chapter, the kinds of writing assessments vary widely from state to state. The legislation and the theories underlying the assessments predict that the kind of writing emphasized also will differ from state to state. The Texas, Kentucky, and Oregon theories allow for the inclusion of literary writing in the assessments, whereas Illinois excludes it, and New York does not test it. Three states call explicitly for persuasive writing; Kentucky includes it under the broader category of transactional writing, but New York does not mention it. So there are clear differences in the kinds of writing to be tested and likely to be taught.

There are clear and important differences in the actual methods of assessment prompted by legislation. The state legislatures in Oregon and Kentucky require both on-demand writing and portfolios or samples of writing developed in class. The other states call for on-demand writing only. Later this book will examine what effects these various differences have for instruction and for testing.

CHAPTER 4

A Test Is Not a Test

People tend to think of a test as a list of questions or a prompt to which people must respond in order to reveal what they know or can do. The questions or prompt constitute an important dimension of the test, but it is only one part. In and of itself, the questions or prompts have little meaning. For us to make sense of a test, we need to know not only the character of its questions, but what counts as a right answer, and what counts for acceptable or passing performance. Other variables also make a difference in the character of a test: the time allowed, the number of questions or pieces of writing, the procedures for scoring, who does the scoring, and feedback to teachers and students.

THE TESTS OF WRITING

The variables above will play important roles in determining how writing is tested and, in turn, how it is taught. But the assessment process itself adds another layer of variables to the differences we already see among the state assessments. These variables include the grade levels of testing, kinds of writing tested, the nature of the writing prompts, their number and variety, the conditions for writing, and the criteria for judging the writing. The remainder of this chapter will examine these variables in some detail. Ensuing chapters will return to them as we examine how combinations of variables in different state assessments work together to affect instruction.

The grade levels tested are ordinarily determined by the state legislature, with most states testing at several different levels. The levels tested vary from state to state. For most of the 1990s Illinois tested at 3rd, 6th, 8th, and 10th grades. Kentucky originally tested at 4th, 8th, and 12th grades, but shifted to 4th, 7th, and 12th, because officials decided that 8th graders were overloaded with assessments. Texas tests at 4th, 6th, 8th, and 10th grades; New York at Grades 4, 8, and 11. Most other states exhibit comparable patterns of testing writing, although some do not test high school writing. The grades tested appear to affect the writing curriculum in the contiguous grades. In Illinois, for example, some school systems begin preparing students for the 3rd grade test in the 1st grade.

KINDS OF WRITING TESTED

It is important to consider the kinds of writing tested, because we have known for a long time that in other curricular areas what appears on tests influences what is taught in schools (Madaus, 1988). As we have seen, Texas begins with one of the richest theories of writing among all the states, providing the possibility for 16 fairly broad categories of writing. Yet, when the tests are created, the Texas Education Agency ignores most of the cells in the matrix. Texas test makers select only a few of the cells for use in the fourth and eighth grades. In 1993 and later, for example, fourth graders had to be prepared to respond to prompts that might require what teachers call the "how-to," an informative narrative that explains how to make or do something. In addition, they were responsible for writing the persuasive descriptive, the informative descriptive, the expressive narrative, and the classificatory. (Informative descriptive was later dropped from the testing program, leaving four possible prompts.) Fourth grade students received only one prompt on test day, but it might be any one of the four. Eighth graders also prepare for four different prompts of similar types. Tenth graders prepare only for persuasive writing, which can be either descriptive or classificatory persuasive.

The theory underlying the assessment, originally intended to encompass the universe of writing, loses its breadth and vigor in the process of designating specific types of compositions. Perhaps that loss is due to the pressure to perform on the types that are tested and perhaps by pressure on the state to make the testing more predictable. Whatever the reason, we are left with a relatively narrow list of certain types of compositions upon which teaching will inevitably focus.

In Illinois and Oregon, with simple underlying theories, the kinds of writing tested are comparable in all grades tested. In Illinois, students prepare for writing narrative, expository, and persuasive. In the 1990s, tests were structured so that each year, students would write on two of these types. In Oregon, students must produce at least three of the four types at a passing level. There is no disjuncture between the theoretical level and the level of selection of types for testing. But then, the theoretical levels are barely developed.

In Kentucky's portfolio assessment, the State Department of Education establishes requirements for what is to appear in the portfolio. Portfolios at fourth grade originally included six pieces of writing but have been reduced to four, one of which must be a letter to reviewers reflecting on the writer's own work. At the fourth grade level students may include one or two personal expressive pieces, one or two literary (imaginative) pieces, and one or two transactional pieces. One of the pieces must have its genesis in a subject other than English. At seventh grade the requirements are comparable with the exception that two or three pieces may be transactional. At the senior level the portfolio is to include five pieces plus the letter to reviewers: one personal expressive, one imaginative piece, and three transactional pieces. Of the five, two must originate in subjects other than English. The state expands on these types of writing, presenting lists of genres that qualify under each of the broader categories. Clearly, the spectrum of writing used in the Kentucky assessment is far broader than in any other state examined in detail in this study and broader than that in any of the other states with writing assessments.

Kentucky also uses an on-demand writing test as well. These tests focus on narration, persuasion, and responses to a "text, graphic, or chart" in "the various forms (letter, article, editorial, and speech)" (KDE, 2001).

In New York, the types of writing tested in 2001 are what other states would call expository. At the 3rd, 8th, and 11th grade levels, all writing in the language arts/English assessments involves responses to passages that are read aloud, read by the student in the testing situation, or recalled. Thus the types do not conform to the patterns found in other states. We might expect the writing programs in New York to be quite different from those in most other states.

PROMPTS, CRITERIA, AND BENCHMARKS:
CLARIFYING THE NATURE OF THE WRITING

Labels such as expository, narrative, and persuasive do not in themselves stipulate the kinds of tasks to be performed for the sake of assessment. Even narrative, which may seem fairly specific, encompasses everything from fairy tales and fables to novels, epic poems, some writing about history, and even directions. Persuasive writing may encompass an even greater breadth. We can argue that most pieces of writing intended for public consumption involve persuasion. Even a poet must persuade an audience to accept the conventions and assumptions if a poem is to work its magic on a reader. But the term also has extensive overlap with expository writing. In school parlance, persuasive writing ordinarily includes anything intended to convince someone to do something. In some circles, convincing others that some scientific principle is superior to other principles dealing with the same phenomenon is regarded as expository, because the writer's attention is focused on the subject matter, even though the subject is controversial. However, rhetoricians have begun to analyze the persuasive characteristics of scientific writing. Bazerman (1988), for example, has demonstrated the rhetorical and persuasive features of Newton's treatise on optics. What, then, is to count as persuasive, narrative, expository, or any other kind of writing in testing situations? The prompts, criteria, and benchmark papers clarify the real nature of the kinds of writing tested and the level of quality expected.

Writing Prompts

Prompts may be analyzed in terms of what they specify and do not specify: discourse type and/or discourse structure; topic and/or subject matter; data (not specified, specified, or provided), and audience (not mentioned, general, or specified). Sometimes prompts for the writing assessments examined in this study specify only the general discourse type. For writing portfolios in Kentucky, the state indicates only the general type of discourse to be included: transactional, personal, and literary or imaginative writing. Reflective writing is the exception. This requirement specifies the discourse type (a letter), the topic (growth as a writer), subject matter (your growth as a writer), and the data (pieces in the portfolio), but does not provide the data. The circumstances of the portfolio make it possible and necessary for students to collect their own data for all their writing. It does specify an audience, if only generally (a reader).

Texas prompts vary in these respects. Prompts for the "how-to" writing indicate the general discourse type by specifying the structure: "how to make." It specifies the topic (making a present), but not the subject matter, allowing the student choice of the specific present to write about. It provides no data and mentions no audience. Prompts for persuasive writing in Texas have much in common with those in other states. The following prompt from New Jersey is comparable to those in Texas and Illinois.

WRITING SITUATION

This year your school's soccer team won the state championship. When your team won, students ripped up pieces of the soccer field and cut the goal nets to keep as souvenirs of the game. As a result, the school principal has announced that any money raised this year by all the school clubs will go toward repairing the playing field and replacing the soccer equipment.

The principal's decision has created a controversy in your school. You decide to write to the editor of your school newspaper about this decision.

Writing Task B

Write a letter to the editor of your school newspaper. Explain your views on the principal's decision requiring that money raised by school clubs be used to repair the field and replace soccer equipment. Use examples, facts, and other evidence to support your point of view. (New Jersey Department of Education, 2000, p. 22)

This prompt specifies the discourse type (persuasion), the topic, the subject matter, and an audience. It tells students to "use examples, facts, and other evidence to support your point of view," but since it does not provide such information, students will have to pull that from their own experience if they can. In prompts for persuasive writing, Illinois does not ask the student to give evidence of any kind, only to "explain the reasons" that will convince someone. This may be an important distinction that leads to a difference between making a case and simply expressing wishes. However, it may be that New Jersey does not really pay attention to evidence. Only the scoring guide and benchmark papers will tell. It is, after all, almost impossible to produce evidence from memory on a relatively unfamiliar problem.

In a New York Regents examination, on the other hand, students have passages before them and must find what they think is evidence to make a case. As the tests are now constructed, two of the four prompts include passages that students must read in the test situation. A third prompt includes a passage that is read aloud to them, and a fourth prompt asks them to write about literary texts they have read in the past. One would expect that this feature of the New York tests would result in significant differences in instruction.

Criteria and Benchmark Papers

Most prompts make what students are to do generally clear. But while some prompts call for evidence, most do not explain what will count as evidence or what the quality of the evidence must be. If unconfirmed generalizations count as evidence, the writer is confronted with one kind of task. But if the writer must find concrete evidence that is confirmable and show how it supports the case being made, then the writer is faced with quite a different task. The demands of information processing in the second are much higher. Most writing prompts do not, perhaps cannot, make that information clear themselves. Sometimes, writing tasks are not as clear as those in the prompts above from New York and New Jersey.

For example, one kind of writing eligible for testing in fourth and eighth grades in Texas is the informative narrative. Writing in this category obviously includes news stories, descriptions of processes in science, or histories of an event. Presumably, this category of writing could include something as complex as Harvey's *Circulation of the Blood,* but in Texas the prompts do not request anything so complex. The following is a prompt for what Texas teachers have come to call "how-to" writing.

Think of something you could make as a present for a friend or a member of your family. Tell what you could make and explain all about how to make it. (TEA, 1993h, p. G5)

This prompt sets out the kind of task to be performed and suggests some of the boundaries of what counts as that kind of writing. But it does not explain "all about how to make it." The scoring guide for grade 8 states that the best papers, those receiving a score of 4, "contain a thorough presentation of a sequence or set of steps/stages in a process or activity. The responses are specific and well-elaborated, and the process or activity as a whole is presented in such a way that it can be clearly understood by the reader" (p. G21).

At the other end of the scale, the criteria for scores of 1 are these descriptions of failure:

- Responses that use the wrong purpose/mode; that is, they do not include the requisite components of informative/narrative writing. In these responses the writer does not order sequentially and/or delineate the steps/stages needed to complete a specified process or activity.
- Responses that are informative/narrative ("how-to") but are unsuccessful in their presentation. Responses that attempt to address the specified process or activity but are not successful [because they fail to present adequate information in a variety of ways]. (TEA, 1993h, p. G6)

The statement further explains that pieces at this level may lack clarity because they "contain incomplete or illogical thoughts, making the meaning unclear," because they "lack explicit connections between ideas, causing confusion," or because "the expression of the writer's thoughts is so confusing that the reader is left wondering what the writer is attempting to say." Further, "these responses may be poorly organized. The writers may present steps/stages in a random or repetitive fashion" (p. G6).

To demonstrate the need for benchmark papers to clarify the nature of the task, examine the following two responses. Consider how you might score them given the criteria for the two extremes.

For my sweet loving parents I'd make a special, long-lasting present. There present would be a beautiful, devine, and flying Stretch Mercedes. I would built an everlasting motor and engine, so they would never have a tragic and expensive problem. The other parts would be the same as the parts in other cars. The mercedes would be painted an elegant Cherry Red. I would trim their Cherry Red Mercedes in dazzling gold. I'll place gold rims on the Mercedes popular, new tires. The sparkling rims will have my parents initials placed in them. I would drop the Mercedes low with tinted windows for that young appeal. The inside will be eye-catching and glamorous. First of all, I would make suede, Cherry red seats to place in the Stretch Mercedes. The Stretch Mercedes will have three rows of seats, but the second and third row is further apart than the first and second row. I'll have several buttons built in for easier management. The buttons would be for the hot bubbling jakoozee, an ancient gold table, a luscious lunch, a breathtaking breakfast, a devine dinner, for the tinted windows to rise, for the sun roof, button to open the brand new trunk, button to play CD's and button to play records and tapes. This is what I would make my beloved parents. (TEA, 1993h, p. G7)

Here is the second paper. Would you score it higher or lower than the one above?

If I had to make something for my Mom and Dad I would make them a coupon book. The reason they need this coupon book is for chores. The book would consist of about 30 coupons. Coupons might say clean your room, kichen, bathroom, vaccum, dust or scrub toliets. Each coupon would have a price on it. When my parents need a chore done they would tear off a coupon and give it to me. They would pay me the price on there. I would need to make a coupon book each month if I wanted money.

   Making the coupon book is easy. All you need is 32 sheets of small paper, marker and a stapler. First put all the chores on 30 sheets of paper. (One per page). Then stack all the papers together. Put one sheet of paper on the bottom and one on the bottom. Label the P COUPON BOOK. Last, staple everything together. This is very easy and it's a fast way to make money on your own. (p. G17)

If you thought the first might be a 2, 3, or 4, you did not agree with the raters in Texas. They present it as an example of a score 1 paper. The comment recorded beneath the paper in the scoring guide explains why:

This response gives an elaborated and detailed description of the gift, the flying Stretch Mercedes. It also includes an explanation of the purpose of some of the features. However, there is no information on the process of assembling the Mercedes. (TEA, 1993h, p. G7)

In a sense, there is information about assembling the Mercedes. The writer presents a series of abstract steps that do not provide detail about how actually to install the various items, but he or she does present a general process. If we were to ask a congressperson how to get elected to the House of Representatives, she would likely give us a set of things to do such as finding a group to help us, raising funds, finding ways to have our views aired, meeting our proposed constituents, identifying issues that our constituents think are important, proposing ways to resolve those issues, and so on. Each one of these is a process in itself, which our congressperson would most likely leave unexplained, unless we asked a more specific question, how to go about raising funds, for instance.

The second response receives a higher score, 3. The comment following the paper explains as follows:

This response is a tightly controlled presentation, organized by stages. The first part of the paper explains what the gift is (a coupon book) with elaboration on what the coupons represent. The second stage, the actual construction of the book, provides specific details about supplies needed and the stages involved in the assembly. (TEA, 1993h, p. G17)

The piece of writing has some problems. It is questionable that the coupon book is a present, a condition that the prompt appears to require. The steps in making the book are not clear (e.g., size of paper, placement of the staples). There are other problems that are not addressed. How does one determine the cost of each chore? Why would parents use such a coupon book? So why does this paper score 3? It seems to me that the answer is not at all clear in the writing prompt and the criteria.

However, the illustrative papers in the scoring guide clarify these issues. The keys to success in the Texas "how-to" task are choosing a limited, concrete process and presenting the steps unambiguously enough for a reader to follow successfully. It has to be a concrete, Martha Stewart kind of task, not the assembly of a Mercedes or the process of thinking through a difficult problem. The benchmark papers clarify the task.

Criteria, Benchmarks, and Quality

Criteria and benchmark papers have another function, that of defining and making distinctions in quality. Scales for judging writing in state assessments are criterion- or standards-based rather than normative. That is, they are based on levels of performance that can be described and identified with considerable clarity. With a normative test, achievement is relative to the achievement of others taking the test; so we talk about falling above or below the mean or average performance. With standards-based tests we can talk about achievement in relationship to a set standard. With the normative test, we say that Johnny has a higher score than Sam, but we cannot say what Johnny's strengths or Sam's weaknesses are, only that their scores are higher or lower. A standards-based test is designed to indicate what a student's strengths and weaknesses are. Thus a score of 3 on a writing test will have a reasonably specific meaning as revealed through the criteria and the benchmark papers. With criterion-based tests, teachers will work to help all students achieve the highest levels possible for them. Teachers will be delighted if all students cluster at the top of the scale. A normative test used in a school would be deliberately designed to show wide differences among those tested. If scores clustered near the top of the scale, the test makers would scurry to include more difficult items in order to spread out the cluster. If student scores clustered together at the high end of a standards-based test, the test makers might break out the champagne first and then consider including more difficult items to provide a higher level of achievement for all to attempt.

Criteria and benchmark papers clarify what the standards are in criterion-referenced assessment. For the New York prompts, there are six levels of accomplishment based on five categories of criteria: "meaning, development, organization, language use, and conventions." Each of these is defined for teacher use in scoring the student responses.

Meaning: the extent to which the response exhibits sound understanding, interpretation, and analysis of the task and text(s).

Development: the extent to which ideas are elaborated using specific and relevant evidence from the text(s).

Organization: the extent to which the response exhibits direction, shape, and coherence.

Language Use: the extent to which the response reveals an awareness of audience and purpose through effective use of words, sentence structure, and sentence variety.

Conventions: the extent to which the response exhibits conventional spelling, punctuation, paragraphing, grammar, and usage. (NYSED, June 18, 1999, n.p.)

The teachers who rate the student responses are to use all these dimensions of quality to make an assessment of any paper. The actual criteria related to these dimensions mark the cut-off points between one level and another. New York presents a matrix for each of the four writing tasks in which criteria appear by level and category. The criteria vary slightly to conform to the different writing tasks. For the task entitled "Reading and Writing for Literary Response," the category of development includes the following criteria for the six levels of responses:

Level 6: develop ideas clearly and fully, making effective use of a wide range of relevant and specific evidence and appropriate literary elements from both texts.

Level 5: develop ideas clearly and consistently, with reference to relevant and specific evidence and appropriate literary elements from both texts.

Level 4: develop some ideas more fully than others, with reference to relevant and specific evidence and appropriate literary elements from both texts.

Level 3: develop ideas briefly, using some evidence from the texts—may rely primarily on plot summary.

Level 2: are incomplete or largely undeveloped, hinting at ideas, but references to the text are vague, irrelevant, repetitive, or unjustified.

Level 1: are minimal with no evidence of development. (NYSED, 1999, June 23b)

These criteria remain quite ambiguous. Could we ever know when something is "fully developed?" It seems to me that an idea would only be fully developed when nothing else could be added to it, when it would no longer be possible to detect additional nuances, applications, implications, and so on. Almost certainly, the criterion does not mean "fully developed." Rather, it means developed to some considerable extent, given the time available to the students. Key to the differences among these criteria are the statements about evidence. Level 6 calls for the "effective use of a wide range of relevant and specific evidence." Level 5 reduces the demand to "reference to relevant and specific evidence." Level 4 maintains the level of "relevant and specific evidence" but only as applied to "some ideas" that are developed "more fully than others." Level 3 includes only "some evidence," while evidence is absent from levels 1 and 2. While these distinctions are relatively clear, they cannot stand alone without examples. The benchmark papers provide those examples.

The benchmark paper illustrating score 5 is concerned with the proposition that "Both passages showed a teacher who made the lives of their students' better." Here is the section that deals with the poem:

Through a violent storm, passage II showed a teacher's attempts to calm the nervousness and anxiety of her students. After one student screams, "A tornado!" Mrs. Wells insists "it's just a drill." Her reassuring words are all the students need to perform the drill that's routine to them. Despite hard rain on glass, lightening in the stairwell, and the shuddering building, the children remain calm and focused. Their teacher is their savior as she instructs them to "Hang on!" With that the storm is over. With the help of Mrs. Wells the students have survived the first storm of their lives, perhaps making the ones to come somewhat easier. (NYSED, 1999, June 23b)

The score 5 writer quotes from the text twice and alludes specifically to several lines without quoting them. All of the data are cited in support of a claim, making them evidence. All are confirmable.

At the 4 level, the benchmark paper does not refer to the text in as much detail and with far less specificity. This paper promotes a proposition similar to the one above: "Teachers create a positive experience in some shape or form on the lives of their students." The writer specifies this claim a bit more in a later sentence: "mostly they teach their students about life and about themselves." The writer of the score 4 paper is succinct about the poem:

Mrs. Wells has a positive influence on the life of the narrator of the poem. During a tornado she reminds them of a drill in essence saving their lives. After the storm has passed she takes the students back to class to continue to learn. The narrator calls this a "mystery of love." Mrs. Wells teaches her class the importance of learning. (NYSED, 1999, June 23b)

This writer uses the events of the poem as evidence but does not cite the language of the text except for one phrase. None of the lower score papers quote the language of the text, and as the scores become lower, they present less and less evidence.

As we will see, other state assessments do not require evidence. The Illinois guide defines *support* as focusing on "the quality of the detail or support illustrating or explaining the reasons" for accepting or rejecting some policy (ISBE, 2000a, p. 153). Under support the *Sample Writing Materials* for Illinois states that for the highest score of 6, the best papers will reveal "extensive, in-depth development of Support using multiple strategies (e.g., explanation, evidence and example)" (ISBE, 2000a, p. 153). Some of the sample papers illustrating the criteria are responses to the following prompt:

The State Legislature thinks it is important for graduating high school seniors to have high quality knowledge and skills for college or the work force. To guarantee this, they are proposing a high school graduation exam. Students would be required to pass the exam before receiving a high school diploma.

Write a persuasive paper stating whether or not you agree that students should be required to pass an exam to graduate from high school. Give reasons why you think as you do. (p. 157)

It is interesting that the Illinois testing people saw no need to request any more than reasons, despite the fact that their own criteria call for more than reasons. Needless to say, students give no more than reasons. The following paragraph is from a top-ranked paper by a writer who rejects the idea of such an exam.

The State would like a high school graduation exam to be added to the many graduation requirements, but are they willing to accept the costs? Unfortunately, every high school will have an exceptionally large amount of student who don't pass the test and it's going to cost the state more money to put them through another year of high school. The students who don't pass the test are going to become majorely discouraged and may only become a burden to our society when we are paying for them while they are on welfare. (p. 172)

This paragraph is representative of the other four. The "support" is not support. Rather, it consists of additional claims that themselves require substantiation. The predictions that many students will flunk the test and cost the state huge sums of money for another year of schooling or that the flunkies will become discouraged and go on welfare are mere speculations that raise questions but do not present evidence in support of the writer's main contention. In fact, the predictions might be used in support of the opposite claim. If so many people are so poorly prepared as to flunk the test in large numbers, then that might be construed as evidence that a test is needed.

The point is that to understand what a state means by its criteria, we must examine the sample papers. The benchmark papers illustrate the criteria by making them concrete. They provide explicit examples of what the criteria mean. Generally, states use the criteria in combination with the benchmark papers to illustrate to teachers what they should strive for. The benchmark or illustrative papers become the guide to teaching.

Standards for Meeting State Expectations

All states provide, in addition to the scoring rubrics, standards for passing or meeting state expectations. In New York the standards are complicated by the use of the score on multiple-choice items in conjunction with the writing scores. The chart for interpreting scores on this combination indicates that if the total essay score over the four required essays is 8, or a 2 on each essay, the student fails, even if he or she has correct answers on all multiple-choice items. A total score of 9 makes a pass possible if the student has all multiple-choice questions correct. A total score of 12, or an average of 3, will allow a pass if the student also has at least 20 of 26 multiple-choice items correct. (The scoring guides do not explain how these combinations were determined.) We can assume from this that a score of 3 is the standard for passing the writing in New York.

Other states have standards even when the tests have no teeth (as in Illinois). In Texas the standard for meeting expectations is a score of 2 along with passing a certain number of multiple-choice questions on usage. At 10th grade level, this level of performance allows students to graduate. Schools are evaluated on the basis of the percentage of students reaching the level of 2 in writing along with the percentage reaching passing levels in other areas. These scores are grouped together along with those on other tests in a formula to determine school improvement over the course of a school year. A similar approach is used in Kentucky, with writing counting for a large proportion of the whole measure, but with the portfolios counting for far more than writing-on-demand.

In several states, the results of such formulas produce rankings which determine bonus money for principals and sometimes teachers or increased funding to schools. In the states using such a system that I know about, the school systems do not have to compete with each other for increased funding because there is no arbitrary limit as to how many schools or systems can reach a certain level of performance. That, of course, is regarded as an important virtue of standards-based testing.

Other Variables

Other important variables include the length of time that students have for writing, the amount of or access to information for the writing, scoring procedures, and the stakes involved. While Kentucky students have a school year and sometimes more to produce their writing for assessment, Illinois students have only 40 minutes, and Texas students have a school day. In New York, students have information provided to write about, while Illinois and Texas students do not. Kentucky and Oregon students have unlimited access to information for at least some of their writing. In New York and Kentucky, teachers in the buildings score the writing. In Illinois, and Texas, the student compositions go to Measurement Incorporated for scoring. Finally, the stakes differ considerably. In Illinois, how well students do on the test has no ramifications for them personally. In Oregon, students who pass receive a Certificate of Initial Mastery, which is recorded on the high school transcript. In New York and Texas, students must pass the tests to graduate from high school. These differences are almost bound to have an impact on the ways teachers prepare for the tests.

These, then, are the important variables that make the differences among tests and lead me to say that a test is not a test. The character of a test of writing is dependent, to some extent, on all of these variables. And there is a good chance that they are responsible for what students learn about thinking and writing. In the next eight chapters we will turn to those variables in greater detail and to the effects they have.

CHAPTER 5

High Stakes and Mediocrity in Texas

The Texas Assessment of Academic Skills (TAAS) in writing takes place in March at the 4th, 8th, and 10th grades. Other subject areas are tested on those grade levels as well. Because TAAS is a high-stakes assessment, several conditions come into play that do not appear in other states: writing tests and all other TAAS tests are handled under very high security measures; students must pass the 10th grade exit-level test to graduate from high school; schools must offer extra no-credit TAAS review classes for those who do not pass; and a system of rewards and punishments operates for teachers and administrators. All of these conditions add to the gravity surrounding the TAAS program.

The writing prompts arrive at the school under very high security. Mrs. Addison, the district TAAS coordinator in one suburb, tells about the hierarchy of authority responsible for maintaining the security:

> Every district has a district [TAAS] coordinator. Every campus has a campus coordinator. And then the teachers are the test administrators. So the test administrators are under the campus coordinator; the campus coordinator is under the district coordinator; and I, as the district coordinator, am under our superintendent, who also signs an oath of security that the whole district is secure. And then he's under the Texas Education Agency.

Mrs. Addison says that the "TAAS is the most highly secure test that we have ever seen." When the tests arrive, they are "sealed," and "numbered."

> The numbers of the test booklets are assigned to a teacher, who is the test administrator. Assigned, checked out to her officially, on a piece of paper, the morning that she gets them. They're checked back in the minute that she brings them back. She does not keep them—they're kept in a secure place, locked storage.

Every student must take the writing test unless exempted by Admission, Review, and Dismissal Committee or the 504 Committee, which Mrs. Addison explains refers to

> number 504 in the state policy which talks about the silent disabilities, which are dyslexia and those types of learning disabilities where a child would not be able to do a paper-pencil test. . . . So that committee also addresses whether he is able to take a group standardized test. And they address that once a year. Maybe he can take the math portion, but he can't take the language arts or the reading. So they make him exempt from that, if he takes any portions.

In order to meet minimum state standards and, at the 10th grade level, to graduate from high school, students need to pass writing with a score of 2- on a 4-point scale, complicated by the necessity to achieve a higher score on the objective test for mechanics and usage with that score than is required for a higher score in writing. This arrangement is similar to that in New York where the lower the writing score is, the higher the multiple choice score on reading comprehension must be (see Chapter 3). One Texas teacher explained that

> if they get a 4 then all they need to get correct on the objective [test] is eight questions. If they get a 3, they have to get eighteen questions correct. If they get a two, which is passing, they have to get 28.

Some districts do not allow students who fail the writing test to participate in commencement ceremonies. Other districts allow students to go through the ceremony of graduation but without receiving a diploma. For students who fail at the 10th grade level, most schools provide a TAAS review class to prepare students for taking the test again. Students do not receive credit for such classes.

There was a statewide push to have 90% of students pass by 1999. This push was tied to a system of rewards and punishments. One high-level official in an urban district told me that his superintendent had received a very large bonus because scores on TAAS had risen across that system as a whole. In the same system, all but a handful of principals had signed contracts in which they had given up their rights to legal recourse if their contracts were not renewed if their schools did not achieve the academic goals. Under that contract, however, they would be eligible for several thousand dollars in bonuses if the scores went up by some expected proportion based on past achievement and future expectations. In some districts, teachers would be eligible for bonuses if certain proportions of their students passed the writing assessment.

At the same time, the state board of education may place school districts under supervision and may even dismantle a given school district on the basis of low test scores, assigning the students to surrounding districts. Or the board may send in an "expert" educator whose task is to turn test scores around. We have interviewed in schools which had been taken over by an expert sent in by the state because of failure to improve. In one instance, that person had been in the process of releasing 10 teachers by early spring of the school year. Understandably, these conditions provide a tension-filled environment in many school systems.

Partly because of the high-stakes environment in Texas, the writing test is not timed. Texas administers only one prompt at each grade level, but students may take the full day to write the required composition. And teachers in several districts say that some students at each grade level sit until 4:00 P.M. working on the piece of writing.

THEORY OF WRITING, KINDS OF WRITING, AND CRITERIA

Chapter 3 shows that the theory of writing in Texas is complex and rich in contrast to theories underlying writing assessments in other states. The theory promised to produce a rich curriculum in writing including so many possibilities for use in schools. However, one needs to examine the assessments themselves to see the extent to which that promise was fulfilled. To do that I will turn to the prompts, the criteria for evaluating, and the benchmark papers that define the official state goals for writing.

From Theory to Practice in Testing

The Texas objectives for writing are loosely tied to the theory of writing. The first objective, for example, states that "the student will respond appropriately in a written composition to the purpose/audience specified in a given topic." Responding appropriately to an audience using forms appropriate to the task at hand is important to effective writing. The remaining Texas objectives have to do with organizing ideas (Objective 2), demonstrating control over the English language (Objective 3), and generating a "written composition that develops/supports/ elaborates the central idea stated in a given topic" (Objective 4) (TEA 1993a, p. 2).

The scoring guides for 1993 and later eliminate the literary purpose. They present three remaining purposes, persuasive, informative, and expressive. In all cases the definitions are somewhat simplified from the statements in the *Framework* (TEA, n.d.). Concerning informative writing, for example, the *Framework* states that the "language primarily explores questions, provides information, and produces verifiable evidence for given questions." The scoring guide states simply that in informative writing, "The writer selects facts so that information can be conveyed." The difference is that the processes of exploring and verifying have disappeared, an important loss.

Likewise with persuasive writing, the emphasis in the *Framework* statements is on "language [that] generally attempts to change the thinking of individuals or groups." This statement implies that all the language of a persuasive piece is involved in changing the thinking of others. The scoring guide statement seems far more simplistic: "The writer presents reasons in support of a point of view with the intention of influencing a particular audience" (TEA, 1993a, p. 2). This shift means that the writer is no longer responsible for the language of the whole, but only for some "reasons in support of a point of view." We will need to ask what constitutes a reason.

Another diminution in the scoring guides is their exclusion of evaluation as a mode of writing, leaving only the three remaining modes of writing: narrative, descriptive, and classificatory. The definitions of these modes also are simplified. Narrative becomes "events in a particular order." Gone is the entire emphasis on "the logic of chronology to relate activity or change in the subject" (TEA, n.d., p. 10). Classificatory writing becomes "group[ing] elements on the basis of their characteristics." Gone is the *Framework* emphasis on "giv[ing] order to images and situations through comparison of their characteristics" (p. 10). One can group things on the basis of characteristics without giving much order to them and without explicit comparisons or contrasts.

These changes from the *Framework* statements of the theory have the effect of simplifying the writing tasks involved in the assessment. In addition, the vision of writing that appeared in the *Framework* is significantly reduced from four purposes and four modes to three of each, with perhaps the most challenging gone. But the number of cells in the matrix, the types of writing available, is cut nearly in half, from 16 to 9.

As the tests are created, most of the cells in the matrix are ignored. In fact the tests require that students be prepared for the kinds of writing in only four of these cells in the fourth and eighth grades. In 1993 and later, for example, fourth graders had to be prepared to respond to prompts calling for informative narrative, persuasive descriptive, the informative descriptive, the expressive narrative, and the classificatory. (Informative descriptive was later dropped from the testing program, leaving four possible prompts.) Fourth grade students received only one prompt on test day, but it might be any one of the four. Eighth graders also prepare for four different prompts of similar types. Tenth graders prepare only for persuasive writing.

In most cases, that writing is usually specified further. For example, the fourth-grade teachers know to prepare for the "how-to," the only representative of informative narrative. In both fourth and eighth grades, classificatory writing is reduced to writing about the good and bad things about rainy days, recess, TV commercials, summer vacation, and so on. The examples provided in the *Framework* for classification include comparison, contrast, and definition. Comparison and contrast are chief strategies in almost any inquiry. Medical researchers study new diseases by comparing as many instances of the disease as they have data for. They look for similarities and differences that may provide insight into the infectious capacities of the disease. Social scientists study the behavior of groups of people through comparing and contrasting what they do under varying conditions, or they compare and contrast different groups under similar conditions. When we read a novel, we understand changes in characters by comparing and contrasting their reactions at different times and under various conditions. In a class that I studied a few years ago, students were actively engaged in comparing different features of a pair of Hogarth engravings to come to some understanding of what these eighteenth-century pictures conveyed (Hillocks, 1999). Any inquiry involves comparison and contrast as a means to understanding new problems or old ones reconsidered. Such work is a very important part of learning how to learn. However, in Texas, comparison and contrast has been reduced to making lists of good and bad things, lists which require only unsupported opinions. There is no reason to compare or contrast to develop an interpretation.

Another type of writing in eighth grade is "persuasive descriptive." The topic in one of the scoring guides for helping teachers learn the rubric is illustrative.

The principal of your school is thinking of starting a program in which eighth graders would help second and third graders who are having trouble with their school work. Write a letter to your principal in which you state whether or not you think this program is a good idea. Be sure to give convincing reasons for your position and to explain your reasons in detail. (TEA, 1993j, p. G5)

Why this is called persuasive-descriptive rather than evaluation, I am not sure, except that evaluation has been removed from the list of modes. It is interesting to note that while a strong persuasive letter would explore both the strengths and weaknesses of the principal's plan, this assignment calls only for "whether or not you think this program is a good idea," a presentation only of one side or the other, but not both. A more sophisticated prompt might require that the writer provide both sides of a case or acknowledge the other side and argue a choice for one. By contrast, the persuasive descriptive requires that the writer support only one side of an issue.

In the process of test making, the theory of writing originally intended to account for the universe of discourse is substantially reduced to the point where it deals with only a fraction of that universe. My guess is that the narrowing of the possibilities is due to the exigencies imposed by the time for testing and the fear of making the test too demanding. Politicians who wish to demonstrate their capacities as educational leaders will not want a test that is too demanding. One goal of the test makers is a test that will easily demonstrate change in students achievement, not one so demanding that it results in further deterioration of scores. Test makers are restricted by their own lack of knowledge and that of teachers for whom the legislature has failed to provide significant funds for professional development. That is, they have to work with the status quo of teacher knowledge. For a variety of reasons, Texas school children are left with a very narrow range of writing. And in the 10th grade, the state tests only persuasive writing. It is predictable that, in some schools, persuasive writing of the kind required on the tests will be the solitary focus of attention to writing in the 10th grade.

Criteria

The criteria for judging student writing in Texas reported in the scoring guides are called "focused holistic" criteria. They include the following: (1) "writing to the purpose/audience specified in a given topic," (2) "organiz[ing] ideas in a written composition on a given topic," (3) "demonstrat[ing] control of the English language," and (4) writing a composition that "develops/supports/elaborates the central idea stated in a given topic" (TEA, 1993j, p. G2).

The guides go on to explain these criteria and to differentiate among the scores of 1 to 4. The scoring guides make the point that the prompt must be addressed (Objective 1). If not, the composition will not be scored and the writer will receive a score of 0. They call for a response to have a consistent organization. They also call for "consistent control of the English language." They recognize that students are writing under pressure without chances for feedback or much reflection, and that, even in the best papers, some "conventions" may be violated. The student is not penalized for these kinds of errors "unless they are so frequent or severe that they interfere with the reader's ability to understand the response" (TEA,

1993a, p. G2). The scoring guides claim to be more concerned with ability to present ideas clearly so they flow smoothly from word to word, sentence to sentence, and paragraph to paragraph. High-level responses are also relatively free of awkward phrases; choppy, simplistic sentences; or usage errors that may distract or confuse the reader. In addition, they are often characterized by "effective, precise choice of words" (TEA, 1993a, p. G3).

The scoring guides devote the most space to discussions of elaboration, such as the following:

An essential part of successful writing is the effective use of support or elaboration, which requires the student to develop clearly, logically, and completely those ideas that lead the reader toward an understanding of the writer's purpose in the response. The degree to which support or elaboration is achieved, therefore, is dependent not only on the student's ability to generate ideas, but also upon the extent to which the student provides the reader with a detailed explanation of those ideas. . . . The more thoroughly and precisely each idea is developed with specific details, the stronger and more complete the support or elaboration will likely be. (TEA, 1993a, p.3)

While we can hardly disagree with this statement, it will be necessary to see what it means exactly, to see what actually counts for the "detailed explanation of . . . ideas." Fortunately, the guide presents examples of reasons given at different levels of elaboration. An example of the Texas analysis of least to most developed ideas appears in Figure 5.1. The examples are based on a response to the following exit-level prompt:

Some people believe that all teenagers should be required to perform one year of unpaid service for their community right after they graduate from high school. This community service might include helping to clean up parks, delivering food to the elderly, or working in a hospital.

What is your position concerning this issue? Write a letter to your senator in which you state your position and support it with convincing reasons. Be sure to explain your reasons fully. (TEA, 1993a, p. G5)

The wording of this prompt is important and is reflected in the analysis of what counts for elaboration: "convincing reasons" and "explanations of the reasons."

Consider, for a moment, what the Texas guide calls the "fully elaborated reason." When we talk about an argument that something should or should not be done, we may have a major claim about what to do and several reasons for doing it or not doing it. The reasons may be called subclaims, which themselves require some kind of support. If, for example, a teenager is arguing to a parent the need for buying a used car, she might

FIGURE 5.1. What Counts for Elaboration

Exit Level—Persuasive

BARE REASON

I am against the idea of making all high school graduates serve the community since it will <u>interfere with our plans</u>.

EXTENDED REASON

I am against the idea of making all high school graduates serve the community since it will interfere with our plans <u>to go to college or work to pay for things</u>.

SOMEWHAT ELABORATED REASON

I am against the idea of making all high school graduates serve the community since it will interfere with our plans to go to college or work to pay for <u>necessities like a Nissan 80 ZX. Also, some people have to help their parents with rent and grocery bills</u>.

MODERATELY ELABORATED REASON

I am against the idea of making all high school graduates serve the community since it will interfere with our plans to go to college or work to pay for necessities like <u>$350.00 a month car and insurance payments</u> on my Nissan 280 ZX. <u>Making your payments is important on your first loan so you can establish good credit.</u> Also, some people have to help their parents with rent, groceries, and <u>medical bills</u>.

FULLY ELABORATED REASON

I am against the idea of making all high school graduates serve the community since it will disrupt and interfere with our plans to go to college or work. <u>Students who plan to go to college will forget most of what they have learned if they spend a year away from school. Their chances to achieve a high GPA will be hamstrung. As far as plans to work go, some graduates, like me</u>, plan to work for necessities. I have to pay $350.00 a month car and insurance payments on my Nissan 280 ZX. Making your payments on your first loan is important so you can establish good credit. Also, some people have to help their parents with rent and groceries, and medical bills.

(From TEA, *Exit Level 1993–1994 Writing Collection Scoring Guide For Persuasive Writing* [1993a], p. G6.)

claim that they should buy a particular 1996 Camry because it is in good condition, it is priced appropriately for the budget available, the Camry has a reputation for low rates of mechanical failure, and she can expect to get 5 or more years of use from it. Each of the four reasons is itself a claim that requires support. When we provide support for the subclaims in an argument, we usually provide evidence, hard data about the "facts of a case" that are purported to be true. Evidence that our used Camry is in good condition, might include the depth of tread on the tires, the sound of the engine as it starts and idles, an inspection of the body for past accidents, and the results of an inspection by a trained mechanic.

Sometimes such an argument also includes statements that serve to explain why data support a claim. These are general rules that parties in a discussion can accept as true or at least are willing to agree to tentatively. One indirect piece of evidence that the Camry is in good condition is that the current owner is a 67–year-old grandmother. With such evidence we almost always need to explain why it supports the claim. In this case, it is the general rule, our belief that older women tend to drive carefully and take good care of their cars. Such a statement is called a warrant because it explains why data are appropriate in support of a claim. That is, it warrants the data. (See Toulmin, 1958, for a complete treatment of this analysis of argument.)

If we use the framework of major claims, subclaims, evidence, and warrants, we can analyze the "fully elaborated reason" as follows:

Main Proposition: I am against the idea of making all high school graduates serve the community since it will disrupt and interfere with our plans to go to college or work.

Subclaim 1: Students who plan to go to college will forget most of what they have learned if they spend a year away from school. (Therefore, the writer implies)

Subclaim 2: Their chances to achieve a high GPA will be hamstrung.

Subclaim 3: As far as plans to work go, some graduates, like me, plan to work for necessities.

Evidence: I have to pay $350.00 a month car and insurance payments on my Nissan 280 ZX.

Warrant: Making your payments on your first loan is important so you can establish good credit.

Subclaim 4: Also, some people have to help their parents with rent and groceries, and medical bills.

There are other ways to analyze this "fully elaborated reason." What it suggests is that most of the subclaims remain unsupported, which in turn leaves the major claim open to serious question. The strongest part of the argument is subclaim 3 which is followed by evidence of a sort and a warrant that helps to establish the need to pay bills for what the writer calls necessities. (It is, of course, problematic that the Nissan 280 ZX is a necessity.) But that is clearly the closest that the elaboration comes to presenting evidence. Subclaims 1, 2, and 4 remain totally without support.

What is disturbing about this example, provided so that teachers will understand what is meant by elaboration, is that it is likely to become the standard toward which teachers push. The example says in effect that evidence is not necessary. When such examples are presented as exemplary, they effectively lower the standard for persuasive writing, even, I suspect, when the persuasive writing in the classroom is not for the writing tests.

Part of the problem is the structure of the writing prompts. Two directors of writing assessments told me that they could not hold students responsible for content. Therefore, the prompt writers strive to find issues about which students will have opinions that they can state in the form of reasons in support of the major position adopted in their writing. However, only when writers know the data surrounding an issue in some depth can they present truly solid arguments.

On the other hand, many Texas teachers tell us that they tell their students to "make up evidence." The following piece from the TAAS *Exit Level Writing Collection Scoring Guide for Persuasive Writing, Musical Lyrics* (TEA, 1993b) is an example of a writer's taking that advice seriously or an example of someone whose cousin and best friend both had the ill luck of doing what the music told them to do and ended in very serious trouble. The prompt sets up the following problem: "There are people who do not like the lyrics of some of today's music and believe that music with these lyrics should not be played on the radio. What is your position on this issue?" The directions tell students to write a letter to an editor of a newspaper. Here follows the response from the most unfortunate cousin and friend, whom I will call Ronald.

Dear Editor,

It is thought by many people that music with unacceptable lyrics promotes unacceptable behavior, therefore the music should be banned from the radio. I happen to be one of those people and I think that all vulger music and lyrics should be banned from the radio and music video television stations.

First of all MTV reporters have been reporting that at least 25 cops have been killed in the Los Angeles area. The cause of this has been from listening to the fairly new release of Ice T's "Cop Killer." Kurt Loder, an MTV reporter, has been researching the causes of the cop killings. It has been reported that 3 out of 5 cop killings were committed by teenagers who are fans of Ice T. Most of the alleged murderers were listening to the radio which just happened to be playing "Cop Killer" just before the homicide occured. Jake, my 18 year old cousin, is a megafan of Ice T. He believes in the cause that Ice T stands for and will do anything that his songs say is cool. I found out last week that Jake has been arrested for the killing of a police officer. He will go to trial in December and will plead guilty to 1st degree murder of a public official. This could get him fifty years to life imprisonment. If songs like "Cop Killer" are banned from radio it would keep a lot of kids like Jake from being influenced to commit illegal acts such as killing cops or anyone for that matter.

Another song with unacceptable lyrics is "O.P.P." which was released by Naughty By Nature. This song promotes premarital sex and affairs outside of marriage. It has been proven that 4 out of 5 girls who have premarital sex or affairs result in pregnancy. Five out of every 8 women who have premarital sex are teenagers who listen to Naughty By Nature. My best friend, Beth, lives in Miami, Florida. She got pregnant last year at a party while listening to "O.P.P." She now has a beautiful set of twins, but she is on welfare because her parents disowned her and her boyfriend left her. Her doctor has treated many teenage girls who have got pregnant at parties and who were listening to "O.P.P." by Naughty By Nature. If music like this could be stopped then this would not be a song listened to at parties and then maybe the teen pregnancy rate would go down.

Banning music with unacceptable lyrics from the radio is an excellent idea. I urge you to go along with me on this issue for the sake of the children and for our country. (pp. 25a–25b)

Even if Ronald created the evidence, it is apparent that he learned what kind of evidence is necessary to make the case: statistics about the relative frequencies of the problems, personalized examples of specific cases, and testimonies from people with specialized knowledge. I suspect that Ronald may have intended the piece as a satire of the prompt or the attitudes of some people toward the issue. Or perhaps the writer simply thought to make it soap-opera comic. Certainly, he could not believe that any thoughtful reader would be convinced with his data. I have found no other essay among the Texas examples that is as concrete in elaboration as this one.

Texas prompts for 10th grade (the exit level) always involve arguments of policy, in contrast to those in Illinois which may be arguments either of policy or of judgment (e.g., best relative). Arguments of policy, however, almost always entail arguments of judgment, the results of which become the basis for whatever policy is being argued. In the example above, the writer argues that certain lyrics have evil effects; therefore, they should be banned. Since he has chosen to use as evidence the murders of police and unwanted pregnancies, he does not have to argue that they are evil.

He can assume that we will accept that. But he does have to show that the effects exist. If he does so successfully, we may accept his claim that such music should be banned.

Another writer, Claudette, takes the opposite position, that the effects of such music are not maleficent. She will have two strategies open to her. Either she will have to argue that censorship of lyrics is unconstitutional under the First Amendment or that the lyrics in question have no evil effect. For different reasons, either one of these choices is quite difficult. To elaborate fully on the first, she will need to know a good deal about First Amendment law and precedents, areas with which most teenagers of my acquaintance are unfamiliar. To elaborate on the second, she will have to prove that there are no evil effects. But proving that something does not exist is even more difficult than proving that it does, especially something as abstract as an effect. When charges of witchcraft were brought against people of Salem, they were unable to prove their innocence. How can you prove that you do not engage in a practice? What would the evidence of its nonexistence be? You can only disprove evidence brought against you.

Yet we can expect most teens to stand for what we might call freedom of lyrics. When they make that choice, they almost necessarily are driven to material that is, at best, only peripherally relevant. Claudette begins with a definition claiming that "censorship can be summed up by saying that a limit or restriction is being put on someone's idea, thought or action. Is that anyone's right? I think not!" Claudette goes on to a paragraph of revisionist history that claims that the revolutionary war was fought to gain

independence to speak and say what we please, to do as we wish and worship as we would like. Now, the tables have turned and in 1992 we then turn our nose up at those who speak their opinions freely and in some cases try to indict them. The point I'm trying to get across is that this country's ancestors shed precious blood just for the basic right such as an individual saying what's on their mind and it's not right for some conservative government to say "Shhhh!" (TEA, 1993b, pp. 23a–23b)

This essay continues with a paragraph concerning the necessity of being "blunt." Claudette tells us that "with such catastrophes like drugs, teen pregnancies, and AIDS you can't hold anything back, whether it be a statement of total ignorance or helpful knowledge that would keep someone from *being in* total ignorance." In a fourth paragraph, Claudette comments that anyone so weak as to let "a song influence them to the point of shooting a cop, killing themselves, or taking drugs," that person should get psychological help" (TEA, 1993b, pp. 23a–23b).

Nearly the entire essay is composed of material that is irrelevant to the issue, not to mention misinformed. But the prompt is surely the culprit. If Claudette is to produce an elaborated essay, she either has to make up evidence as did Ronald, or she has to present whatever she can think of that is a bit related to the task given in the prompt. If she organizes what she has to say about the prompt issue and writes enough sentences related to each point, she receives a high score.

My grandmother used the Scots word *blether* as a noun or verb to indicate talk that was unfocused, rambling, and more or less thoughtless. It strikes me that *blether* is a good word to indicate the kinds of writing that these state prompts invite. Students cannot be held responsible for content. There are no criteria for judging the relevance of the subclaims supporting the main claim or the accuracy and relevance of the evidence supporting the subclaims. Texas presents several sample papers given the highest scores. Teachers use these papers along with the criteria to help their students learn how to become evaluators of writing.

A book by Fuller (1994), intended for exit level TAAS preparation, explains that scored student samples appear in the *Handbook* (TEA, 1991c) and comments:

Teachers around the state are teaching the criteria of "0" through "4" papers by having students read these student samples, studying [*sic*] them against the criteria in the guide, discussing [*sic*] the critiques, and then becoming [*sic*] the grader by evaluating them. In becoming good evaluators, they are writing on target for TAAS. (It works!) (p. 9)

However, in every paper provided, the support and elaboration is irrelevant, facetious, inaccurate, or sometimes false. When teachers use these papers as models of good writing, irrelevancy, facetiousness, inaccuracy, and falsehood become the standards for good writing. Worse, my guess is that students learn to view writing as a nonserious enterprise, a matter of form without content, the domain of "blethering."

While elaboration appears to be the most important criterion, there are several others. Figure 5.2 presents the criteria for a score of 4 on the persuasive prompt. This guide clearly emphasizes elaboration. At the same time, it does recognize the need to attend to consistent organization, control of written language, effective word choice, descriptive detail, and so forth.

It is apparent from these criteria and the writing prompts that the focus in Texas is on the form of the writing rather than the content. The writer needs to have enough sentences on a particular point to suggest elaboration, even though it does not really mean support. And while Texas begins with Kinneavy's theory of writing, it significantly reduces it to something clearly more akin to current traditional rhetoric that focuses almost exclusively on form.

FIGURE 5.2. Texas Criteria for a Score of Four on Persuasive Writing at the Exit Level

SCORE POINT 4

4 = RESPONSES THAT ARE CONSISTENT, ORGANIZED, AND ELABORATED
ATTEMPTS TO ADDRESS THE PERSUASIVE TASK. THESE RESPONSES
ARE UNIFIED AND EASY TO READ. THE INCONSISTENCIES THAT MAY
OCCUR ARE OVERWHELMED BY THE OVERALL QUALITY OF THE
RESPONSES.

- These responses contain <u>specific, well-elaborated</u> reasons. The reasons are
  presented in such a way that they provide convincing support for the writer's
  stated position.

- These responses are characterized by most of the following:

    - A consistent organizational strategy. Although minor inconsistencies may
      occur, the responses have a clear sense of order and completeness. If
      otherwise well-written responses end abruptly because the writers have run
      out of space, the papers are still eligible for a 4.

    - A consistent control of the written language. Though the writers may not
      incorporate all of the appropriate mechanics or conventions of language,
      the responses are nevertheless effective by virtue of their overall clarity of
      expression and fluency.

    - Highly effective word choice, including especially apt or striking words,
      phrases, or expressions.

    - Particularly descriptive details or illuminating illustrations.

    - Especially thoughtful reason or reasons that offer an unusual perspective or
      a broader view of the situation.

    - An unusual persuasive strategy that is carefully carried through.

(From TEA, *Exit Level 1993–1994 Writing Collection Scoring Guide For Persuasive
Writing*[1993a], p. G 23)

The State Standards

But we have not examined the standards for meeting state expectations.
A score of 2 is sufficient to pass the exit-level test. We need to examine a
benchmark paper to see what a 2 is. The Texas Education Agency prompt
concerning community service contains no information about community
service, the legality of such a program, or data about real or fictional com-

munity service projects. The student responding to this prompt must pull all reasons and explanations from his or her own experience. The prompt, however, calls only for reasons and explanations, not evidence. Here is a response rated as 2, passing.

Dear Senator,
As a teenager about to graduate from high school, I think it is rather unfair to do these services without being paid for it. Therefore, I believe we shouldn't have to do these services right when we get out of high school.
First of all, when people graduate from high school, a majority of the people will either go to a junior college or college. During the summer break, most of them will get jobs to help pay for college. Another reason is, it takes money to drive around town and do these services.
Personally, I think you all should use all of the unemployed people that re-ceive unemployment checks because they're the ones that have nothing to do.
These are the reasons why I think we shouldn't have to do these services.
Sincerely,
(TEA, 1993a, p. G14a)

The first reason given for opposing the community service proposal is that "it is rather unfair to do these services without being paid for it." Focusing on pay evades the problem of requiring service of teenagers, which given required school attendance and the military drafts of the past is not automatically dismissible. In addition, there is no argument as to the unfairness of not being paid. The writer must assume that his assertion of unfairness is true *prima facie*. This is probably the strongest reason that the writer presents, but it remains unsupported and unex-plained. The second reason presented is that "when people graduate from high school, a majority of the people will either go to a junior college or college." If there were a law requiring that high school graduates had to provide full-time community service during their first year out of high school, it would be challenged not because "the people will either go to a junior college or college," but because it is considered an infringe-ment of human rights. There will be arguments on the other side as well, since it is already the case that some schools require community service for graduation. The final reason is "it takes money to drive around town and do these services." This reason assumes that the service will require personal transportation and that expenses will not be paid. However, it simply fails to address the central problem. The response is shallow, totally devoid of evidence, and certainly fails to persuade anyone of anything.

The Texas scoring guide commentary on the paper makes this evaluation:

This controlled, organized response takes a clear position against requiring community service. The section discussing the necessity of working for pay is somewhat elaborated while the solution adds elaboration by offering a ready alternative (the unemployed) to employing high school graduates. In total, a minimally sufficient amount of evidence is provided, and the response demonstrates minimal success with the persuasive task. (TEA, 1993a, p. G14a)

The scoring guide does not contain any explanation of what counts as evidence. So there can be no explication of the phrase, "minimally sufficient amount of evidence." While the commentary praises the "ready alternative (the unemployed)," the suggestion simply evades the central question. Is it just or appropriate to select any defined group of people in the community and require that they do anything? Suggesting the use of the unemployed implies that the idea of conscription for unpaid work is just and appropriate, the very idea that the writer opposes.

This sample of student writing and its commentary indicate that Texas accepts a very low level of performance as passing. What we really have is a badly stated proposition supported with three generalizations that are themselves poorly explained and unsupported, along with the statement of an alternative that serves to undercut the writer's main contention. But it meets George W. Bush's standards for excellence. In 1999, he boasted:

> In 1994, there were 67 schools in Texas rated "exemplary" according to our tests. This year, ther are 1,120. We are proud, but we are not content. Now that we are meeting our current standards, I am insisting that we elevate those standards.

When Bush calls for higher standards, he is not insisting that the criteria for judging the writing be upgraded. Rather, he is demanding that greater percentages of students be brought to the passing level, the level exemplified by the piece of writing above. To make the boast a bit more honest, we might restate it this way:

> Now that we are meeting our current very low standards, I am insisting that we bring more and more students to meet this same low standard.

The kind of writing prompt and the attendant criteria that reward organized blether are not necessities of life. One alternative involves the presentation of data relevant to the issue, evidence that will allow the support of several different positions on the issue on which a prompt focuses. We have seen one example of such a prompt in New York in Chapter 3. In Texas, with virtually a full school day to write the response, such data sheets could be a feasible part of the writing test.

Materials for Teaching

Early in the development of TAAS, the Texas Education Agency published *TAAS and the Composing Process: A Composition Handbook, Exit Level, Grades 9 through 12* [1991c]. The introduction states that the handbooks were developed as a result of "numerous requests" during the 1989–1990 school year "to provide schools with additional information concerning the written portion of the Texas Assessment of Academic Skills" (p. 1). The *Handbook* has four announced purposes: (1) "to show the connection between classroom writing and the TAAS writing test"; (2) "to provide information on the writing process and how this process can be applied by students when writing for TAAS"; (3) "to offer detailed information on scoring"; and (4) "to provide sample papers, along with detailed annotations, for each type of writing eligible for assessment on the TAAS test." Over half the *Handbook* is taken up with presentation and explanation of the criteria and the presentation of sample papers at each level of accomplishment along with commentaries.

One section of the *Handbook*, however, presents the writing process and how it relates to writing for TAAS. This discussion and attendant examples are related to limiting the use of water by Texans. The idea is that students begin with a prompt, do brainstorming, focused free writing, webbing, and so forth to develop a store of ideas so that "their compositions will more likely reflect the degree of specificity, elaboration, and organization required for success."

A short section on drafting emphasizes the need for students to elaborate during this phase of the writing. However, it does not provide specific strategies either for the teacher to use in teaching elaboration or for the writer to use in elaborating. It simply stresses the importance of elaboration and explains certain misconceptions about writing.

The all-too-common belief that errorless writing is "good" writing has prevented some students from recognizing the relationship between thinking and writing. Although these students possess the language mechanics to write well, they have not acquired the thinking "tools" necessary to improve the quality of the elaboration in their writing." (TEA, [1991c], p. 17)

However, the book does not go on to explain how students can be taught those thinking "tools."

The text further explains that in the "prewriting stage" students should "generate and record as many ides as possible without consideration for whether they will be ultimately useable," but during the drafting stage, "adopting a critical frame of mind becomes necessary." This has two advantages for the writer:

The writer who adopts a critical frame of mind will be able to
(1) focus on what is "good" about the development of each idea so that he or she can shape each one into something that creates meaning and
(2) discard any idea that is irrelevant, general, or vague and replace it with one that is relevant and specific. (TEA, [1991c])

However, the text does not explain how to help students develop this "critical frame of mind." Given what we have seen in the sample papers awarded the highest scores and what passes, this is a crucial omission.

The section on writing process also deals with teaching revision. We have long known that when students revise, they tend to make only what are called low-level revisions. These include cosmetic revisions and changes in spelling and mechanics. Changes in the content of the writing or in its structure are far less frequent (Bridwell, 1980). Students need to learn to revise at higher levels of content and structure. The *Handbook* briefly reviews techniques such as modeling the revision process using a piece of writing to revise on an overhead projector with input from students, conferencing with students stressing the strengths of a piece before examining one or two areas for improvement, minilessons about specific problems, and peer revision. The text makes plain that all of these techniques are dependent upon knowing what questions to ask about a piece of writing. Clearly, these questions will necessarily reflect the critical frame of mind. Once again, however, the text provides no suggestions about helping students learn to ask the critical questions.

So, why is the critical frame of mind present only by allusion? (Of course, some states do not even allude to it.) I suspect that there are many reasons. One of the major reasons we have simplistic tests is that politicians running on a platform of educational improvement want a test capable of demonstrating gains quickly, so that they can claim that the gains are a result of their leadership (e.g., Bush). If we believe that writing involves more than just blether, that it actually requires thinking, and if we believe that writing tests are important, then we need a more sophisticated test, one that will be more complex and less conducive to showing quickie gains. More sophisticated tests, however, would necessitate more money, time, and expertise to produce workable and reliable writing tests and far more money to train teachers in how to develop writing curricula that would meet their demands.

Part of the deficiency of the Texas assessment of writing lies in the inadequate theory of writing left after most of Kinneavy's theory was discarded and, in the case of persuasive writing, a totally inadequate theory of argument. The criteria speak of "reasons some of which are clearly and logically developed," but what counts for logic is not defined, and there is no talk of data, evidence, proof, demonstration, and certainly, no talk of relevancy, accuracy, or warranting.

If the test makers had a clear idea of what counts for logic, it would be possible to be clear about what constitutes a critical frame of mind, at least for the Texas tests. For example, if we were to adopt the Toulmin (1958) model of argument, it would be a simple matter to explain what a critical frame of mind entails. We would know to ask questions such as the following: What evidence supports the claim? To what extent is the evidence relevant (warrantable)? To what extent is the evidence accurate or open to challenge (rebuttal)? Are the claims appropriately qualified? When students are engaged in the kind of dialectical processes we have seen in Ms. Levine's classes, they appear to acquire the critical frame of mind through use. But the Texas materials mention no such instructional processes.

Commercial Materials

The TAAS *Handbook* specifically warns against the use of the five-paragraph theme as a formula that leads students to believing that knowing and using a formula can produce meaningful writing by "following predetermined steps" (TEA, [1991c], p. 17). The *Handbook* points out that writing requires careful thought. Despite this caveat, published materials recommend five paragraphs for persuasive writing and for narrative and other kinds as well. In a booklet intended for fourth-grade students, Fuller (1994) provides box diagrams for narrative, "how-to," "informative by classifying," and persuasive. Only the "how-to" diagram suggests the need for more than five paragraphs, depending on how many steps are involved. The others all suggest five paragraphs. In the eighth-grade volume, the same writer provides the same diagram and recommends, in a list of "tips," that students "have at least three well-elaborated reasons" and that they be equally elaborated. At the same time, the fourth-grade book commends the *Handbook*, referred to above, that carries the caveat against the five-paragraph theme. It may be that the five-paragraph theme is so ingrained into our traditions of school writing that no mere caveat from a state department of education can end it.

In addition to providing schematic diagrams to guide the writing of students, scoring tips, and sample prompts for each kind of writing at a grade level, the commercial texts present many pages of exercises for testing conventions of writing: punctuation, subject-verb agreement, spelling, capitalization, and sentence structure. The help on writing is very thin. Despite the de-emphasis on mechanics in the *Handbook* and other TEA documents, the commercial publishers thrive on exercises on mechanics. They are easy to produce, teachers like them because they are easy to administer and grade, and many teachers probably still believe that mechanical correctness is the most important criterion for judging writing.

CHAPTER 6

Teachers and Administrators Under Pressure: The Case of Texas

WITH VERA L. WALLACE

How do administrators, supervisors, and teachers respond to the demands of high-stakes assessment in the particular environment that Texas has put in place? We will examine responses to the theory of writing and the kinds of writing tested, especially the ways in which teachers prepare students for the assessment in the various types. We will be particularly concerned with how the assessment affects writing instruction generally and with administrative responses to the assessment. In addition, we will examine attitudes toward the assessments, its impact on other parts of the curriculum, and the impact of the interplay of the theory of writing, the kinds tested, the criteria, and administrative and teacher perceptions of writing. The chapter will close with two case studies of administrative responses to the assessment in districts of different economic advantage.

THEORY OF WRITING

The teachers and most district supervisors of language arts interviewed did not know about the original Kinneavy (1971) theory of writing. Teachers tended to talk instead about the kinds of writing in one word, indicating that they have not identified a class of writing based on ideas about purpose and mode. Rather they refer to highly specific writing tasks: the "how-to" piece; the comparison-contrast, and the persuasive piece. The teaching goal becomes that particular writing task and its features, rather than the class of writing to which the task belongs.

At the same time, the writing tasks tested tend to represent the universe of writing for most teachers interviewed: 61% believe that the state writing assessment supports the kind of writing program they want for their high school; only 27% believe that other kinds of writing should be included in the curriculum, and nearly all of these teachers suggest that creative writing and writing about literary works be included. Forty-seven percent feel that the assessment has helped to improve writing in the schools. Nearly all of these believe that the testing has forced attention to writing. Several teachers commented that "teachers simply were not teaching writing much before the testing went into effect." Twenty percent think the tests have not improved writing. The remainder were noncommittal. Nearly all administrators to whom we spoke believed that the testing had improved writing among students because teachers were paying more attention to writing than they had been prior to the assessment.

Taken together, these attitudes suggest that teachers and administrators see the testing program as successful in improving writing. In addition, they indicate that the testing program becomes a kind of surrogate theory of discourse for most teachers. It tells teachers the boundaries of knowledge about composition and stipulates what should be taught. It tells teachers how to judge writing and what features are important for what the state says is good writing of certain limited types.

The research also reveals that language arts teachers at all levels have had little course work in writing. In Texas, of the teachers we interviewed, only one had had graduate work in writing (rhetoric) or the teaching of writing, but 31% had attended a Writing Project session, usually a summer session lasting several weeks on the teaching of writing. Far more, 76%, had attended workshops related to the TAAS writing assessment. Most of these were oriented to learning the criteria for judging writing and using them in a systematic way.

Since most teachers have never engaged in the analysis of criteria for judging writing, they tend not to analyze criteria set by the state. In fact, only 16% of teachers we interviewed disapproved the Texas rubric for judging writing. On the other hand, 58% approve it and see it as useful. Many comment that the rubric is what they need to move ahead with writing.

One of the messages that the test conveys is that writing should be approached by learning to meet the state criteria for each type. As might be expected, 84% of teachers interviewed in Texas were classified as having adopted current traditional rhetoric. Only one had adopted an expressivist rhetoric, one an epistemic, and three a focus on grammar. When the teachers talked about their teaching of writing, 98% gave evidence of focusing on the structure of writing as opposed to the content. So while some had adopted a rhetorical focus other than current traditional rhetoric, even they displayed strong tendencies to focus on form or structure. In short, the types of writing and the criteria of the state assessment have very largely become the basis for theories of rhetoric and writing pedagogy that guide the teaching of most of the Texas teachers included in this research sample. We will look at those more closely.

THE CRITERIA AND TYPES OF WRITING

Of the Texas teachers we interviewed, 58% approve the rubric used in TAAS. Thirty-one percent actually use the rubric with their students. Only 16% disapprove it. Some teachers were noncommittal about it. But nearly all used it as a guide in their teaching, even when they disapproved it. Only the teacher who had adopted an expressivist rhetoric and who was not teaching at a tested level did not seem to be influenced by it. She was not teaching the kinds of writing that have much connection to TAAS.

They all know that organization and elaboration will count heavily for whatever the task is. Most believe that elaboration is the most important criterion. The very first teacher interviewed before this project began said that "the most important thing is to get them to elaborate. Nothing else really matters." Well, not quite. The writing had to be organized and reasonably free of error. But without some elaboration, a piece would not pass. The district language arts supervisor in a large urban system told me that she encourages students to write more as they take the test. "Just do whatever you can to get them to write more," she said. At the same time, it is clear that a majority of Texas teachers see organization through the five-paragraph theme as one way of assuring basic elaboration, so that students have at least three reasons to make a persuasive point.

We have known for many years that length in word count correlates with quality ratings (Hillocks, 1986a). That is, at school levels, the more words students write, the better the writing is likely to be. However, as several researchers point out, the gross number of words is probably not in itself responsible for quality (O'Donnell, Griffin, & Norris 1967), accounting only for between 9 and 25 percent of the variance in quality scores (Hillocks, 1986a). The elaboration must at least be also relevant and forceful.

As we have seen, sometimes when students elaborate, they create a series of statements that all relate to the same topic but show little more than what we might call topical relevance. Recall, for example, the compositions about community service in the previous chapter.

While most Texas teachers in this sample recognize the importance of elaboration for higher scores, many of them appear to believe that topical elaboration, in the framework of a five-paragraph theme, will enable students to pass the test and even achieve a high score. As we have seen, nearly every teacher interviewed (98%) attends to the structure of writing and leaves content alone except for initial brainstorming. Only 10.9% show any evidence of using inquiry, the kind of processes that Ms. Levine's class uses in Chapter 2. Most of those put structure first. Indeed, 54.6% adopt the five-paragraph theme as the structure they teach with 52.7% using schematic diagrams to emphasize the structure. Elaboration is developed within this structure.

For example, Mrs. Steele, a teacher in a large urban high school, asks students to begin their writing with some sort of brainstorming, "scatter diagram," or webbing. Such brainstorming sessions appear to be relatively brief and involve listing ideas that students may have about a topic. Mrs. Steele believes that such brainstorming helps students locate positions they can take in writing persuasive pieces.

She says, "I give them the pros and cons, the organizer, and then this template that shows them how to drop in the information in each paragraph, what they should be putting in each paragraph." A *T*-diagram is the organizer. On it, students list the pros and cons of the issue on either side of the *T*. The side of the issue for which they have the most reasons is the side they should choose to argue, not the side of the issue about which they feel most strongly. Then comes the template, which, as you might guess, has five boxes with indications of what should go in each box, each representing a paragraph. The opening box is labeled "Issue, Background, Position." The second is labeled "First Reason, Four sentences of Elaboration," and the third and fourth paragraphs are labeled in a similar way. Other teachers in the same high school and elsewhere in Texas call this the 3.55 composition: three reasons, five paragraphs, five sentences in each paragraph. (It is interesting to note that this 3.55 composition nearly always is preceded by a definite article, "*the* 3.55 composition," a generic form, comparable in stature to the sonnet, the short story, the novel.) Mrs. Steele explains how she uses the template:

> In the first paragraph, okay, I teach them this. You must define the issue. In other words, assume the reader knows nothing. So you can't just say I oppose smoking cigarettes. You have to give me a little background so I can figure out why I should even care whether you oppose it or not. So then, a lot of this information is in the prompt, and I'm going to go back to that. Cause we, we also spend about a week or two on just analyzing prompts. Okay, and then you must put your position statement in the first paragraph. So I must see those elements in there, and that's what I check for, organization, and I see that.
>
> In the second paragraph, I'm looking for transitional words, . . . you must organize your arguments, that means you need to num-

ber them. So I know when you're moving from one to the other, in some kind of a way, you need to move me directional, working on transitional direction. And then you must have one, . . . main idea or a reason (in a paragraph).

The same holds for the third and fourth paragraphs.

The final paragraph, she says, should "restate the position statement."

I need to have a conclusion, okay, and then I gave them some elaboration strategies just for the concluding paragraph: Tell a little hypothetical story, go back and relist what it is that you've already told them, and ask questions. Tell them why it would benefit, you know, why supporting your position would benefit everybody: the world, the country, whatever, that kind of thing, but you must restate that position statement, whatever your position is.

When asked directly if she expects students to produce five paragraphs with five sentences each, she replies,

My main point is that they need to do two pages because I've seen some very well written shorter work turned in that was graded low, and so I understand now that part of the game is we want to see two pages, we need to know that these students can take this thing, take an idea and manipulate it. Work with it.

Mrs. Steele teaches elaboration strategies to develop what she calls arguments. These include the typical newspaper story heuristic, "the five W's and one H, the who, what, where, when, why, and how, the way we were taught." These are for students to use when "they are in trouble." The problem with this theory is that the answers to the questions of the newspaper heuristic are not equivalent to arguments. For Mrs. Steele, being in trouble has to do with having nothing to say. Asking the "5W and H" questions generates something to say. But consider the kinds of ideas likely to come out of asking these questions. In dealing with smoking, Mrs. Steele explains

You know, when they deal with who [what, when, why, where, how], then it forces them to think and organize their ideas. . . . But start with these if you can, you know. Why does [smoking] cause a problem? . . . . What kind of medical problems do you have? When do you get them? Do you get them later in life or just from being exposed? You know, if you can't answer that, go on to how. How does it cause medical problems if that's the way you understand it, you see. Anyway, I teach them that. That's the simplest technique, then dig out with a why. And then if you run into trouble, make up a story, (laughs) that makes your point. The reader doesn't know. Ask a series of questions. I give them about ten little strategies that they can use.

If I were to answer the questions posed above, I would have answers such as the following:

Why? Smoking causes health problems because cigarettes deliver nicotine to the human body, and nicotine is a poison that has pernicious effects. (I cannot be more specific, because I do not know why nicotine has these ill effects.)

What kind of medical problems? Nicotine affects the heart, lungs, and circulatory system. Smoking has been strongly associated with lung cancer and heart disease.

When do you get them? The results of smoking tend to strike later in life (I think). The effects take time to build up (I think), but there is also evidence that people can suffer effects from exposure to cigarette smoke.

How does it cause medical problems? Once again, I cannot answer more than I already have for the why question.

If I try to make use of the answers above in writing a persuasive composition, I will have a few fairly vague sentences and not much else, unless I make up evidence and stories as this teacher recommends and as did the writer on how the lyrics of "O. P. P." cause premarital sex (see Chapter 5), or unless I have resources and time to find out what I do not know. The "5 W and H" strategy does not work well for persuasive writing in a testing situation.

In Texas, there are separate learning standards for mechanics and usage that are brought to bear on writing and examined through multiple-choice items. As we have seen, the lower the writing score, the more multiple-choice items one must pass. As a result, for most teachers we interviewed (85 percent), grammar, mechanics, and usage becomes the second major focus of attention. This does not mean working with mechanics and usage in the context of student writing but rather using many sets of multiple-choice or other objective items to rehearse for the test, a practice that many studies have shown to have no impact on the quality of writing. Indeed, many studies have strongly recommended against this kind of direct teaching of "grammar" as a means to improving writing (Braddock, Lloyd-Jones, & Schoer, 1962; Hillocks, 1986a).

Mrs. Steele says that she has spent the first 8 weeks of school on usage and mechanics, including sentence structure. Her class meets 90 minutes per day for a semester, after which her students are finished with English for the year. For a total of 8 weeks, Mrs. Steele's students spend 90 minutes per day doing the kinds of grammar exercises presented in the many supplementary booklets available commercially for TAAS preparation.

The pressure of meeting the TAAS objectives is great, especially in a large urban school at which test scores are traditionally low. In this context, Mrs. Steele believes that she does not have time to teach students new things. She reasons that because they have been talking, they can write.

> All I have time to do is work on prior knowledge. All I have time to do is find out where they are and show then how to use what they already know and make it work for them. And I tell them I'm your coach; I'm not your teacher. I'm not going to try to teach you something. No, it's too late. What we want to know is, how do we get in a huddle and figure out how to get across . . . the goal line for TAAS.

Scoring the touchdown on TAAS, passing the test, is the main goal. Ironically, although Mrs. Steele uses simplistic formulas to teach persuasive writing and believes that she cannot teach students anything new and boasts of not using a text, she speaks idealistically about teaching persuasive writing in a democracy and warmly about the usefulness of TAAS:

> But in 10th grade we live in a democracy, you ought to be able to take a position on an issue and articulate it in writing to other people. That, that is *so* basic to me. I understand why persuasive. We live in a society where the art of persuasion should be the rule that governs social relationships, and one ought to be versed in that. I'm a strong supporter of TAAS. I really am.

In light of everything that had preceded, this a very curious statement of faith in what she is teaching and in TAAS. On the one hand, Mrs. Steele believes that she cannot teach the students anything new because there is not time. She provides strategies that are almost certain to produce superficial persuasive writing, and she requires weeks of pretty useless exercises. On the other, she claims the most noble purposes for education and testing. Such contradictory positions may well be the result of idealism supported by too little learning caught in the mesh of poorly considered state-mandated criteria applied to the results of prompts to which no one could write intelligently. The testing program appears to be conducive to a kind of intellectual schizophrenia.

MODE OF INSTRUCTION

Most teachers we interviewed in Texas (82%) are presentational in their teaching. Mrs. Steele above is a good example. Even at the elementary school level, teachers we interviewed are predominantly presentational. The focus on the structure of writing, the use of schematic diagrams (referred to by some teachers as visual organizers), and the emphasis on the five-paragraph theme are all part of the presentational mode.

However, there are some signs of movement away from the strictly presentational classroom. Five teachers use a workshop method and two use environmental methods in which students are regularly engaged in structured, interactive learning situations. All but one of these seven teach in economically advantaged districts, with the two environmental teachers in the same school. There is evidence of other more advanced teaching of writing among others as well. At least occasionally, 11% of teachers interviewed engage their students in examining data as part of preparation for writing, as does Ms. Levine in Chapter 2. In addition, 18% use some activities that engage students in invention or imagination, activities in which students invent an original character, a dialogue between two or more characters, or a new perspective in trying to see a situation. Although these kinds of methods have been shown to be among the most effective in the teaching of writing (Hillocks, 1986a), they are not a major dimension of instruction for most teachers in our sample, but they do represent a movement, though small, toward an epistemic rhetoric.

WRITING PROCESS

Many teachers interviewed in Texas tell us that they use several of the process elements: brainstorming and related prewriting, 80%; peer feedback, 64%; teacher feedback during writing, 26%; revising, 55%; editing, 80%; and publishing, 38%. The differences among these figures suggest that teachers use pieces of the writing process. A majority of teachers focus on brainstorming and editing; but only 25.5% provide feedback during the writing process. Curiously, only 54.5% stress revision. The brainstorming and other prewriting is often directed at dealing with prompts comparable to those students will receive on the test. While our teachers in Texas report using parts of the writing process, few use it as a whole as a usual means of developing writing. Still the writing process emphasis we find in Texas is certainly far greater than it would have been at the time of Applebee's (1981) survey.

ADMINISTRATIVE DIRECTION IN SCHOOLS OF CONTRASTING ECONOMIC STATUS: TWO CASES

by Vera L. Wallace

In conducting this research, we could not help but notice that schools and school systems with high and low socioeconomic status appeared to deal with test preparation in quite different ways. The case studies that follow attend to the administrative practices in two elementary schools in Texas, one in a large urban center with 95.5% of students classified as economically disadvantaged in 1996, the second school in a suburb of the same urban center, but with only 5.2% of students so classified. The following looks at differences in both policies set by administrators and practice as reported by teachers.

Case 1

Driving though the crude business area of a large city to our targeted elementary school, we see the prosperous downtown section of the city that lies beyond the dismal and haggard shops around us. The business section suddenly gives way to a residential area. The buildings edging the sidewalk resemble structures that belong to an era long past. The raw, weather-beaten siding on the exterior of these dwellings screams for several layers of the paint that had been sucked into invisibility. We cautiously navigate the turns that were indicated on our map. As we wind our way through several more turns, we conclude several times that we were, once again, lost. How is it that a school on the fringes of such a large urban center is difficult to find?

Finally, straight ahead, the street upon which we are to make a left turn approaches. There, just ahead, appearing out of no place in particular, stands a beautiful, brick, two-story building with Kelly green trim. Close to this building is a perfectly appointed playground enclosed by an 8-foot-high chain-link fence. In the center of the playground stands a majestic 10-foot-tall silver rocket, complete with red nose cone, which seems to serve as sentinel for this building.

The interior of the school is bright and clean. There are many bulletin boards laden with samples of student work, signs and notices, slogans with TAAS reminders and catchy phrases. We ask for directions to the office. A tall, immaculately dressed and professionally composed woman asks if she may be of assistance. I assume she is the principal and inform her that my colleague and I are here to interview her and two teachers. She smiles softly, demurely registering the inadvertent compliment—or my stupidity—and informs us that Dr. Jayne is not in her office. We wait in the comfortable seats in the front of the office.

Presently, I hear a lilting voice answering questions, giving directions. I am aware of brisk movement, floating, skipping, turning, a flurry of motion. Suddenly, the office door snaps open and a glimmer of pink whizzes by. She reaches the area behind the counter in what appears to be two strides. She speaks to each of the women behind the counter one at a time at the same time, it seems. She inspects her memos, rattles off a list of instructions, the whole time in motion. She notices us sitting there, wondering. She comes to the counter and waves us in.

Dr. Jayne escorts us into her office. She arranges comfortable leather wingback chairs closer to her desk and asks if we would like refreshments. She graciously serves us juice. Dr. Jayne is the driving force around which this totally African American school functions. This principal, with a doctorate in education, appears determined to increase performance as measured on TAAS assessments. Her expectation for writing is to achieve scores in the mid-eighties, meaning that 85 percent of students would pass the test. She indicates that the school has been working very hard to increase writing skills this year, and because of new policies she has initiated, felt that a score of 85 was a realistic goal.

Schools with TAAS performance levels at the lowest end of the ratings (Unsatisfactory) function under the very real possibility of shutdown. Also, administrators can be replaced and teachers either reassigned or terminated. These schools are also subject to scheduled and unscheduled visitations from a team designated by the Texas Education Agency. The task of the team is to monitor what is going on in classes and the kinds of training teachers receive and to provide listings of inadequate teacher competencies complete with a timeline, observations, and suggestions to ensure that teacher weaknesses have been corrected. They also teach classes in order to demonstrate how to teach skills being tested on the TAAS.

Dr. Jones is one of the principals brought in by the state to replace the principal of a failed school. She told us that her school was currently undergoing remediation. She said that the expectation for performance in Texas is a 5% increase each year. If school performance in any given year is substandard, that school, with the help of the state intervention team, has one year in which to raise scores. If a school is 5 points below expected achievement levels, the following year the total gain would have to total 10% in order to avoid remediation. Dr. Jones felt there was little hope that underachieving schools would be able to meet such demands. She admitted that Texas does not know what to do if a school, after remediation, still fails to meet state standards.

Dr. Jayne, however, does not share the view of Dr. Jones. Like other principals in this district, she has signed a contract that surrenders her right to recourse if she should be removed from her job in the event that test scores fail to go up in her school. The good news about this contract is that she will be eligible for a sizeable bonus if the scores go up. She is adamant about the need to improve all scores on the state assessment. As a result, Dr. Jayne has developed several paths to remediation in writing.

First, she backs the policy of curricular alignment that comes from the district superintendent's office, apparently in oral form only. Curricular alignment, teachers report, is the policy that subjects such as science and social studies, which are not tested, may not be taught until late spring when the year's assessments in reading, writing, and math are completed. One fourth-grade teacher complains:

> I mean, you can spend all year on wonderful science, but unfortu-
> nately, that's not tested. And so, in some schools where the chil-
> dren are not so critically at risk, you could probably afford to do
> that. But in our school, we couldn't justify it. I mean, I would be
> questioned if I did that. So you have to tie it—they want to see
> justification for why we're teaching everything. And it has to be
> tied to TAAS. It has to be the objectives. You know, we have 13
> math objectives, we have only 7 writing objectives.

She indicates that the pressure about what to teach and when to teach it are tied to threats to job security.

> I mean, our supervisor . . . has said, you know, I mean, all their jobs
> are on the line. Supposedly ours are, too, but—you know, "Forget
> science and social studies until after the TAAS! Even the math and
> the reading. Forget it!" I mean, our scores are so low! After that,
> you can do all those wonderful things.

Second, the writing curriculum demands restricting attention to the types of writing eligible for testing: narrative, persuasive, "how-to," and classificatory. There is no time for other kinds of writing. Attention to these tasks means learning the specific features that will permit passing scores. One teacher explains that there is not time for writing process because it takes too long and does not necessarily contribute to learning the necessary features. The policy of concentrating on formal features of the writing tested is reinforced by the school principal and appears to result in the teaching of writing as declarative rather than procedural knowledge.

Dr. Jayne reinforces these macrolevel policies by a variety of changes at the microlevel, the level of planning specific lessons. She is developing a visual to help fourth graders understand the concept of a composition with an introduction, body, and conclusion.

> I have a little developmental person in my mind, with a comb on his head, a triangle, red, which means an introduction, and then I have a body that I'm going to put on, with arms, and the body's going to say some things. So I'm going to develop him over the summer, and every classroom is going to have one of those. So when they get ready to write—and African Americans are visual learners, by research. And you don't have to tell that to me, because I knew I was visual! [LAUGHS] But if they say, "Think of your little man, and write your story, what is going to go on the top? That's his head. It's going to be an introduction. What is going to go in the middle? That's his body. And what is a body filled with? All kind of things. That's all our information, in the middle. And at the end, we're going to put his legs on, so he can move." I'm thinking of how to develop a person, or a robot, or something that is gonna stick in their minds, as a visual. So when they see it, they'll say, "I can write anything."

Further, Dr. Jayne teaches some of the lessons, by taking her students through various prompts to show them how to develop and elaborate a topic. She sometimes meets teachers and their classes in the cafeteria. She tells how she teaches:

> "Okay, today's prompt is this. How would you introduce this if you're beginning to write a paragraph? What would you say?" Then they give their little thing. Then I say, "What would you say?" Then a teacher may say, "I would start mine like this. How did you start yours?" So they can get an idea of the introductory sentence, what that should look like. . . . Maybe 10 percent can't come up with an introductory sentence. One of the things we tell them is to go back to the prompt. "Did the prompt say, 'How well did you like your Easter break?' In your introduction you could say, 'I did not like my Easter break because—.' Or, 'I liked my Easter break because—.' Or 'My Easter break was fantastic. It was because—.'" And we give them an idea of how to go back to the prompt, if they

can't think of something original or creative, and give it [the prompt] back to them. And then we talk about the middle of it, the body part. "Now, what are you going to say about it? What happens next? You liked it because it was fun. Now, why was it fun? Because you saw your uncle, your aunt, your cousin, you played with your favorite friend—what did you do?" That's the body. And then, "How you gonna close it out?" So we talk about all that in the big group workshop, we call it a little workshop for the kids. It's actually giving them a workshop on what they already know, and focusing their attention on it even more heavily. We tell them, "When you see it on a test, if you cannot be creative and come up with something on your own, go back to the prompt! And remember you need the three basic parts: introduction; a body—where you're going to tell me about it; and then how you're going to close it out. If you can't do anything else, do those three."

In short, Dr. Jayne concentrates on the basic parts of the formula that she believes will be successful in a response to the test prompt. These involve attention to the form of the writing, the properties that a successful piece is thought to exhibit, but not to the development of content.

Dr. Jayne's third policy involves what she calls "WIT Friday", "Winning in TAAS," a policy that calls for everyone in the school to be working on what will be assessed on Fridays. During the first phase of WIT Friday, from the beginning of the school year till about a month before the test, teachers must work on TAAS objectives all day on Friday. Dr. Jayne monitors individual classrooms to be sure that such work goes on. In the second phase, beginning about a month before the test, all fourth graders go to the cafeteria for the kind of TAAS instruction Dr. Jayne describes above. This provides her a clear window on exactly what the teachers have been teaching and what they have not. Her questioning is aimed at what the teachers are supposed to have been teaching during the preceding days. When she asks students from a particular teacher's class about how to start a composition, she gains what she sees as firsthand knowledge of what students have learned about introductions. WIT Friday is not simply a means of insuring that the forms deemed appropriate for the tests are taught, but part of a system for monitoring what is taught in the classroom.

A fourth policy involves an accountability system that enables her to pinpoint the performance of a particular teacher's students on specific state objectives. She explains that she can go to a teacher, point to a result on a particular objective for a particular student, and call that teacher to task. She says,

I want to be able to put my hand on the objective, and a student, and then test on it every 3 weeks. Whatever the objective you worked on for 2 weeks, on the 3rd week you test on it. I want to know, did they master it? "You taught it during the week, or had overlap teaching of some sort of it, and then on Friday, if you didn't overlap, at least you focused in on it, and exposed them to it. And then after they've been exposed, and sometimes taught during the week as a follow-up, you expose them more and you test on it. . . . Whatever that objective is, and you tested it," and I say, "I would like to see his test on objective #7." I look at it, and I say, "He only scored 45. What are you doing to change this so that when we retest this, this is going to be better than 45?" Then the teacher will say, 'cause she already used one resource, "He already had exposure to that." You can't teach it the same way, and use the same material, and expect to get a different result. So now, you gotta get a different resource. You gotta say, "I'm going to use *this* resource now, I'm going to let him team with a friend, I'm going to send it home as homework, I'm going to use overheads that I didn't use before." You gotta do something!

The fifth policy instituted by Dr. Jayne is Saturday school, in which all of the students who have failed to meet the state's standards are compelled to attend several 4-hour sessions of writing instruction in which cheers and chants are used to "pump up" the students. Dr. Jayne says that she requires parents to attend these sessions with their children. She tells us that she calls parents and informs them that their children are failing and that she will pick them up herself if necessary. Dr. Jayne is sincerely, vigorously attempting to elevate writing scores. However, we suspect that identifying failing students, requiring leisure-time, weekend writing sessions for learning mechanical formulas for writing, and mandating that parents accompany their children to such sessions places extreme pressures on a population already burdened by daily survival exigencies and depressed levels of self-esteem due to such labeling.

As the test approaches and on the day of the test, other policies go into action. She tells us,

Like, we even had a pep rally when they did the writing. The day before the writing test, I had cheerleaders out, *I* was out cheering, I made up cheers about the teachers, cheers about the students: "We can do it!" Pumped them up. Went through, when they were writing, when it was getting the toughest, in the afternoon. They were tired around one o'clock. I could tell they were just worn out with that test, the kids.

So Dr. Jayne "pumped them up." These policies appear to result in a rise in the test scores in writing during Dr. Jayne's first years of principalship. She is pushing for a greater rise, to 85% passing. It is clear, however, that in the process of doing this, attention shifts from the substantive to the formal, from the generation of complex ideas to incorporating cues that indicate the presence of an introduction, a body, or a conclusion, from the thoughtful elaboration of ideas to the inclusion of sentences to fill up the space that is expected. Much of the instruction is focused on the kinds of multiple choice items that appear in the mechanics and usage portion of the test. That will be enough to pass TAAS writing. In fact, scores have gone from 69.2% of all students passing in 1994 to 86.5% passing writing in 1999. Her school is "recognized," a designation of merit in the Texas system.

Case 2

As we drive toward the affluent school, we see no buildings at all for a while and are left wondering if we are lost again. Finally, we realize that homes are set off from the road, hidden behind stands of trees and bushes. When the school does appear, it is a modern one-story building of yellow brick with large windows decorated with student art. The first hallway we see has a display of student work, almost like a museum with student writing and art mounted on colored paper set neatly in patterns for the viewer. As we enter the spacious office reception area, we note that here, too, children's work decorates the walls. Mrs. Richardson, the principal of the school, does not hold a doctorate, but she has been a classroom teacher, an associate director of a Writing Project, and a team leader for writing in the school system. Sixty-nine percent of the teaching staff have between 6 to 20 or more years of experience in the school even though the compensation in this district is not as great as in other outlying districts. The teachers choose to teach here in spite of that. Mrs. Richardson encourages many types of writing, examples of which are displayed on the hallway walls. Students write plays and poems. They write about works of art, interpreting them or writing an imaginative response to them. She says,

> This year, wanting to move our kids to a higher level, I had a lady come in and do art with our kids, taking a piece of work, and artists are storytellers, and they're telling a story with their painting. And she worked with my teachers on how to get kids to write a story about that. And [this produced] some of the best writing that we have received this year. It is incredible! Incredible! We get the teachers to see how we develop the setting, what's the setting for

that story? What's the problem or the task or what's the author trying to convey there? What's his purpose for painting that?

The students at this school have a variety of writing experiences throughout the school year in all subject areas. They do the "how-to" and the other tested tasks but go well beyond in a very rich writing program. Mrs. Richardson appreciates the value of extending the writing opportunities of her students by extending curricular studies and integrating all subject matter into a writing opportunity instead of neglecting or omitting the study of various subjects.

Writing is integrated into all aspects of the curriculum. Mrs. Richardson detailed one teacher's approach:

> In our GT [gifted and talented] Program, writing is a part of everything, from the first unit that she taught this year, robotics, which is where they're using computers to manipulate arms and things like that. But they had to write and describe those experiences, so that writing is naturally integrated into everything the kids are doing. And we use many of the same concepts, we use the same materials for our GT kids that we use for our Tower One kids, our special ed population.

In contrast to Dr. Jayne, Mrs. Richardson does not isolate the slower students. Tower One students are exposed to the same instruction as the gifted students.

Mrs. Richardson's leadership and knowledge about writing motivates the writing curriculum's rich, nonrestrictive practices.

> I truly believe that writing is the highest level of thinking you can be involved in, because you have to use both sides of your brain as you write and create and do those kinds of things. I believe that you need to expose lots and lots of literature as good models of writing if you're going to expect kids to be able to write.

In contrast to Dr. Jayne's marathon cafeteria sessions immediately preceding the test, Mrs. Richardson would engage the students in procedural activities to elicit ideas from the students' imaginings.

> You might see me presenting the topic that you were going to write, but typically if I'm going to present, let's say classificatory writing, I would talk about rainy days for instance, and we might read poems and brainstorm all the things we can think about on

rainy days. We might talk about what do we like about rainy days? We would brainstorm all of those things. And then we talk about what we don't like about rainy days, and we brainstorm all those. And we write, the whole board might be, or you might have tables, charts filled with all those things. And you do all that writing and they're simply giving you. So you've just done a lot of brainstorming. That's prewriting. And then we say, you know, let's compare and contrast, or let's talk about what we like and dislike about rainy days. And then the next time, they do it on their own. So that you'd done the prewriting together, but they're doing the writing on their own."

Mrs. Richardson also has an accountability policy similar in some ways to that of Dr. Jayne. She feels that this system allows her to be aware of problem areas which affect the entire campus.

So this student came to this teacher at this (level). They left this teacher at this. So you can look and say, "Jodie, your kids came to you and they were about 95% in math and addition but they left you and they were only about 78%. What do you think happened here, Jodie?" . . . So I know where they came, and I know where they left, so I can show growth cause it's the same kids. . . . And, I met in conference with every teacher . . . at the end of the year, I will know what they've done. I also . . . look at data based upon multiple years, and then I can see if they're going up or down, or problem areas. And when you look at it for your campus it's scary. I mean I could pick out problems right off the bat for my campus.

Teachers at this school feel free to explore a variety of writing opportunities and activities. They report being very secure in their work and say they find it very rewarding. Mrs. Richardson's system of accountability is geared toward maintaining high expectations and student growth, and encouraging teachers to maintain their focus.

Mrs. Richardson's version of Saturday school takes on a tone decidedly different from Dr. Jayne's. Teachers are invited to participate in staff development sessions devoted to some component of the writing process. They are not paid to attend. Mrs. Richardson makes it clear that all teachers hired in her district must go through at least 1 or 2 days of staff development in writing.

In all interviews at this school, it was obvious that the emphasis was on developing thoughtful ideas and not on the outward form of the writing. Teachers worked with mechanics and usage primarily as problems arose in the students' writing, not in isolated multiple choice formats. Students were often engaged in inquiry (as they studied paintings and interpreted what they saw as stories) and thoughtful recall of experience. Writing results at this school vary between 94.9% and 98.1% passing from 1994 through 1999.

Our interview records indicate that 31% of Texas teachers we interviewed told us about having attended one or more of the Writing Projects in Texas. Of these, 67% teach in the two economically advantaged suburbs in our study. In the economically advantaged elementary school, two teachers and the principal have been associated with Writing Projects. On the other hand, 78% of Texas teachers interviewed report attending workshops related to TAAS writing tests, usually on how to score writing, learning and using the criteria. In the affluent suburbs studied, 70% report attending such workshops. Thus, it seems that while teachers have approximately equal experience with test-scoring workshops provided by their districts, they do not have equal experience with more advanced thinking about writing. Attending such summer workshops usually results in teachers having far more knowledge about writing and the teaching of writing than teachers usually gain in a single college language-arts methods course.

Our interviews reveal that teachers in inner-city schools, largely without the benefit of Writing Project experience or other advanced training in writing, tend not to have the knowledge base of teachers in suburban schools and, therefore, tend to teach more directly to the tests. In every state, when teachers have little knowledge of writing, the testing system tends to become the knowledge base for teaching writing. When the urge to do well on the tests is high and the students are deemed unlikely to perform at satisfactory levels, the knowledge base becomes even more restricted by administrative directives indicating what should be taught, how long, and in what order. Further, many administrators tend to see what needs to be taught in more strictly test-oriented, formulaic terms. Although one goal of state testing may be to decrease the achievement gap in order to leave no child behind, the state testing program has a powerful effect on increasing the gap by restricting what students are allowed to learn in many poorer districts.

CHAPTER 7

Locking-In Formulaic Writing: The Case of Illinois

In contrast to assessments in Texas, those in Illinois are frequently described as low-stakes because they cannot result in catastrophic failure for schools or students. The Illinois State Board of Education (ISBE) cannot place schools on academic probation, prevent students from graduating high school, or take measures to disassemble a school or school district. However, in the 1990s, test scores were published in newspapers by grade level and subject. Administrators in advantaged districts told us of their competitions with nearby districts to attain better scores. Administrators and department chairs encouraged teachers to prepare students for passing the tests at a high level. For several weeks before the exam, administrators sent out announcements about the importance of doing well, and visited the classes of 10th grade teachers to ascertain if they were teaching the writing skills they thought the test represented. Teachers generally were eager for their students to do as well as, or better than, the students in the affluent districts nearby. Elementary school teachers in small schools felt as though everyone in the district identified them personally with low scores, especially when there were only one or two classes tested.

People assume that when a team is losing, the coach is not coaching well. So, they assume, it must be with teaching: When students do poorly on a test, it must be that the teachers are not teaching well. In several communities, realtors publish the test scores in their guides to area property. Thus, even though teachers are not in danger of losing their jobs or having their schools disbanded or seeing their students fail to graduate from high school, teachers feel considerable pressure about the tests.

According to *Write On, Illinois!* (ISBE, 1994), Illinois began testing writing by collecting actual writing samples in the late 1980s. The fact that the state moved from multiple-choice to writing was a welcome change to many teachers. By 1993, writing tests were scheduled to be administered at Grades 3, 6, 8, and 10. Those tests focus on narrative, expository, and persuasive writing at all grade levels. At the third grade level, students receive only one of the writing prompts. At other levels, they receive one prompt in one session and two in a second from which they must choose one, for a total of two of the three types in the two sessions.

Write On, Illinois! asserts that responding to two prompts "produces a more reliable profile" and meets the state goal that "students will be able to write 'for a variety of purposes.'" It claims that two prompts "will give all students a better chance for success by allowing them to choose something to which they can respond" (p. 7). As the test works, however, there is no choice on one of the testing days.

The book does not explain the testing conditions. However, teachers reveal that on 2 days in March, students receive prompts and have 40 minutes to produce the required texts. In most schools, the tests are given at the same time periods to all students so that the teacher in charge of any group of students is not likely to be the English teacher. In one school the tests are given in homeroom groups. In another school, English classes stay together, but the test administrator is unlikely to be the English teacher.

To keep the test honest, teachers have no access to the prompts before they are administered. The state requires that all testing materials be returned to the state. Teachers are directed not to copy student responses and therefore have no opportunity to examine what their students have written. But some schools report that they have begun to make copies. Through 1999, scores were returned to the school in the following school year. In the first few years of the assessment, only the school scores were returned, but more recently, individual scores were returned in an alphabetical list. In one suburban district, if teachers want to know how well their students did, they must go to the office and sort through the list to find the scores of their students. The chair of the English department of that school reports that "teachers do not go to all that trouble." In an urban high school, individual scores go to the homeroom teacher in the year following the test. In short, teachers have little or no involvement with the test, other than preparing students to take it. And they receive essentially no feedback.

As already stated, Illinois divides the universe of writing into three domains. This focus appears to have been borrowed from the National Assessment of Educational Progress writing tests or Warriner's famous *Grammar and Composition* series. Until the 1993 edition (Kinneavy and Warriner, 1993), this series of texts paid little heed to the strategies necessary for developing ideas or content. By 1993, the editions had begun to pay some attention to writing process, but not to specific strategies for producing the content of essays, for example, how to generate an argument.

WRITING PROMPTS

Write On, Illinois! explains the kinds of writing prompts that students can expect to encounter in Illinois Goals Assessment Program [IGAP] assessments. Although the guide maintains that there are three domains of writing, it allows for different kinds of writing prompts within those domains.

Narrative Prompts

There are two possible types of prompts for narrative: "the paper in which students recount and reflect upon a personally significant experience OR the paper in which students report and record reactions [*sic*] to an observed event" (ISBE, 1994, p. 119). These two appear to be quite different. The former sounds as though it would be highly subjective, using concrete detail, imagery, and language aimed at achieving an empathic response, while the latter appears to elicit objective writing of the kind we might find in a newspaper. The power of the former lies in its ability to let us enter and imagine the reconstructed experience of the narrator, while the power of the latter lies in its reconstruction of an event so that the reader understands and can judge it in an objective fashion. We value the former in so far as it engenders vicarious experience. Its correlation to actual events is secondary at best. We value the latter in so far as it presents actual events reliably. If it evokes vicarious response at the expense of veracity, it is open to severe criticism.

Despite these differences, *Write On, Illinois!* presents only one set of criteria for judging the writing, implying that there are no differences among the writing tasks involved. Curiously, the sample prompts in *Write On, Illinois!* are all of the first category: "a time when you were surprised" (p. 137), "a time you did something that made you feel good" (p. 124), "a time you learned or experienced something for the first time"(p. 155).

Expository Prompts

Write On, Illinois! presents the following description of expository prompts: "Students are asked to explain, interpret, or describe something based on background experiences or information provided in the prompt." It goes on to explain, "These assignments differ from the narrative in that the writer does not include personal reaction or feeling in describing or presenting information" (p. 65).

Two of the sample prompts in *Write On, Illinois!* provide a list of possible topics under a superordinate category: "workers" and "historical periods." Topics under worker include mechanic, doctor, waitress, and so on. Students are to choose one of those or any other and write a composition explaining how the work is "important to your school, your community, or the country as a whole." The prompt listing historical periods suggests "the time George Washington lived," "the time of the Wild West," and "more recent times when your parents were young." Students are to choose a time from the list or one of their own and write a report in which they name the time, "give reasons it is important," and "explain what people did and/or the things that happened during that time and why those things are important." Students are told to "be sure to report about things that actually happened" (p. 70).

A third sample prompt, for sixth grade and higher, reads as follows:

Your science class has been discussing the problems in our environment such as littering the land and water, using products that cannot be recycled, burning toxic chemicals and other waste products, cutting down trees, filling in the wetlands, and killing rare kinds of birds and animals. Your science teacher has asked each of you to choose one problem in our environment and explain why it is a problem and suggest things that can be done to solve it. (ISBE, 1994, p. 102)

The prompt goes on to tell students to "name and describe one problem in our environment" and then to "explain *why* it is a problem and how it hurts the environment" (p. 102).

All of the supposed expository topics involve "explaining" why something is important or a problem.

Persuasive Topics

In one prompt already alluded to, students are asked to pick a person who should win the best relative of the year award. Others involve persuading someone about the best place to live, and whether to support a proposal for Saturday school. Two of these are quite similar, making a case that something is the best. The third, however, is different in kind. It goes beyond making a judgment to deciding on a course of action and supporting that decision.

These persuasive prompts are representative of two of the three types of argument discussed by Aristotle in the *Art of Rhetoric*: the argument concerned with praise or blame (epideictic) and that concerned with policy, or what to do in a particular situation, which Aristotle calls deliberative. (His third type has to do with establishing the facts in a case and is referred to as forensic argument.)

Establishing praise or blame (the best relative or the best place to live, or the worst for that matter) necessarily requires establishing or assuming some definition of the terms of the praise or blame (e.g., what are the essential characteristics of a good relative and why are those characteristics essential). On the other hand, deciding what to do in a particular situation has to do with examining the moral, educational, economic, or other principles that come into play and resolving the conflicts that are likely to exist among them as a result of the situation. Almost inevitably, arguments of policy require arguments of praise or blame. If we wish to argue for Saturday school, for example, it may be necessary to argue that the additional time for education is a good thing and that the existing calendar for schooling is bad or inadequate. If we can establish that the additional time is a good thing, then the next argument is whether to put a new schedule into effect and whether the additional time should be added on Saturday or in some other way. This argument will depend on a host of exigencies inherent in the particular situation: the community's ability and willingness to pay, teacher union rules, parental wishes, and so forth.

Both kinds of prompts demand quite complex thinking. Consider the argument of judgment as an example. Deciding on the best relative or the best place to live or the best or worst of anything demands considering which qualities permit such a decision. Those who rank the "most livable" cities in the United States spend no little effort in determining what are the most important qualities, weighting, and justifying them. We can imagine that they begin by asking what are the most important qualities communities can develop for the good life of their citizens. They would have to ask what constitutes a good life. They would have to engage to some extent in considering the philosophical dimensions of the qualities they use. Further, each quality will involve a scale of some sort, quantitative or qualitative, that will allow for a comparative analysis of cities in terms of that quality. Finally, they will have to show how each city judged to be among the most livable meets some criterial level of excellence on each quality.

Of the expository prompts presented in *Write On, Illinois!*, one calls upon students to "explain" why some type of work is important, another to "explain" why an historical period is important, and a third to "explain" why some sort of pollution is a problem. Each calls for an argument of judgment.

To make a thoughtful case in dealing with these topics, the writer needs a definition that will make it possible to distinguish the important from the unimportant or the problematic from the nonproblematic. When and under what conditions is something important or unimportant? When and under what conditions is something a problem or not a problem? My students and I have been working in a high school in Chicago teaching 10th graders how to write argument. One problem had to do with a shopping mall's proposal to institute a new and restrictive security policy to reduce theft and injury on mall property. Students had to determine whether there was a real problem. Raw statistics suggested there was a great increase in arrests for theft, 292% among teens. However, examined in proportion to increased patronage at the mall, there was no increase. Rather the arrests remained constant over the years for which statistics were available at a rate of approximately 3 for 10,000 patrons. The 10th graders argued that for a significant problem to exist, there would have to be a significant increase in arrests. Without that increase in proportion to patronage, there was no problem, and, therefore, the new security policy was unwarranted. This is an argument with a claim, evidence and a warrant intended to influence the thinking and policy of the audience, in this case, the mall management. It is not simply an explanation requiring no argument.

Assessments in many states pretend that topics like those in Illinois are expository. They use the direction *explain* to differentiate them from persuasive writing topics. In effect, the term *explain* reduces the thinking necessary to complete the assignment. It suggests that no argument need be made, that all is self-evident, that no persuasion is necessary.

KINDS OF WRITING AND THEIR SCORING

Write On, Illinois! (ISBE, 1994) explains that all three domains of writing are evaluated using a 32-point scale made up of four analytical scores plus a holistic score for each piece of writing. The analytical scales provide scores on focus (1–6), support and elaboration (1–6), organization (1–6), and mechanics (1–2). The holistic score (1–6), called integration, is based to some extent on the success of students on the preceding scales. If students score at least 2 on mechanics and 3 on the others, integration may be doubled. The criteria that must be met for a score of 32 in persuasive writing appear in Figure 7.1. Interestingly, for a score of 32, expository pieces must meet the same criteria.

The Five-Paragraph Theme

Perhaps the most important criterion in shaping what will be taught appears in the focus scale. For a score of 6 on focus, both the persuasive and expository rubrics, require that the "subject/issue is clear and maintained," that the "position(s)/ opinion(s) are explicitly announced in the opening and maintained throughout the paper," and that "major points of support are explicitly previewed in the opening." If the writer does not wish to write such an explicit opening, but prefers to be somewhat more subtle, perhaps to keep the reader in suspense, the score will go down to a 4, for which the "position(s)/opinion(s) . . . may be arrived at inductively" (ISBE, 1994, p. 16). But clearly, doing it this way does not result in a top score.

FIGURE 7.1. Illinois Guide for Scoring Persuasive Writing: Score 32

All features of writing of the Illinois Guide are scored on a 6-point scale, except for conventions of writing, that is, mechanics, and sentence structure, which can receive a score of 1 or 2.

Focus: Rating 6
> Subject/issue is clear and maintained.
> Position(s)/opinion(s) are explicitly announced in the opening and maintained throughout the paper.
> Major points of support are specifically previewed in the opening.
> Paper must have an effective closing (not necessarily a separate paragraph).

Support/Elaboration: Rating 6
> All support/elaboration of the position(s)/opinion(s) is ample and developed by specific detail.
> Elaboration for each key point shows evenness or balance with that of other key points.

Organization: Rating 6
> The structure of the paper is evident.
> For multiparagraph papers, the opening, closing, and <u>all</u> major points of support/ elaboration are appropriately paragraphed.
> For multiparagraph papers, opening and closing paragraphs must contain more than one sentence.
> Coherence and cohesion are demonstrated by transitional devices. (Coherence can be effected by developing the pattern announced in the beginning.)
> All points are logically presented and interrelated.
> There are <u>no</u> digressions.

Conventions: Rating 6 (Although this is called a rating of 6, all ratings of 4–6 receive only 2 points.)
> There are few or no minor errors. There are no major errors. (The guide stipulates lists of major and minor errors.)

Integration: Rating 6 (The scoring guide indicates that this holistic rating is dependent on the scores above to some extent. To receive a score of 4 or higher on integration, it must have received scores of 4 or higher on focus, support/elaboration, and organization, as well as a score of 2 on conventions. If the score on integration is 4 or higher it is doubled. See p. 12.)
> A fully developed persuasive paper.
> Each feature is evident.
> There is a clear position; lines of reasoning are identified and coherently developed by logical reasons throughout the paper.

(From <u>Write On, Illinois!</u>, pp. 16–20, by ISBE, 1994.)

What is a "major point of support?" For that we need to turn to the benchmark papers. The following is the first paragraph of an Illinois paper receiving a top score of 32.

My grandmother deserves the "Best Relative of the Year Award" because she has done a great deal of things. She is a very hard worker, a kind and considerate person, and has done many things. (ISBE, 1994, p. 35)

Write On, Illinois! explains that this receives the highest score for focus because it explicitly announces the position in the opening ("grandmother deserves the . . . award") and maintains it (i.e., repeats it in the conclusion). The guide points out that this piece of writing explicitly reviews the major points in its opening and quotes them: "hard worker . . . kind and considerate . . . done many things" (p. 35). According to the guide, these are the major points of support.

What is the sense in which these points support the main claim of the essay? They are not evidence. They are not conclusive by any means. Each makes a claim about Grandmother. Even supposing that the writer can make the case that Grandmother has "done a great deal of things," does doing a "great deal of things" make one the best relative? It seems to me that the number of things done is irrelevant. That, however, is not a concern for *Write On, Illinois!* Apparently, the term *support* does not really mean support in Illinois. What is clear is that for the highest score, a writer must preview something that might be construed as support in the opening. Illinois presents no means of evaluating the quality of the support.

These criteria predict that teaching writing of exposition and persuasion for the Illinois writing test will focus on what has come to be known as the five-paragraph theme. *Write On, Illinois!*, of course, never mentions the word *five* in connection with these criteria. But three "points of support" or simply three points has been conventional for decades, since long before Janet Emig attacked the five paragraph theme in 1971. Teachers appear to believe that one or two reasons in support of a position are simply inadequate. Three reasons, however, provide a solid foundation, perhaps like the three legs of a tripod or stool. One, two, or even four might wobble, but three will not. Any three points of support generate a five-paragraph theme, along with the introduction and conclusion.

Homogenization of Writing

For the same score of 6 on focus in the narrative rubric, the language changes slightly requiring that the "subject/topic is clear and maintained" and that "the central theme/significant or unifying event is explicitly stated in the opening or closing, OR the reader is drawn into the event with the central theme/significant or unifying event commented upon at the end." In addition, narrative requires that "key reactions and episodes are specifically previewed in the opening or specifically addressed holistically throughout the paper" (ISBE, 1994, p. 120).

The message is clear that, to obtain the highest scores, teachers ought to teach students to write the explicit opening paragraph that outlines what is to come for exposition, persuasion, and narrative. But how many effective short narratives provide a summary of events at the beginning? To be sure, the *Odyssey* and the *Aeneid* present brief forecasts of what is to come, but nothing like a summary of events or episodes. Commonly, effective short narratives begin with the action, some *in medias res*. All other descriptors in the focus scale for narrative are the same as those in the focus scales for exposition and persuasion. The similarities in focus are typical of the similarities in other scales in the rubric. With the Illinois criteria in operation, we can expect narratives to look very much like expository pieces.

The criteria concerning support/elaboration, for example, are differentiated only slightly for the three domains of writing. For a score of 6, the persuasive and expository rubrics stipulate that "All support/elaboration of the key position(s)/opinion(s) is ample and developed by specific detail" and that "Elaboration for each key point shows *evenness* or balance with that of other key points" (pp. 17 and 67, emphasis in original). The narrative rubric varies only slightly: "All major narrative components and the theme or unifying event are explained and elaborated by specific details" and "Elaboration for each key point shows *evenness* or balance with that of other key points" (p. 121, emphasis in original).

However, the support required for an argument is quite different from that required in a narrative. In a persuasive piece, support will include details selected to support a claim or proposition (evidence), warrants (statements that explain how or why evidence supports the claim), qualifications, and counterarguments. But the rubric makes no mention of such particulars.

On the other hand, elaboration in a narrative that is supposed to tell "about a time when you were surprised" is likely to include details that convey the nature of the surprise, the feelings of the character who experiences it, and so forth. Although these details have some evidentiary impact, their main function is empathic, to enable the reader to feel some of the elements of surprise with the character. When the distinction between empathic and evidentiary detail disappears, narrative begins to look even more like exposition and persuasion.

Support in Persuasion

In persuasive writing, top papers receive scores of 6 on elaboration and support because, the marginal notes say, "all support [is] specific" with "numerous examples." What counts as specific and numerous? The writer need have only three reasons to construct the kind of five-paragraph theme appearing as examples of best papers. As we have seen in the "Grandmother" paper, there is no check on the quality or even relevance of the reasons or points of support. While IGAP requires support and elaboration for the major points of support, there are no criteria for assessing whether the support at that level is either supportive or relevant. For example, the third paragraph from the "Grandmother" composition is supposed to provide support for the claim that grandmother is kind and considerate.

My grandmother is a kind and considerate person. My grandmother is nice to everyone. I have never heard her yell. When my mother was a child, she was nice to many people. Now, my grandmother is still kind and considerate. About last year, my grandmother gave a whole bunch of money to my two cousins, my brother, and I. She had been saving it since my oldest Cousin was born. It was a special account just for us. (ISBE, 1994, p. 35)

The marginal notes in the rubric point to this paragraph as an example of support that should receive the highest score. Yet, the sentences do not really make a case for the judgment "kind and considerate." The second, third, fourth, and fifth sentences do little more than reiterate the topic sentence. The final sentences, concerning the gift of money, present a single piece of evidence. However, a gift of money does not necessarily indicate that the giver is kind and considerate. Many people give money without being kind or considerate. The evidence needed might be an anecdote illustrating the essential kindness of a deed. The point is that this paragraph presents only a superficial elaboration of the opening sentence.

Figure 7.2 presents my favorite of the "best" (32-point) papers written in response to the "best relative prompt." It is a very clever piece of writing. But it clearly illustrates an interesting problem with the criteria used in scoring. There is no way of evaluating the character of the support provided. The writer uses the fiction of an unreliable narrator. He pretends to be naive about all of Grandpa Dulong's dishonesty and peccadilloes and pretends they are worthy of great praise. Of course, the evidence, which we are meant to see through, cannot support the contention that Grandpa Dulong is generous, helpful, and caring. On the contrary, it demonstrates that Grandpa is a rascal at best, not a person worthy of

FIGURE 7.2. A Perfect Five Paragraph "Persuasive" Theme from the Illinois Scoring Guide

My Grandfather, Milton Dulong, deserves to win the Relative of the Year Award. He deserves to win the award because he makes everyone around him happy. He's generous, he's helpful, and he's caring. With all of these characteristics, he is the ideal relative.

On one occasion, he gave me $100 for my birthday. He knew how much I needed it, and he went all out. Thanks grandpa! Another example of his generosity was when he gave (donated) a large sum of money to our gang in the 4th grade. We were called the "Stingrays" and we needed a tree-house. So, my grandpa paid for construction workers to come and build a house in one of our trees. Thanks grandpa! One last example of his generosity was when he loaned some money to a group of businessmen, who needed the money in order to invest in some horses. Even though something seemed "fishy" my grandpa loaned them the money. What an idle!

Secondly, my grandpa is very helpful. On one occasion, he helped an old lady across the street. It was so nice and helpful. The one thing I couldn't understand was why the old lady slapped him across the face. Another example of his helpfulness was when helped me study for a big test I had to take in Math. He gave me a calculator and told me to hide it in my pocket. He said to punch out the numbers so the test wouldn't take me so long. I ended up getting an A+ on the test. What a guy! And again, my grandpa showed he was helpful when my mom was mixing drinks for a party (meeting) she was giving for one of her woman's clubs. He added a little bit of everything. WOW! Did that punch taste good! What a great grandpa!

Finally, my grandpa is very caring. One example of his caring was when we were walking down Rush Street and there was a young girl on the corner. She looked like she needed love. So, my grandpa offered to give her some money and a place to stay. He went to the nearest motel with her, and he came out after a half-hour. He really cared about her! Another example of his caring was when he bailed some men out of jail. They were the same men that borrowed money from my grandpa. Even though they owed him money, my grandpa still bailed them out. What a caring person! Finally, he was a very caring person when his rich mother was in the hospital. He was the heir to her $10 million, but he loved her till the end. He cried when she passed away, and even gave her a huge funeral. Everyone one was there. It was just like a huge party..... Well, anyway he was devastated. What a guy!

In conclusion, my grandpa Dulong was the most helpful, caring, and generous relative I've ever heard of. And I hope you think so too.

(From *Write On, Illinois!*, p. 34, by ISBE, 1994.)

the relative of the year award. The evidence could not be taken seriously by even the most obtuse judge. But the paper is a beautiful example of the five-paragraph theme.

The marginal commentary that accompanies the composition praises it for its opening, support/elaboration, and organization and cites the paper as having a "clear position logically developed." What, we have to ask, counts for logic? This paper is logical much in the same way that Swift's

"A Modest Proposal" is. I am told by state officials that the essay was removed from *Write On, Illinois!* (ISBE, 1994), not because it fails to illustrate logical support, but because a state legislator regarded it as off-color.

It is ironic that the essay in Figure 7.2 is a brilliant piece of writing that cannot be categorized as persuasive, nor as expository or narrative for that matter. It is a parody of the sugary content and form of the kind of school writing that the test elicits. No piece of writing in *Write On, Illinois!* can compare. The scorers and those who put the book together recognized the five-paragraph form, but they apparently missed the satire. There is no allusion to the humor in the marginal comments.

Restrictions on Testing

Why develop these criteria or these prompts? In part, the answer lies in the circumstances imposed by the state legislature. In part, it lies in the superficiality of the theory of writing adopted from the start. Further, according to the director of the Illinois writing assessment, the Illinois State Legislature sets the limit on how many classroom hours the state may use for testing during a school year at 15. Because the time is restricted, the prompts must be manageable in 40 minutes, another factor affecting the complexity of the writing. In addition, prompts must be developed so that students will be able to draw information from experience because the state believes it cannot hold students responsible for content. Presumably, then, out of these restrictions of time, writing theory, and content, the kind of assessments (prompts and scoring rubrics) are born. Prompts must be such that students are able to respond even in a short period of time and write passingly well. Thus the ISBE produces prompts that engender vacuous writing and thereby sets a very low standard for teaching writing.

I sent an early draft of this chapter and the next to the Illinois State Superintendent of Instruction for comments. The official who responded, the Chief Education Officer, claimed that many of my statements about the Illinois testing program are "erroneous or misconceptions" (M. L. Dunn, personal communication, June 15, 2001). This letter also indicates "disappointment" that I did not mention the change in the scoring rubrics in 1999 until the end of Chapter Eight. In 1999, Illinois did change the rubric. It is no longer mandatory for the highest score to preview the major points of support in the first paragraph, thus eliminating the criterion that helps to prompt teaching the five-paragraph theme. However, the criteria for the focus scale state that the opening paragraph "may or may not include specific preview" (ISBE, 2000, p. 152). The only paper presented illustrating a perfect score on a persuasive/expository essay at the high school level is a five-paragraph theme with a preview of the major points of support in the opening paragraph (pp. 172–174). The criteria for elaboration/support for the top score require "extensive, in-depth support using multiple strategies (e.g., explanation, evidence and example)" (p. 153). The new rubric calls for "all points [to be] logically presented and interrelated" (p. 154).

The sample paper illustrating the highest score according to the new rubric is in response to a prompt that tells students that the state legislature is considering making a high school exam a requirement for graduation. It states, "Write a persuasive paper stating whether or not you agree that students should be required to pass an exam to graduate from high school. Give reasons why you think as you do" (ISBE, 2000, p. 157). The author opens with the following paragraphs:

I strongly believe that students should not have to take an exam and pass it to graduate. Students who don't care what happens in their life after high school aren't going to start caring now because of the exam they have to pass. Students who strive to be burger flippers after high school aren't going to care whether or not they pass. Teachers are already testing the seniors of their knowledge in almost every class. What a high school course teaches an individual is important, but is it important enough to affect whether or not they can go to college?

The state would like a high school graduation exam to be added to the many graduation requirements, but are they willing to accept the costs? Unfortunately, every high school will have an exceptionally large amount of students who don't pass the test, and it is going to cost the state more money to put them through another year of high school. The students who don't pass the test are going to become majorely discouraged and may only become a burden to our society when we are paying for them while they are on welfare. (ISBE, 2000, p. 172)

The second paragraph begins with a rhetorical question that carries an implicit claim, that the state will not want to accept the costs. This is supported by three subclaims that large numbers of students will fail the tests, that this failure will require another year of high school, and that those who fail will become so discouraged that they will go on welfare. All of these generalizations are pure speculation with no support. How they can be called support for the main claim about costs escapes me. But the scoring manual states that this paper is exemplary because it "features reasons that are fully and evenly developed through specific detail and multiple strategies" (p. 175). Recall also that one of the criteria for the highest rating calls for "all points [to be] logically presented and interrelated."

The two paragraphs above do not pass the test of logic. If so many students do not care about their lives after high school and aspire only to be "burger flippers," why should they be greatly discouraged by failing the test? Why would failure of an exam put them on welfare rather than in a burger kitchen? The remainder of the piece of writing holds up no better under scrutiny than the first two paragraphs. The third paragraph explains that teachers are testing in classes all the time, while the fourth develops the third point in the introduction that the graduation exam could keep certain people from attending college. The first point in the introduction, about the low aspirations of students, is never developed.

Someone might contend that students cannot be expected to do better than that, that the circumstances of the testing limit their writing. That is exactly the point. The test limits what students can do. The scoring rubrics cannot be too demanding. The limited time for writing and the inaccessibility of information relevant to the issues in the prompts must allow students to respond in vague generalizations. By the same token, it is also predictable that writing in vague generalities will become the standard to which schools and teachers aspire.

TEACHING MATERIALS AND
THE TRANSFORMATION OF THEORY

Given the emphasis on the particular organizational framework, the lack of concern for content, and the similarity among the scoring rubrics for "all three domains of writing," it should not be surprising that the three domains become homogenized. We see the transformation of narrative to five-paragraph theme. In its guide to teaching, *Write On, Illinois!* (ISBE, 1994) presents diagrams illustrating an unfocused paper and a focused one. The focus in these diagrams depend on the idea that the major points must be previewed in the opening paragraph. The diagram uses a triangle, a circle, and a square to represent the three reasons that will be presented. In the unfocused diagram these figures appear on different lines of the paper. In the focused paper, the figures appear in the first line of the paper followed by their appearance in the same order but on lower lines of the paper (pp. 214, 229). In conjunction with the rule that the paper have a closing, these diagrams clearly indicate that a five-paragraph theme is appropriate, even called for, as a response to the writing prompts.

The five-paragraph theme motif is picked up by independent firms for the production of commercial materials, for example, by a booklet called *The IGAP Coach: Grade 10, Writing,* (Crowell & Kolba, 1996). This book, purchased by one of the schools we visited for use by every student and referred to by many teachers we interviewed, applies the five-paragraph theme to the narrative as well, even though most of the top-score narratives in *Write on, Illinois!* have fewer paragraphs than five. *The IGAP Coach* explains that "whenever you tell someone what happened, you're telling a story" (p. 89). It tells students that they will learn to write a story and proceeds to an example. However, the example is not a story by any definition that I know. Nor is it a narrative for that matter. It begins as follows:

I always enjoy a visit from my Aunt Joan. When she comes to visit from her home in New Jersey, it's like a vacation for all of us, but especially for me. Aunt Joan is very energetic and out-going, and she always plans special things for us to do. Even when we don't go out, she makes everyday life seem special. (p. 90)

The piece presents four more paragraphs, three of which provide information about the kinds of things that Aunt Joan does when she visits: catching up on family news, doing things with the computer, and visiting an amusement park. The final paragraph acts as a conclusion. There is no plot line, not even a chronological sequence, the absence of which appears to be a violation of the insistence in the scoring guide that the narrative structure be evident.

Far from being a narrative, this model is a five-paragraph theme with an evident structure of the sort required by the scoring rubrics for persuasive and expository writing. Three body paragraphs support the claim made in the first paragraph that a visit from Aunt Joan is " like a vacation for all of us, but especially for me." The final two sentences of the first paragraph serve as the "preview" of "major points of support" required for the top score on focus for both persuasion and exposition.

The booklet then goes on to redefine narrative for the student. It explains to students that they will learn to write a story, "the kind of narrative that you may be asked to write for the writing portion of the IGAP" (p. 89). Immediately following the model, it states, "A narrative tells a story. It answers questions like these: Who? What? Where? When? Why? How?" The text announces that "Rob's paper is a good example of a narrative because he tells in detail what happens when Aunt Joan comes to visit" (p. 91). In fact, Rob presents no narrative at all. Rather, he presents an argument in support of his claim about the joys of Aunt Joan's visits.

In the same book, the treatment of exposition comes close to being a treatment of persuasion. *The IGAP Coach* tells its readers that "In a persuasive paper, you tell others what you think. Then you try to persuade them to think as you do or to take some action" (p. 49). It tells the reader that "expository writing is writing that explains or answers questions like these:

- What does this mean?
- How does this work?
- Why does this happen?

Why these questions are thought to be typical of those answered in exposition is not clear. Any one of them might well involve persuading someone to think as you do about what this means, how this works, or why
this happens.

Indeed, *The IGAP Coach* is unable to maintain the distinction consistently. For example, the first model of expository writing is "an essay explaining why so many teenagers work after school." It opens with a sentence citing adults as complaining that teenagers work too many hours in
after-school jobs and proceeds to provide "good reasons that students work
full-time while going to school" (p. 10). What follows is an argument
emphasizing the goodness of the reasons for which teenagers work. The
apparent intention is to persuade adults that they are wrong in their assessment of the working teenager. *The IGAP Coach* calls the piece exposition because the writer "explains why so many teenagers have after-school
jobs," as though the statements made have a status that puts them beyond doubt or question.

The epistemology underlying current traditional rhetoric, which provides this typology of writing, assumes that knowledge is directly apprehensible through the senses and, therefore, need not be argued and allows the
distinction between exposition and persuasion. When the text introduces
expository writing, it implies that exposition deals with known facts about
which there is no need to argue or debate. When *The IGAP Coach* uses the
term *reason* in explaining expository writing, it refers to reasons that explain.
Later, in the section on persuasion, the book refers to reasons that persuade.
The text never appears to recognize the need to differentiate these. I suspect that it is simply not possible to make that distinction, that the reasons
to explain are always reasons to persuade. This confusion is the result of
the underlying epistemological stance which is untenable. We are left with
a collapse of distinctions that are claimed in the rubric but that cannot be
made clear. *The IGAP Coach* completes the homogenization of the three
domains of writing that *Write On, Illinois!* began.

We see a comparable homogenization in a series of books by Hamilton
(1996) to which I will refer as the Power Writing series. It is based upon
what the books present as four levels of power: the Level 1 sentence that
"must serve as the main statement, idea, or thought"; the Level 2 sentences
that "provide the major details or specifics"; the Level 3 sentences giving
elaborating details; and the Level 4 sentences providing more elaborating
details. Each of the levels beyond Level 1 is introduced by "power" 2, 3, or
4 transition words. Interestingly, nearly every power 1 sentence provided
for practice in producing the major supporting details contains the word
three, thereby forcing in place the five-paragraph theme, whether the task
be persuasive, expository, or narrative.

The writer of these books has fastened on the call for transitions in *Write On, Illinois!*, which states that "coherence and cohesion are demonstrated by transitional devices" (p. 68). The most advanced workbook, *The Higher Power Writer Within Me*, (Hamilton, 1996) tells students to use the following transition words to introduce the main supporting details: "First, second(ly), third(ly), to begin with, above all, also, next, besides, then, in addition, furthermore" as well as the expressions "one is, another is, and the other is." These in conjunction with the Level 1 power sentence, provide the framework for the opening paragraph of a five-paragraph theme. It produces models for imitation such as the following "Terrible Bad Day" composition, which the book calls a narrative. Numbers appear in parentheses to indicate the power level involved.

(1) Friday was one of the worst days I have ever had. (2) First, my gym locker was vandalized. (2) Secondly, my date for the school dance could not attend. (2) Thirdly, I did not make the cheerleading team. (p. 38)

Of course, each of these Level 2 sentences provide the topic for a following paragraph, each of which is to be developed using a set of "power (3)" transition words that include "specifically, for example, for instance, restated, in other words, translated, to explain, to describe" and that introduce "minor elaborating details about power (2)" (p. 26). Another group of transition words, "power (4) words," introduce details about the "power (3)" level. These, the book says, can be used interchangeably with power (3) words (p. 26). At any rate, the use of words at these levels produces model paragraphs for students to imitate. The second paragraph in the "terrible bad day" paper provides an example of the use of these transition words:

(2) To begin with, I eagerly entered the school because I have gym first period. I went to my gym locker and found it had been vandalized. (3)Specifically, my locker was empty and my gym clothes were gone. (4)To explain further, I was not able to dress properly for gym.

In *The Higher Power Writer Within Me*, we see the ultimate homogenization of narrative, persuasive, and expository tasks. Each may be developed with the same transition words and "power levels." There is no need to distinguish among them. Further, it does not matter that the transition words make the writing stilted. They serve simply to cue the need for additional sentences.

One might hope that this stilted writing would not do well on the state writing test, that its mechanical, shallow nature would be detected and scored as unsuccessful. Apparently, however, that is not the case. According to the author, the system was used in Harvey, described as the "third lowest poverty stricken district in the state of Illinois." Because of the Power Writing Workshops the district was able "to score state level and above in writing" (p. 43).

SCORING

The papers that students write in March are not scored in Illinois. They are shipped to a firm in North Carolina for scoring. The firm scores for several states. As any English teacher knows, commenting on compositions is an important part of the process of learning how to write, and it is extremely time consuming. But scoring commercially is less complex because the scorers need only assign a score without explaining it or making any recommendations for change.

In fact the firm, according to a former employee I interviewed, is concerned with speed and reliability in scoring. According to my source, the speed expected of scorers is at the level of 60 compositions per hour, a minute apiece. The firm seeks retired English teachers, graduate students in English, or others with some background in writing. The scorers work in the basement of a store located in a shopping mall. The firm trains them over a few days during which they learn a particular state's criteria, practice scoring a sample of the papers, receive feedback on their scoring, and as they become familiar with the scoring criteria, they push the speed up until they reach the acceptable level.

My source said that the scoring was a rigorous experience, because all knew that if they failed to remain reliable or if they failed to maintain the speed, they would be fired. Raters in this situation are not allowed to use their own judgment about a paper. They must try to get the "right" score using the official criteria. The effort is to minimize disagreement, that is, to remain reliable. Reliability in such situations is often maintained by circulating a subsample of the papers to many raters in a given session. The goal is for all of them to agree. When they do not, the process may be halted for retraining. When a rater cannot maintain reliability, the rater is removed from the team.

That seems reasonable, because it is only fair to score students on the criteria that supposedly have been taught. However, the need for strong reliability and for high speed have the effect of drawing attention to the most obvious features. My guess is that a rater would not have had time to realize that the paper about Grandpa Dulong presents no evidence that Grandpa should receive the award. They must be looking at the amount of writing and skimming for certain features that appear in the opening and are followed up in the paper. Because teachers know about the scoring processes, it may be that they are afraid to teach anything more subtle than the five-paragraph theme.

FIVE-PARAGRAPH THEME AND THE TESTING OF TEACHERS

In Illinois all prospective teachers must pass a basic skills test created by National Evaluation Systems. To enlighten teacher education institutions about changes in the test, the ISBE has distributed copies of a booklet entitled, *Enhanced Basic Skills Test: Elements of the New Assessment* (Illinois Certification Testing System, 2000). An accompanying letter from the Deputy Superintendent for Professional Preparation states that ISBE is "committed to restructuring the system of preparation . . . to ensure that all Illinois public school students have access to quality teachers" (F. Llano, personal communication, December 6, 2000). The booklet announces that a key characteristic of the test is that the "skills measured . . . are closely aligned with the Illinois Transferable General Education Core Curriculum" (p. l). What that means in everyday language is that the teachers have to know and be able to do what the students are supposed to learn.

That appears to be a very reasonable goal until we realize that it entails the same kind of vacuous writing that we find in *Write On, Illinois!* and in the ISBE 2000 guide. Even the rating scales are comparable though not precisely in the same language. However, the criteria for a top score are parallel to those for elementary and secondary students. The prompts for writing are comparable: "Should all young men and women between the ages of 18 and 25 be required to perform one year of military or civilian service?" (p. 14). The sample response in the booklet illustrates the kind of five-paragraph thinking that we find in the exemplary papers from students. It includes the standard introduction, complete with the magic word *three*:

I believe there are three important benefits of requiring young men and women between the ages of 18 and 25 to perform one year of military or civilian service: restoring the idea of citizenship, providing young people with valuable work and life experience, and helping young Americans learn to live in a democratic society. (p. 15)

These ideas are developed in the following three paragraphs. Then the writer adds a fourth paragraph of two sentences indicating that such a program might encounter problems.

To develop the point about "restoring the idea of citizenship," the author claims that "before and during World War II the idea of citizenship was an important part of American life." Then, apparently, that idea began to fade away because, she claims, John F. Kennedy had to revive it by telling us to ask "what you can do for your country." Then she adds,

In recent years, however, the idea of citizenship seems to have faded away. Requiring young people to devote a year of their lives to their country or their community would restore the concept that our society depends on the contributions of all of its citizens.

Perhaps we can commend this writer for ingenuity in saying nothing about something. But what we have is still only pretentious blether, designed to elude the necessity of supporting the proposition that compulsory service is capable of "restoring the idea of citizenship." In fact, all propositions remain unsupported even though this piece of writing is touted as an exemplification of high Illinois standards for teachers. In doing so, it locks shoddy thinking and writing into the Illinois goals and the curriculum they generate.

CHAPTER 8

Schools, Teachers, and the Illinois Assessment

How do administrators, supervisors, and teachers respond to the demands of the writing assessment in Illinois? This chapter will examine responses to the various dimensions of the writing assessment. It will close with a look at responses to the assessment in one Illinois district.

THEORY OF WRITING, KINDS OF WRITING, AND CRITERIA

The state administrator in charge of the writing assessment, Carmen Chapman, claims that "since educators can use writing to stimulate students' higher-order thinking skills—such as the ability to make logical connection, to compare and contrast, and to adequately support arguments and conclusions—authentic assessment seems to offer excellent criteria for teaching and evaluating writing" (1990, p. 1). The Illinois assessment does indeed "offer . . . criteria for teaching and evaluating writing." Unfortunately, as I argue in the previous chapter, the criteria are anything but "excellent." As we have seen, although the Illinois revised criteria mention logical connections, the illustrative writing samples reveal that the criteria do not actually deal with the logic of the writing. The Illinois criteria do not, for example, require evidence in support of claims; they permit general unsupported claims to suffice as support.

Chapman claims that the Illinois assessment is an example of authentic assessment, which she defines as "getting beyond writing as an isolated subject unto itself" (p. 1). She claims that assessment is authentic when it reflects "various types of writing as well as levels of complexity related to the task assigned in the prompt." The Illinois assessment does include a version of "various types of writing," which we have seen have a tendency to merge into one narrow conception of writing, the five-paragraph theme. But it remains unclear what the "levels of complexity" are or what their relationship is to the "task assigned in the prompt" (p. 2). The writing involved, however, can hardly be authentic in the sense that the prompts

123

and test situations represent writing that actually takes place outside test situations. No real writers must deal with issues about which they have only extremely limited information in 40-minute time slots.

In claiming that the Illinois assessment is authentic, Chapman states that the "founders of the Illinois Writing Program are philosophically committed to integrating instruction and assessment." She says that

to accomplish this, their assessment specifications require
1. representing defined writing skills, status, and growth,
2. verifying that the methods used to construct, conduct, and verify the assessment meet technical standards, and
3. implementing an information network, for classroom and district personnel to use test results to improve instruction. (p. 2)

There are several problems with this statement of philosophical commitments. First, as we have seen, the definition of *writing skills* is weak in all three domains of writing. The definition of *status* (does that mean the scores?) appears to be badly misleading, and there is no definition of *growth*. Perhaps the scoring of the compositions meets technical standards, but there is no useful information network that permits "personnel to use test results to improve instruction." Principals and teachers do not receive the school scores until the following year. The view of the state authorities is that the assessment is perfectly appropriate and Chapman can argue that, since the test is a good one, "teaching to the test is O.K." (1989).

TEACHING TO THE TEST

Teachers we interviewed in Illinois are ambivalent about the test. Only 41% believed that the assessment had contributed to the improvement of writing across the state, while under 8% disagreed. The remainder were noncommittal. However, 55% viewed teaching to the test positively, while 30% did not. At the same time, 57% approved the scoring rubric, while only 28% disapproved it. And 51% felt that the state assessment supported the kind of writing program they wanted in the schools, while 32% did not. Some 28% thought the attention to the testing displaced other important parts of the curriculum, mostly practice on conventions and grammar. Some teachers (13%) believed that the testing brought too much pressure to bear on them. This seemed especially true of teachers in smaller schools who believed they would be identified with the scores reported in the papers. Clearly, the teachers we interviewed are not in agreement about the usefulness or benefits of the assessment. Nevertheless, most of the teachers interviewed teach to the test.

Rhetorical Stance

At the same time, nearly all of the teachers in our interview sample are firmly entrenched in current traditional rhetoric. Slightly over 83% take CTR as their primary rhetorical stance, while another 15% show some evidence of such a stance. Only one teacher could be classified as using an expressivist stance, and only one as epistemic, although another two showed some evidence of epistemic and two showed evidence of expressivist stances. As a general rule, then, their teaching is in line with the Illinois assessment that focuses on the structure of three kinds of writing.

As we might expect, given this orientation, many teachers talk about their focus on the five-paragraph theme (72%); many (38%) use schematic representations (diagrams with boxes that students fill in, one for each of the five paragraphs); many (59%) ask students to read models of writing as a means of learning the structure, most often drawn directly from *Write On, Illinois!* (ISBE, 1994), *The IGAP Coach* (Crowell & Kolba, 1996), or *The Higher Power Writer Within Me* (Hamilton, 1996). A few teachers (26%) claim that they model how to write compositions for the students by going through the process of writing using the chalkboard or an overhead, a procedure widely believed to be useful to students.

One administrator, who worked on the writing assessment and has conducted many training workshops for teachers, explains that it is not a five-paragraph theme at all. It could be six or seven or even four.

> No, it is not a five-paragraph theme, and, in fact, that's one of the things when I do workshops that I share with people! I tell them that there is a formula, and the formula is that in your introduction you determine the number of reasons, the number of paragraphs that you have are the number of reasons plus two, your introduction and your conclusion.

In other words, while the key number is not necessarily five, the structure remains the same. But most of the teachers we interviewed do not push for more than five paragraphs.

In addition, as I argued in Chapter 7, the types of writing have been homogenized in teachers' eyes, and they believe that a similar structure is appropriate for all three types, even narrative. One teacher says that students do not have to study narrative in 10th grade because

> the structure is really the same as far as IGAP is concerned, you know. They still have to have the thesis statement in the introduction and examples. So they're pretty much ready for the IGAP narrative.

That is, students are ready for narrative because they study the same form for persuasive and expository in the 10th grade.

Major tools in expressivist rhetoric and in workshop and sometimes environmental modes of teaching are writing in a journal and free writing. The idea underlying this practice is that students should enjoy expressing their own ideas as real writers do, without any restrictions, that some time should be devoted to these authentic purposes for writing, and that journal entries can be the inspiration for other, more formal writings that may be more fully developed and subjected to peer and teacher review.

Many Illinois interviewees (50.9%) say they encourage writing in a journal by assigning prompts every day for writing. One high school teacher in a large urban high school, which I will call Washington High, claims that the IGAP assessment has made her rethink what she does. In order to prepare students to write narrative, she says,

> My particular approach is, first of all we do a journal, we write every day for 10 minutes, and that is narrative. What I do is give them some kind of a writing prompt, and then sometimes they can choose. And we've been doing that all year. . . . And that's pretty successful.

At the time of the interview, Washington High had a schedule of 40 minute periods, which means that this teacher devoted 25% of classroom time to the journal. While this teacher treated exposition and persuasion more specifically in terms of developing the content of various ideas, she believed that the journal writing sufficed for teaching narrative.

The majority of teachers claiming to use journals provide prompts about which students are to write. Many use the journal to reinforce more specifically what they have done to prepare for the tests. Ms. Donaldson, a third-grade teacher in a rural community, which I will call Farmington, talks about the need to stress the five-paragraph structure.

> They do have to keep the structure, and they're taught that at an early age [meaning prior to third grade]. And then we really, really, stress that and just pound it, pound it, pound it, over and over in the third grade. And so now when we write in our journals it's first, next, and last.

"First, next, and last" is part of the specific formula that Farmington schools have adopted representing the three major points that must be included in the body of every expository and persuasive theme. In short, for many teachers, the journal becomes part of the five-paragraph arsenal.

It is comforting to know that some teachers who teach the five-paragraph theme for the test condemn it and do not allow it to control the remainder of their instruction. For example, Mrs. Barnett, teaching in a blue-collar suburb of a large urban area, says,

> I think that the IGAP is really very, very basic. It's . . . a sort of babyish writing style. . . . It's almost more what people do in speaking than what they do in writing about literature. "Let me tell you about this, this, and this." It's just not that sophisticated. . . . There's not a huge need for kids to know how to write a five-paragraph essay. . . . Basically, . . . all [kids] need to know [is] how to group a topic into three and talk about the topic. And they could say, "My favorite things are apples, oranges, and yesterday's newspaper."

Mode of Teaching

As we might expect with a heavy emphasis on current traditional rhetoric, the mode of teaching that appears to support such rhetoric is presentational. In Illinois, 81.1% of the teachers interviewed described their teaching in ways that led us to believe that they relied on combinations of lecture and recitation for their teaching of writing.

Environmental teaching would be likely to involve students in inquiry and activities that encourage and support imagining. We searched for evidence of the kinds of active inquiry found in Ms. Levine's class in Chapter 2. But only 5.7% described such activities. We also looked for activities that could be described as encouraging students to investigate data or texts, to imagine new situations, or to invent dialogue or descriptions of characters or other group or whole-class composing projects. Only 13.2% of teachers made use of such procedures.

Mrs. Barnett lists a series of activities that she regularly uses when she is not preparing her students for IGAP. She comments that her sophomores work "during the year, with *Lord of the Flies* [and] with *To Kill a Mockingbird*. They're doing trials. They're writing journal entries in the voice of a character. We do a simulation game . . . where they have a running journal in the character and they create newspaper articles and editorials." Together, she and the students develop a journal for a character, e.g., Piggy in *Lord of the Flies*, so that students learn how to write entries in such a journal. The entries require students to imagine how a character responds to situations even though the author only implies the response. At the same time, students must consider how the character has responded in a variety of other situations. Simulation games, she explains, involve students in collecting information through their character journals, developing a case of some sort from the point of view of the character around some issue the class has identified as important, and presenting the case to other students who respond from the points of view of other characters. These discussions focus on the conflicts that the students discover in the book and occasionally on the conflicts that they themselves have with the author's ideas. The simulations engage students in the construction of arguments, thereby enabling them to learn the necessary procedures. This teacher was categorized as using an environmental mode of teaching.

Most Illinois teachers do not describe such teaching. Rather, they tell us what they tell the students. One teacher, we will call him Mr. Adams, in a large urban school with an African American population living below the poverty line, says that students need to know the rules for each kind of writing.

> For narrative particularly, we talk about what you do when you tell a story. And a lot of times I will just toss a prompt out there, without telling them that this is a prompt from the IGAP, let's say. And we'll talk about it, and I'll take notes on the board from there. And I will say, "Okay, now, we're doing this verbally." I tell them, "You know the basics. This is mostly what they're looking for on that IGAP. If you get the chronological part, you're a good chunk of the way there. And you already knew that before I even said a word about IGAP. . . . However, there are a couple of things the IGAP people will go crazy on if you do or don't do, in this narrative writing." . . .
>
> I tell them the most important thing. "They're looking for two things: all the way through, almost in every paragraph, you need to have a reaction to what's going on, as it goes on; and they want to know what you learned from either the event that you participated in, or the event that you witnessed, whichever the case may be. . . . We're going to learn the game." And so we talk about going back and, "Okay, we have all this chronology up on the board. Where can we stick in our reaction? At point A, point B, point C. How can we say, at the very beginning, before we actually get into the actual chronology, how can we give a little introduction that says, in a nutshell, what happened, and more importantly, in a nutshell, what I learned, what did I learn? How can we add that, reiterate that, and expand upon that at the bottom?" And at the point, they've got the basics down on how to do that narrative essay.

Mr. Adams also provides students with models from *Write On, Illinois!*— good ones and weak ones for students to "correct." In short, Mr. Adams presents lectures, possibly with interspersed recitation, models, and opportunities to respond to prompts. He focuses on declarative knowledge, the kind of teaching we found in the vast majority of our interviews with Illinois teachers.

Writing Process

Illinois teachers use the writing process elements, but not in a consistent way. That is, few take students through most of the process for most of the writing completed. Rather, they use parts of the process selectively. About 66% allude to using brainstorming, most frequently in response to a prompt of the kind to appear on the test. One teacher explains that he takes a typical prompt and practices brainstorming for ideas to respond to it, for example a topic like, "why we should have Saturday school." The idea is to help students learn how to generate ideas for writing on the test.

Most provide feedback after students have completed first or second drafts. Fewer (15.1%) report providing coaching and feedback as students write a draft. A good many (53%) provide for peer feedback and response.

Only about half (50.9%) say they have students revise, but for those who do, revision is not a regular part of the process. It is sporadic. A high school teacher at Farmington says that it is too much to do regularly when she has 136 students per day. A high school teacher at Washington High says that her students will simply not revise: "They would *never* revise unless I will stand there and tell them exactly what to do. It's very rare to have someone [revise]—if you say "Okay, revise." She firmly believes that her students are simply not ready to revise. The fact is that students must learn how to revise, and we have evidence that students can learn how to revise at much younger than 10th grade. But we frequently encounter statements from teachers in Illinois that students will not or are reluctant to revise.

A larger percentage (58%) of our interviewees say they have students edit. However, this seems to be simply the request that students take time to look over their papers to correct errors before they turn them in. We do not find evidence that teachers make a concerted effort to teach editing techniques, for example, as in systematically monitoring deviations from accepted formal usage in students' writing and teaching those systematically, incorporating them into a set of conventions for students to think about as they write.

Almost a third (30.2%) of teachers say they publish student writing in some way. Nearly three quarters of these are elementary school teachers.

Perhaps all of this is the result of the horrendous size of classes in certain Illinois secondary schools. In one fairly large urban system, for example, one teacher at the time of her interview said, "I have 140 students, and next year I will have 35 more. We're talking about five full sessions, which will be 175 kids." When I expressed my horror, she told me that she felt it was "pretty impossible" this year. "I spend a lot of time," she said. "I just finished research papers and I spent an hour—and I'm really not exaggerating—I spent at least an hour on each rough draft, and then another half-hour grading the final paper, so that's a lot of hours, and it's all at home."

If anyone is counting, that comes to 210 hours, the equivalent of five and a quarter 40-hour work weeks. When I evinced surprise that a school system concerned with students' test scores would permit such class sizes, she said that larger class size was a way of getting rid of staff to save money. In my opinion, whoever is responsible for class size in this school system ought to be given the opportunity to teach writing carefully for a few years while he contemplates the error of his ways.

FORMULAIC WRITING IN FARMINGTON

What happens when an administration puts pressure on a faculty to increase the writing scores? Farmington provides an example. It is a very small rural community in about the center of Illinois. We spoke with three administrators and several teachers at each of the elementary, middle, and high schools. It was clear that the administrators wished the school to look good on the IGAP tests. The middle school principal, Mr. Grady, said that IGAP was very important because, in Illinois, the only other ways to evaluate school systems are through the school improvement plans, which he believes no one will examine, and the North Central accreditation, which provides only recommendations about the school, no real evaluation. He says, "IGAP . . . is the only accountability in Illinois. . . . What we're doing now is we're putting all the reliance [on] the IGAP scores as indicative of what you're doing in your school." While he feels that the IGAP is a "cookbook approach" to education, and that it is "very one-dimensional," he also believes that without any question, "the IGAP is here to stay, and it's only going to get bigger. And it could get better, but we're pretty happy with the writing part."

> Having a focus on the writing for the IGAP has made our teachers focus on writing more, to get away from a lot of the traditional grammar and traditional type things that . . . really aren't as beneficial as having the kids write. So in that way I think it has helped. As far as the structure of the *Write On, Illinois!* program, I don't think

it's bad. It provides some consistency and then by the time the kids get older they can branch out from that.

On the other hand, Mrs. Stafford, the elementary school principal, takes a different view.

> Our writing scores are not the state average. And . . . there's a big philosophy difference on writing, and I know that's one of the reasons I wanted to talk to [a specific teacher], 'cause she, she's excellent and she believes in . . . an approach to writing that's different from IGAP, and she does wonderful things, and has a very creative approach. Unfortunately, the state of Illinois says there is one way that you can teach children how to organize their thoughts and write. As a third-grade teacher for many, many years, the first year that I taught *Write On, Illinois!* I thought there's no way the children can ever do this.

Mrs. Stafford goes on to tell of her change of heart. But the change seems to be a hesitant one.

> You know, I, we really underrated what they were able to do. I found out very quickly that, yes indeed, third graders can be taught to write a . . . five-paragraph essay, um, the way *Write On, Illinois!* asks for them to do it, and   it's a way that, that helps them organize their thoughts. It's not necessarily a creative way to write, but . . .
>
> So, if indeed they can at least organize their thoughts and get down five paragraphs and understand an introductory paragraph and a concluding paragraph and three detail paragraphs, then I think it's just a beginning point from which they can deal.
>
> But the . . . major problem is that . . . a third-grade teacher cannot do it all in one year. So we . . . have started some curriculum mapping in the field of writing, and . . . we are working with our lower-grade teachers too, you know. For instance . . . maybe even in kindergarten, if they're used to stating the three reasons for something, you know? . . .
>
> In my past experience, it takes about 5 years to really impact. First of all, you have to get people to understand the need to switch. And then once they switch to the format . . . they have to understand that they're not robbing children of their creativity, that you're giving them a framework for organization and until the state changes that framework, then we should follow the framework.

Accordingly, the administration brought in a consultant, a person who had "developed methods that were successful in raising test scores" to help teachers. She presented several ideas but the one that most teachers mention is the "model" which presents a set of five numbered and labeled boxes: (1) Introduction, (2) First body paragraph, (3) Second body paragraph, (4) Third body paragraph, and (5) Conclusion. Within the block for Introduction several lines appear. The first is labeled Main Idea Sentence, the next three are labeled First, Next, and Last to indicate that the sentences on those lines will preview the three main supporting ideas or events. The first line of each body paragraph begins with one of those words in order. The consultant explained that this device provides cohesion. It is this model to which Ms. Donaldson refers above.

Mrs. Stafford comments on the consultant.

> We brought some excited people in who worked with them on, on the *Write On, Illinois!* process. And so, I think, um, we got a lot more people believing than we had prior. But, um, you know . . . if the test is not my year then I will do what I want to do. . . . The point being that . . . you know, until everybody one hundred percent buys into it . . . our scores will not be as high. . . . I'm noticing that the state scores keep going up, up, up. . . . [As a result] it's going to be even more difficult to make the state average.

I have quoted Mrs. Stafford at length to illustrate the process of indoctrination by the state. To give her her due, Mrs. Stafford, when asked directly, agrees that the IGAP does not represent "good writing." Rather, she says it is "good organization." But that distinction is not enough to lead her away from the IGAP guidelines. She is not an expert in writing. She has an undergraduate degree in elementary education, an M.A. in the same, and the appropriate administrative certification. She feels powerless to resist the pressures from her own administration and the state.

Let us turn to a second-grade teacher. Ms. Eggert, who has been teaching second grade for several years, says that

> Last year, oh, January, I started doing some things because of those *Write On, Illinois!* You know, writing . . . an introductory paragraph, uh, just to kind of introduce the problem. First I would do this. In fact, I've already done that this year. You know, I've used the word problem, I don't really want to do that, but . . . Now, what was the problem? Uh, you know, list . . . talk about three things, um, how you feel about this. First I do this, next I do this, then I do that. Or lastly I do that. And I have that written out on a [large chart], you

know. . . . So, we kind of get some thinking about, about that [pause] I don't want to use this word, but that sequence of thoughts.

Mrs. Folsom is a colleague of Ms. Donaldson's quoted above and also teaches third grade. Her plan had been to begin the year with narrative, "a narrative style, um, by the five-paragraph state standards."

> I have come to the conclusion that they're not gonna be ready. In fact, this afternoon we were supposed to work on that some more. I'm not sure that they're going to be ready to indent, and to know where to start a paragraph and where to stop. . . . I'm just not convinced that that is going to be something they are going to be ready for.

She is not happy with the IGAP format. She says,

> I feel like the IGAP is just imposing something upon us that isn't real, and it isn't real to the kids, and it's very artificial. I would almost rather them just give us 20 sentences that the kids have to edit and say, "they need to know where the capitals go, where the periods go." Then for third graders that might be all they need. You know, we would *know* that that's what we have to teach. . . .
> But when they start imposing five-paragraph essays that take a whole semester or a year to teach them how to write, they're imposing *curriculum*, they're not imposing skills, they're imposing *curriculum*. . . . The state is gonna have to find, what do they want. Do they want five-paragraph essay, or do they want mechanics. . . . Personally, I think [mechanics] would be enough for third graders. . . . But . . . I don't see a reason why third graders have to be able to write narrative, persuasive, and expository. I mean, there's no really even authentic *reason* for them to have to do it.

Clearly, Mrs. Folsom does not agree with Ms. Donaldson. She is one of the teachers that Mrs. Stafford mentioned who are not willing to buy into the program, not because she disapproves of the IGAP format, but because she thinks it is too hard to teach to third graders.

At the fifth-grade level, Mrs. Delmonico reports:

> When we started really looking into what we should be doing, . . . we pushed the kids into the five-paragraph writing and they didn't have any problems! . . . I required my class last year to do at least five paragraphs. And it was so easy for them to write it! Not only

was it easy for them to go to the five-paragraph format, but even the assignment itself was not painful.

Mrs. Hart at the sixth-grade believes that students

come to us with a pretty good background, I think, in paragraph form. And then we take that a little bit further, and of course, because of the IGAP test, we are into a five-paragraph real quick. And we basically teach that canned writing, that form, and they do well! . . . We teach that form, because that's how they're graded. . . . We teach the method, the five paragraphs, the developing the three ideas, and giving the support for each idea, and doing the whole thing.

At the seventh-grade level, Ms. Masters concentrates on "sentences . . . sentences and then paragraphs and then, in the second semester, we go to the five-paragraph essay." She says,

I have a worksheet that they start out with, that they list their statements, their viewpoints, what they're defending, and the reasons for that. At least three reasons for that, and then, I think on the worksheet are some details that support each reason. And if they can fill that out, they have a better chance of doing . . . fairly well structured prewriting thing before they write the [final], and it's usually five paragraphs, three reasons.

We interviewed three teachers at the 10th-grade level. They are in quite strong agreement about teaching *Write On, Illinois!* Comments from one will suffice to illustrate the general 10th-grade position. Mrs. Rankin says that in the past, students would just sit down and start writing. "And some of them [were] not taking it very seriously. And as a consequence, our writing scores were just not very good."

So last year we decided, "Well, if we're going to do this thing, and they're [the administrators] telling us we really need to do better on this, we need to make a concerted effort on how it is done." And we had a woman come in and talk to us about the *Write On, Illinois!* program, and basically said, "That's what they're looking for in the IGAP, is the *Write On, Illinois!* style." So she talked to us about basically what they're looking for in the IGAP. And the five-paragraph essay and the introduction and we're given a little outline, that sort of thing. Basically they're looking for a formula, evidently! So we came back and we decided that we would indeed try and talk to them about that and how to use this formula. And all of our writing from then on—throughout the year I adapted to that style. And we practiced writing the three different types of writing, using the outline and developing the five-paragraph essay. . . . And what we saw was them all doing that. All three teachers, when they sat down—and it kind of helped them, because now they had a way to start, they knew how to start. And consequently our writing scores are much higher this year.

Mrs. Rankin has much more to say about teaching the five-paragraph theme, how kids tend to repeat the introduction almost word for word in the conclusion, how she works against this, how the three teachers use the consultant's outline, how they distinguish among the three types of writing, and so forth. She believes that once they taught the form, their "students caught on to that real well."

She adds as a kind of postscript, "I even noticed that with my seniors this year. Evidently, the junior English teacher last year let them try and use this formula, too. And they're doing that, too. So your introduction is almost identical to your conclusion! So I'm trying to get them out of that mode. That's hard."

One of the principals says, "We'd like to foster the idea of . . . the IGAP being part of . . . our normal lives here. But you almost *have* to make it important to get people's attention. And I think we're gonna be doing that more and more. We're going to be doing more things with our kids, because it's so important. We're gonna do more focus on the IGAP. I'm *sure* we will." He urges the importance of understanding "what the state is doing and making sure we're complying with that." He concludes that "there's a lot of good things that have come out of this. I mean, really. You know, we are articulating, we're communicating as teachers more than we ever were. By far."

SOME CONCLUSIONS ABOUT
ILLINOIS' WRITING ASSESSMENT

With the exception of a very few teachers like Mrs. Barnett, who has had two graduate-level courses on the teaching of writing, one a school-based seminar, most teachers we interviewed have no education in the teaching of writing. Only one reports having worked in a National Writing Project program and only two report graduate-level courses in the teaching of writing. Many of the teachers interviewed have had training in using the Illinois scoring rubric, but scoring and teaching are not the same. The result is that most of them do not think much about writing beyond the confines of the IGAP testing program. For the majority, especially at the elementary and middle school levels, the IGAP test and its accompanying rubric represents the universe of writing. For them, the rubric with its three domains constitutes all that is to be found in writing, and especially what is most fundamental.

For testing in 2000, Illinois changed the criteria so that the opening paragraph need no longer preview the major points of support (ISBE, 2000). The criteria indicate that the opening may preview the major points of support, but allows that a writer may develop the writing in some other way. In a workshop I attended on using the new criteria, the leader emphasized that the writing need not be five-paragraph themes. In the spring of the year when schools had received their scores (for the first time that early), I interviewed several teachers and an administrator in an elementary and a middle school in the same blue-collar district. Twenty percent more students in the middle school and over 30 percent in the elementary school had reached state standards than had the preceding year. They claimed that this success was due to their in-service workshops on the five-paragraph theme and the fact that all teachers were using it. It did not matter that the criteria had changed somewhat. Illinois teachers and administrators have learned how to increase scores and, to them, that means teaching the five-paragraph theme.

On the other hand, it is apparent that Illinois teachers are attending more to writing than did the sample in Applebee's 1981 survey. Administrators are nearly in total agreement that the IGAP writing assessment has helped to improve writing instruction in the state because teachers have had to attend to actual writing rather than traditional grammar.

Still, it is abundantly clear that the Illinois "format" does not support the higher level thinking skills that Chapman claims for it. On the contrary, it imposes not only a format but a way of thinking that eliminates the need for critical thought. It teaches students that any reasons they propose in support of a proposition need not be examined for consistency, evidentiary force, or even relevance. Nearly anything goes.

Meanwhile, directors of freshman English at colleges and universities are complaining vociferously that they cannot stop their freshmen writers from writing the simplistic five-paragraph theme. One faculty member calls the form "immoral." The English department at Illinois State University has published a manual for freshman English that explains on one page that while the five-paragraph theme may have been appropriate in high school, it is not appropriate in college and should be studiously avoided because its "artificiality . . . warps the subject at hand." (Neuleib, 1999, p. 5).

CHAPTER 9

Writing About Texts: The Case of New York

At the time we conducted interviews in New York, the State Education Department (NYSED) had just begun to change the assessment. The Regents of New York had decided to eliminate what had been called the Regents Competency Test that had been used as an alternative to the more demanding Regents exams required for a Regents diploma at graduation from high school. In the old state assessment system, writing assessments were given in Grades 5, 8 or 9, and 11 and 12. In the revised assessment program, writing assessments appear in Grades 4, 8, and 11. By 2004, all students will be required to take the Regents examination with its language arts orientation (see Chapter 3). Under the older system, high school students opting out of the Regents exam were required to take the Regents Competency Test, which required writing a business letter, a report, and a "composition" in response to a prompt. The new Regents exams do not include the business letter, report, and "composition." At the 11th grade all writing samples involve writing about texts. Students have two 3-hour sessions on 2 different days for these responses with two prompts in each. In addition, three of the prompts include multiple-choice questions on passages that students respond to in writing. Other grade level assessments are comparable in the types of responses required. These are summarized in Figure 9.1.

The Competency Test is in the process of being phased out during the years 1999–2004. During that period, a score of 55–64 may be used as passing for local schools' diploma requirements, but 65 is a passing score for a "Regents diploma." However, for ninth graders entering in 2000, the passing score for either local or Regents diplomas will be 65, and beginning with ninth graders entering in 2001, students must take and pass five Regents examinations to graduate: English, math, global history and geography, U.S. history and government, and science. These represent the most demanding examination regimen we have seen in this study.

All of these changes are due to a plan approved by the Board of Regents in 1994 to revise the state assessment system to "assess the broader

FIGURE 9.1. Summary of New York Regents Language Arts\English Examinations

Grade 4

Session I: Read 5 passages and answer 28 multiple-choice questions (45 min).
Session II: Part 1: Listen to a passage read by the teacher, write 2 short responses and 1 extended response (30 min).

Session II: Part 2: Write a composition (30 min).

Grade 8

Session I: Read 4 passages and answer 25 multiple-choice questions. Listen to a passage and write 3 short responses and 1 extended response (90 min).

Session II: Read 2 related passages and write 3 short responses and 1 extended response (90 min).

Grade 11

Session I: Listen to a passage read aloud, answer 6 multiple-choice questions, and use information from the passage to write a response for a specific purpose and audience (90 min). Read a text and related graph or chart, answer 10 multiple-choice questions, and use information from both documents to write a response for a specific purpose and audience (90 min).

Session II: Read 2 literary texts, answer 10 multiple-choice questions, and write an essay discussing the theme and the author's use of literary elements and techniques

Interpret a written statement given to them about some aspect of literature and write an essay using 2 works they have read to support their interpretation (180 min).

range of language functions and the more rigorous level of expectation reflected in the new 'Learning Standards for English Language Arts'" (NYSED 1998, p. 1).

STANDARDS

New York's focus on the functions of language for information and under-standing, for critical analysis and evaluation, and for literary response and expression, all imply a concern for processing content that many states do not share in their rationales. It is a concern with the procedural knowl-edge that enables students to analyze, interpret, and conduct inquiry into unfamiliar content. The Regents set high-level goals for elementary, middle, and high school that include mastering "communication . . . skills as a foundation" to thinking "logically and creatively," applying "reasoning skills to issues and problems," and comprehending "written, spoken, and visual presentations in various media," and speaking, listening to, reading and writing "clearly and effectively in English." These goals are followed by another, even more ambitious one:

Goal 2: Each student will be able to apply methods of inquiry and knowledge learned through the following disciplines and use the methods and knowledge in interdisciplinary applications. [English language arts is the first listed of these disciplines.]

The set of nine goals deals with the cultural and aesthetic; the political, economic, and social; the acquisition and use of "skills, knowledge, understanding, and attitudes necessary to participate in democratic self-government"; and personal life management (NYSED, 1994, pp. 59–61). Each of these is laid out in detail.

Taken as a set, these goals call for educating students to lead what Socrates would call examined lives. It is no accident that logic, creativity, and the application of "reasoning skills to issues and problems" head the list. These are basic to the goals that follow. Students are to think critically and creatively about the basic concepts of democracy; about the values necessary to democratic and just living; about economic, political and social institutions and their international interdependence; about the values requisite to living in a just, diverse, even global society that thrives through its understanding and acceptance of all its members. These goals go admirably beyond the standards announced by other states. Will they be reflected in the writing prompts?

SCORING

The exams will be scored "holistically" by trained teachers using "clearly defined criteria in a 6-level scoring rubric" (NYSED, 1998, p. 2). The state provides training for three teachers from districts or regions who, in turn, are responsible for training the teachers in their home districts and regions. The *Information Booklet for Administering and Scoring the Regents Comprehensive Examination in English* (NYSED, 1999) indicates that the administrator in the home school must appoint a "scoring coordinator" whose tasks are to supervise the "training and logistics of the scoring process," including "task-specific training" (on each of the examination problems) and appointing "two teachers to rate each task independently, with a third available to resolve discrepant scores" (p. 2), a standard procedure. Of course, it insures reliability only within a group of raters who work together, not across independently operating groups.

THE PROMPTS

As Figure 9.1 indicates, the Regents Comprehensive English Examination includes four major writing tasks. The *Information Booklet* states that tasks include listening to and using information from a speech to "write a response for a specific purpose and audience;" reading "a text and a related graphic" and using the information from both to do the same; reading two literary texts and writing an essay that discusses "a controlling idea and the author's use of literary elements and techniques;" and, finally, interpreting a given "written statement . . . about some aspect of literature" and writing "an essay using two works they have read to support their interpretation" (p. 1). Such prompts are echoed in the prompts used at lower grade levels.

In the 1999 Regents Comprehensive English Examination, the first prompt asks students to listen, twice, to a "speech" (i.e., an essay read aloud by the teacher) about the "Suzuki method" of learning to play violin. The first part of the essay outlines the methods used originally in Japan and the results, while the second half describes how the method was changed in the United States to become less naturalistic, more rigid and devoid of opportunities for play and spontaneity.

The original Japanese method begins at an early age with parents playing recordings of violin music including simple tunes and complex music by the master composers. While children are still young, it requires that mothers take lessons learning to play the simple music the children have heard on the recordings and taking the children with them to their lessons, waiting until the time a child desires to try to play the violin, at which point the teacher produces a tiny violin for the child to play.

The Americanized version of Suzuki, according to the speech, has little room for children to make decisions or to experiment with the instruments. Rather, it focuses on teaching a sequence of simple movements and phrases and practicing those to some level of expertise before moving on to the next more difficult steps. It stresses practice, instant correction of errors, and tight control of learning.

The writing task tells students to imagine that their board of education has decided to add violin instruction to the music program in the district and that their music teacher has asked them to write a letter to the board "explaining the Suzuki method of violin instruction and recommending whether *or* not this method should be taught in your district." They are instructed to "use relevant information from the speech" to write the letter.

I would expect this prompt to elicit an argument (not simply exposition) recommending the adoption or nonadoption of the Suzuki method. The argument will have to be fairly complex, if it is to take into consideration all dimensions of the Suzuki method. How could an American board of education adopt such a program? It would surely be condemned as discriminatory, favoring children whose mothers had the leisure and money for violin lessons. It seems impossible to argue reasonably for the inclusion of the original Suzuki method in a publicly sponsored program. We will need to examine the criteria and benchmark papers to determine whether the kind of thinking elicited meets the goals set forth by the Regents.

The second prompt to which the students respond in the first session requires them to read a text and a graphic and "use the information from both documents to write a response for a specific purpose and audience." The June 1999 exam uses a passage about child labor of approximately 1,700 words and a graphic providing a summary of the provisions in the New York labor laws relating to minors as of 1993. The passage provides information about the beginnings, conditions, and history of child labor, pointing out the hardships suffered by children and the efforts to end such practices. The graphic provides such specific information as how many hours per day during the school year minors of certain ages can work and the exceptions ("farmwork, newspaper carrier, and street trades").

The prompt asks students to write a report for a social studies class, "summarizing some provisions of current New York State law regarding the employment of children and discussing conditions that may have led to those provisions." The inferences necessary to link the two documents are quite simple since the information necessary to link the history and the actual laws is stated in both. Again, we will have to examine the criteria and benchmark papers to fully understand the kind of thinking the task requires.

In the second session for 1999, the first prompt presents two literary texts, a prose passage and a poem. The prose passage is a memoir of about 1,280 words from *Barrio Boy* by Ernesto Gallarzo (1971) about the narrator's recollection and reflections on coming to an American first-grade class as a Spanish speaker. The narrator tells how his White teachers helped him become a proud American and retain his pride in his Mexican heritage. The second is a poem of 55 lines, literally fairly simple but more complex inferentially, telling of a young boy's feelings about a day that a tornado swept through his school and what he learned through his teacher's actions. Here is the prompt for writing:

After you have read the passages and answered the multiple-choice questions, write a unified essay about the influence of teachers on the lives of their students, as revealed in the passages. In your essay, use ideas from both passages to establish a controlling idea about the influence of teachers on the lives of their students. Using evidence from each passage, develop your controlling idea and show how the author uses specific literary elements or techniques to convey that idea.

This prompt appears to present a far more complex task than those from Illinois or Texas, and more complex than the first two prompts of this exam. It demands reading and interpreting two texts, synthesizing those understandings, and making a case to support a claim about the two selections. It may not really be more sophisticated, however. The sophistication will depend on the criteria used to evaluate the case that is made.

The final prompt asks students to

Write a critical essay in which you discuss two works of literature you have read from the particular perspective of the statement that is provided for you in the Critical Lens. In your essay, provide a valid interpretation of the statement, agree or disagree with the statement as you have interpreted it, and support your opinion using specific references to appropriate literary elements from the two works. . . . Critical Lens: In literature, evil often triumphs but never conquers.

The prompt goes on to provide guidelines that advise students to

- Provide a valid interpretation of the critical lens that clearly establishes the criteria for analysis
- Indicate whether you agree or disagree with the statement as you have interpreted it
- Choose two works you have read that you believe best support your opinion
- Use the criteria suggested by the critical lens to analyze the works you have chosen
- Avoid plot summary. Instead, use specific references to appropriate literary elements (for example: theme, characterization, setting, point of view) to develop your analysis. (NYSED, 1999, June 23a, *Comprehensive English Examination, Session Two*)

The prompt calls for a "valid interpretation" of the "critical lens." What will count as "valid" and what will count as an interpretation? The easy interpretation of the critical lens is that the triumphs of evil are short-lived and therefore are only triumphs, not conquests. Underlying this interpretation is the assumption that *triumph* connotes a somehow momentary phenomenon and *conquest* a more enduring one. Is that a valid interpretation in the minds of the test makers? Or is a valid interpretation more extensive? Would a more valid interpretation include some statement about cause and effect? "Evil may triumph, but it cannot conquer because of the indomitable nature of human beings or because of their innate goodness." Would that interpretation receive more credit?

Another interpretation is that the author of the lens is a Dr. Pangloss, spouting meaningless platitudes to the effect that we "live in the best of all possible worlds." We know how Voltaire would respond to this item. Would his interpretation be deemed "valid"?

After developing an interpretation, the student is to "use the criteria suggested by the critical lens to analyze the works . . . chosen." That certainly sounds impressive. However, what exactly is entailed is not at all clear. According to the OED, a *criterion* is "a test, principle, rule, canon, or standard, by which anything is judged or estimated." All of these are used to judge or estimate the value or quality of or the differences among some set of phenomena.

In what sense can we use criteria to "analyze" a literary work? The only criteria I can think of for the first interpretation above are standards concerning what constitutes good, evil, triumph, and conquest. We can ask two kinds of questions: (1) What are the criteria by which we measure the intensity, quality, or durability of good, evil, triumph, and conquest? and (2) What is the *sine qua non* of each of these? What, for example, is the *sine qua non* of evil, that without which it is not evil?

When I finally arrived at the final question above, I had to think carefully about it. I suppose that some people believe that evil exists independent of human existence. However, it is easier to begin thinking about the problem in relationship to human activity. In our legal tradition, we have generally associated the most punishable actions with deliberation and intention. Thus, if a driver kills a pedestrian who throws himself in front of the driver's car, the driver is not likely to be punished. If, on the other hand, the driver fails to see a pedestrian in a crosswalk and runs him down, killing him, the driver is likely to be charged with negligent manslaughter, a charge carrying a relatively light sentence. The driver's actions were careless, but he had no intent to kill. Assume the same man has a fight with a neighbor and, in a fit of temper, pulls out a handgun, and waves it at his neighbor. If the handgun should discharge and kill the neighbor, the man could be charged with second-degree murder which carries a higher penalty than negligent manslaughter because of the presence of intent. Even though our man pleads that he did not intend to kill the neighbor, the very presence of a lethal weapon may be enough to establish intent and thereby a more serious charge. If sometime after a quarrel, our man were to plan the murder of his neighbor and the evidence of planning were available, the charge would be first-degree murder, because we consider a crime committed with "malice aforethought" as far more reprehensible than one that is not planned in advance. We take advanced planning of a crime as evidence of unscrupulous hard-heartedness. We now have some roughly outlined criteria for a definition of human evil.

We can go through the whole process with human acts of goodness. What is the *sine qua non* of human goodness? For any virtuous act to be truly praiseworthy in our culture, it must be undertaken for noble motives, be freely chosen, and without the expectation of personal reward. We could in a little time work out a set of criteria for judging the relative goodness of various acts.

We need to do the same for the ideas of triumph and conquest. Both are likely to be problematic because the connotations of the words are not so clear. Is there a difference between the two? What is the *sine qua non* of triumph?

Then there is the term *never*. Any statement with *never* in it covers a great deal of territory, everything, in effect. Is this *never* to be taken as a flat-out *never* or one to be taken as an exaggeration? If we take *never* literally, agree with the proposition, and support our position, we have to prove that evil never conquers. This, of course, will not be easy because of the difficulty of proving a negative proposition.

Now that we have some criteria, we can rephrase the prompt in order to develop a response using criteria: In literature, to what extent do the evil actions of humans triumph over good people without conquering them? Not much simpler, but we now have some criteria to use in analyzing the literary works. All this is by way of demonstrating how difficult responding to these tasks is. We will have to look at the benchmark papers to find what counts as criteria, analysis, and supporting a position.

CRITERIA FOR JUDGING WRITING

As indicated in Chapter 4, in New York, written responses are judged on five rating scales: meaning, development, organization, language use, and conventions.

Other states rate compositions on comparable scales. The most important everywhere are those that deal with meaning and development. They are most likely to reveal the kind of thinking a state hopes students will learn to do. In New York, the wording of criteria for meaning and development varies only slightly by prompt, but some slight changes are significant. For example, for a rating of 6 on meaning, a paper in response to the first prompt (the Suzuki method) should "reveal an in-depth analysis of the text [and] make insightful connections between information and ideas in the text and the assignment" (*Regents High School Examination English, Scoring Key and Rating Guide,* June 18, 1999). The wording is the same for the reading for information (text and graphic) prompt, changing to accommodate the third and fourth prompts. The meaning (6) criterion for the third prompt ("reading for literary response"—two literary texts) calls for the writer to "establish a controlling idea that reveals an in-depth analysis . . . " The remainder is the same. Similarly, the criterion for a rating of 6 in response to the fourth prompt (the "critical lens" prompt) calls for a writer to "provide an interpretation of the critical lens that is faithful to the complexity of the statement and clearly establishes the criteria for analysis [and] use the criteria to make insightful analysis of the chosen texts" (NYSED, June 23, 1999).

The level 6 criteria for development for the first 2 prompts call for the student to "develop ideas clearly and fully, making effective use of a wide range of relevant and specific details from the text." For the second 2 prompts the level 6 criteria changes significantly, requesting the writer to use "relevant and specific evidence and appropriate literary elements from both texts."

There are key words that we need to pay attention to: *in-depth analysis of the text, insightful connections, controlling idea that reveals an in-depth analysis, interpretation of the critical lens, criteria for analysis*, and especially the contrast of *details* and *evidence*. We need to know what counts for any of these. These terms are the keys to linking testing to the goals set by the Regents. Do the referents of these terms in student work represent the goals of thinking "logically and creatively," of applying "reasoning skills to issues and problems," and of applying "methods of inquiry" to various problems?

In response to the Suzuki speech, the top-rated paper essentially summarizes the speech providing many of the details. It states that the American version results in "children [who] are not as happy and proficient as the Japanese children were. On the whole, the American method is very rigid." It recommends that "a method similar to that of the original Suzuki method would benefit our children greatly." The commentary in the scoring guide states that the paper

Conveys an in-depth understanding of the speech and task, by analyzing the differences in effectiveness of the original Japanese Suzuki method of violin instruction and the American version of the Suzuki method. The response makes an insightful recommendation to the Board of Education based on this analysis.

In reference to development, the commentary simply reiterates the criterion:

Clearly develops ideas, making effective use of a wide range of specific details from the speech to support implementing a method of teaching violin which is similar to Suzuki's original method.

Let us consider the term *analysis* first. We might begin by asking what is the *sine qua non* of analysis? The OED defines *analysis* first as "The reso-

lution or breaking up of anything complex into its various simple elements
. . . ; the exact determination of the elements or components of anything
complex." Unstated, but certainly implied is the idea that analysis reveals
something not already obvious or even understood. The OED provides
special definitions for several disciplines from chemistry to psychoanaly-
sis. Nearly every one implies that analysis is analysis only if the object is
not already known. In the definition provided for chemistry, this idea is
explicit: "The resolution of a chemical compound into its proximate or
ultimate elements . . . ; or, in the case of a substance of known composition, such as water, of the foreign substances which it may contain." The
same idea is implied in the definitions of analysis relating to logic, mathematics, optics, psychology, and so forth.

The *sine qua non* of analysis is that it reveal something that was not previously known or obvious to the knower. If I list the contents of my kitchen
drawer, does the list constitute an analysis? Does a list of types of TV programs (crime, true crime, reality TV, game shows, sitcoms, and so forth)
constitute an analysis? Do summaries of the contents of newspaper stories
or encyclopedia articles count as analyses? Most of us would say no.

The top-rated paper in response to the speech about the Suzuki method
is not an analysis. It only summarizes the speech, which already is divided
into two parts, and adds a recommendation that "a method similar to that
of the original Suzuki method would benefit our children greatly." The
speech itself does not, of course, recommend that the method be adopted
by some board of education, but it clearly implies a recommendation. It
calls the Suzuki method a "useful resource," decries the American version
of it as too rigid, and then calls for teachers to "put back into music the
exploration, the discovery, the adventure, and above all the joy and excitement that are properly part of it." In short, the recommendation by
the student is very close to being explicitly stated in the text. Yet the commentary on the response calls this an "insightful recommendation."

The commentary also uses the terms *in-depth understanding* and *support*. What would reveal an in-depth understanding of a text? The top-
rated paper presents a summary of the major points with a highly generalized recommendation attached: a method "similar to Suzuki's original
style." Does that count as in-depth understanding? Ordinarily we think
of in-depth understanding as involving analysis of something beyond sur-
face meanings: symbolic content, structural effects, ramifications and implications beyond the obvious. For the Regents examiners, summary qualifies as in-depth understanding.

The commentary on development states that the top-rated essay uses
"a wide range of specific details from the speech to support" the recommendation. What counts as support? The first and final paragraphs open

with the recommendation that a method similar to Suzuki's be adopted. In between, part of the first and the second paragraphs summarize the Suzuki method with its positive results, while the third summarizes the rigid nature of the American version. We can construe this as support for the recommendation. However, the support is incidental to the summary of the speech. It is not selected and structured into an argument in support of the recommendation. Essentially, the source provides support for its own recommendation, which the student uses.

Despite such expressions as *analysis, in-depth understanding, insightful,* and *support,* the student paper is simply a competent summary of the speech with a recommendation attached at either end. It does not provide evidence of the student's ability to think "logically and creatively," to apply "reasoning skills to issues and problems," and to apply "methods of inquiry" to problems.

The second essay to be written on the examination, called reading for information, also makes use of the terms *in-depth analysis* and *insightful connections,* but not *support.* It simply asks that students "develop ideas clearly and fully, making use of a wide range of specific and relevant details." The student will have to match portions of the graphic to the text. But no special inference is necessary. For example, the text says that part of the impetus for reform of child labor conditions was a concern about the lack of education. There is a section of the chart that indicates the restrictions on working hours for minors attending school. Students have to bring such closely allied pieces of information together. Even so, a successful response is little more than a summary, hardly evidence of advanced thinking.

The third essay, however, raises the stakes. It calls for the reading of two literary texts, identifying a "controlling idea that reveals an in-depth analysis of both texts," making "insightful connections between the controlling idea and the ideas in both texts" and "making use of specific and relevant evidence from both text(s)." The first two prompts and criteria called for "specific and relevant details" but not for "evidence." We still have to ask what will count as *in-depth analysis, insightful connections,* and, this time, *evidence.*

The selection of a controlling idea is supposed to reveal in-depth analysis. In this case, the top-rated paper begins with the following sentence: "Throughout the ages the reciprocal influence between teacher and pupil has had profound repercussions on the development of young minds to learn about themselves." This is an unfortunate beginning, which the raters, fortunately for the writer, ignore. First, neither passage is about a reciprocal influence. Both have to do with the influence teachers have over their charges, but not the other way around. Second, neither has to do with repercussions ("the action of . . . forcing or driving back an impinging or advancing body," OED), but rather with helping students advance. Does such a statement reveal in-depth analysis? Hardly. What the prompt really requires is focusing on a thematic element, which the prompt itself presents: "the influence of teachers on the lives of their students." If the thematic element is presented in the prompt, it hardly requires in-depth analysis to discover it.

The idea of insightful connections is treated in about the same way. The writer of the top-rated paper waits until the final paragraph to make connections between the two selections. The writer says, "In each case, the student learned things about himself which were heretofore never lucid: the first about his place in society, the second about confidence in himself." I am puzzled as to why this statement is seen as insightful. Is it the addition of the phrase, "heretofore never lucid"? If what was learned had been lucid heretofore, it need not have been learned.

What seems to count as insightfulness, then, is simply to extend what is already given in the prompt: that both characters learned something about themselves from their teachers. This hardly calls for in-depth analysis.

The development scale calls for specific and relevant evidence. We saw that this word, though used occasionally in the commentaries in Texas and Illinois, was not used in the rubrics. Texas and Illinois call only for support in the form of unsupported generalizations. Refreshingly, New York calls for evidence and the scale uses the term *evidence* at five of the six levels.

Level 6 calls for the "effective use of a wide range of relevant and specific evidence." Each succeeding level reduces the demand for evidence until level 2, which does not call for evidence, while level 1 says there is "no evidence" (NYSED, June 23, 1999. Part A—Scoring Rubric, Reading and Writing for Literary Response). While these distinctions are relatively clear, the benchmark papers help to pin down their meanings.

The level 6 paper presents the thesis, "Throughout the ages, the reciprocal influence between teacher and pupil has had profound repercussions on the development of young minds to learn about themselves." This proposition will require a load of evidence having to do with the nature of the "reciprocal influence," how this influence has "repercussions on the development of young minds," and how that development leads to learning about the self, as opposed to other entities. The language used by this incipient Mrs. Malaprop obscures the real thesis. The question is what evidence does the writer present in support of the major proposition or some simplified version of it. Here is what the writer says about the poem:

In the second passage, a Tornado Alley elementary student recalls how his teacher reacted to a tornado drill, which from his perspective was like being saved from imminent destruction. In poetic form, this passage uses significant dramatic license to illustrate the emotions of six-year-olds in a life crisis: Marion "can't breathe," "snakes of wind slithered around us," "lightening sizzled the stairwell." His teacher was a symbol of strength, direction, courage who inspired her minions to be the same. Thus, through the catastrophic weather event, the narrator was made aware of his noble duties (to save Patti Holmes from "chunks of concrete") and was endowed with a sense of confidence and pride. Under his teacher's tutelage, the narrator learned to believe in his own strength and abilities. (NYSED, 1999, June 23)

The paragraph does not go to the problems of the reciprocity of influence or of repercussions. It deals only with the simpler claim that teachers influence children to learn about themselves, echoed in the final sentence above. However, most of the specific references to the text do not constitute evidence because they do not support even this simpler version of the proposition. Finally, it is interesting to note that this writer says the teacher "reacted to a tornado drill." The poem states that she said to her children, as they began to panic, "It's just a drill," which has quite different ramifications.

The reader will recall the discussion of papers scored 5 and 4 in Chapter 4. The writer of the score 5 paper quotes from the text and refers to it. These data are cited in support of a claim, which, of course, makes them evidence. All are confirmable. Why is this paper rated only 5, when an arguably weaker one is rated 6? The commentary suggests that the raters were impressed by the score 6 writer's use of "language that is fluent and original with an attempt at stylistic sophistication."

As we have seen, the benchmark paper at level 4 refers less to the text and in less detail. It promotes a proposition similar to the one above: "Teachers create a positive experience in some shape or form on the lives of their students," specifying it a bit more in a later sentence: "mostly they teach their students about life and about themselves." But the supporting evidence is sparse. He or she has not learned to use the events of the poem as evidence and to cite the language of the text regularly. The lower scoring papers do not quote the language of the text, and as they become lower, present less and less evidence.

The final of the four prompts requires students to interpret a "critical lens" in such a way that the interpretation establishes criteria for the subsequent analysis, which is, as I have tried to show, a quite complex task. Examination of the benchmark papers will allow us to see what these tasks really require. The language of the criteria for evaluation is comparable to that for other tasks on the exam. The language calls for clearly establishing the "criteria for analysis," using the criteria to "make insightful analysis," and "making use of a wide range of relevant and specific evidence."

The "criteria for analysis" turn out to be not criteria at all, at least, not in any OED sense of the term. In fact, "interpretation of the critical lens" appears only to call for rephrasing in one's own words. The top-rated paper for this task begins by stating the critical lens, affirming that it is true (thus dismissing all the ambiguities suggested earlier), and then claiming that "many works of literature bear this theory out, and demonstrate how evil may win the occasional battle, but not the war." Here we have a clarification of triumph and conquest: One triumphs in battles and conquers in wars. From this point, the essay goes on to demonstrate how *Dracula* and *The Crucible* both support the thesis that good wins in the end. Good and evil remain undefined and the problem of proving that evil *never* conquers is ignored. No real criteria are used in the analysis of the texts. Evidence is at the level, necessarily, of general references to characters and events in the texts.

Since the prompt requires referring to "appropriate literary elements" in support of the opinion, the level 6 writer alludes to such elements.

In addition, Stoker utilizes setting to achieve the mood necessary to the action of his novel. The novel includes gothic elements such as the obligatory castle and atrocious weather. Nature/animal imagery is evident in the traditional nature of Dracula himself; Stoker uses the bat as an image representative of Dracula's mysterious and malignant qualities. [In the next sentence, the writer turns to *The Crucible*.]

This catalogue of gothic elements, however, does nothing to support the opinion about good winning in the end. Nor does it show "how mood [is] necessary to the action of the plot." So while the prompt tells the student "to support your opinion using specific references to appropriate literary elements from the two works," support turns out to be unimportant. Students can receive a high rating as long as they show that they have some knowledge of what "literary elements" are and make specific reference to some. The criterion at the highest level makes that clear: "develop ideas clearly and fully, making effective use of a wide range of . . . appropriate literary elements." In other words, literary elements need not support the opinion as the prompt says, but simply show the knowledge required.

All these problems indicate considerable ambiguity surrounding the New York Regents Comprehensive English Examination. The exam analyzed above is the first to be given under the new 1994 standards presented in the New York *Framework* (NYSED, 1994), a fact that does not excuse the ambiguity. There is omnipresent language calling for in-depth analysis in all four prompts or sets of criteria. But no analysis is necessary for two of them and only low-level analysis for the other two. One prompt calls for students to interpret a "critical lens," in order to establish criteria for making an in-depth analysis. But the benchmark papers reveal that no criteria need be involved. The writer need simply identify two explicit thematic elements in the lens and use two works that illustrate both. It requires no critical reflection about the content of the lens itself.

Another prompt asks writers to read two literary texts, "use ideas from both passages to establish a controlling idea," and then use evidence to support the idea. Even this prompt, responses to which are actually rated for evidence, belies the necessity for in-depth analysis. The controlling idea is virtually supplied in the prompt. As we have seen, it is the controlling idea adopted in most papers, with only slight tweaking.

We have to ask why this great chasm exists between the expectations we see in the language of the prompts and criteria and the reality of their application as seen in the benchmark papers. It cannot be that this clear disparity has gone unnoticed by players in the New York state assessment. I suspect the gap is intentional.

Why? As in other states, there is a need to convince citizens that the state assessments are as demanding and rigorous as the Regents' goals suggest they will be. Politicians need to claim that their educational efforts will lead to excellence. At the same time, if the assessments do not or do not seem to demonstrate improvement, they become a liability to political careers. If the testing program is really rigorous, it is likely to reveal weak performance, a disaster for any politician claiming education as his chief priority. For the politicians and bureaucrats, it will be far safer to claim high standards and rigorous assessment, and cut a great deal of slack in the implementation. The pompous language of the prompts and criteria, while undoubtedly confusing for students, give the impression of living up to the goals set by the Board of Regents.

RESPONSE TO THE ASSESSMENT

Interviews were conducted in New York in 1997 and 1998. To our surprise, many teachers and administrators, especially in large urban districts, were unaware of the impending change from the far simpler Competency Exams to the Regents Comprehensive Exams. This change will affect large proportions of students who traditionally had not taken the Regents high school diploma. But a version of the Regents Comprehensive Examination had been in effect for many years. Many teachers were accustomed to preparing their students for it.

Rhetorical Stance

It should not be surprising then that most teachers we interviewed do not
see themselves as teachers of composition in the same way that teachers
in other states do. Only 29% of teachers could be classified as taking current traditional rhetoric as their primary rhetorical focus, intent on teaching a variety of forms of writing as forms, and only 37% had CTR as a
secondary focus. Taken together, this is a lower total than in any other
state, all four of which have totals above 90% for primary and secondary
focus on CTR. Only two teachers were classified as expressivist (both
below high school level) and none as epistemic. The latter is curious because of the research evidence showing that an epistemic stance is more
powerful in helping students learn how to write the kinds of arguments
and analyses that New York requests in certain of the Regents prompts.
More teachers than in any other state, 10%, focused primarily on grammar, and another 58% adopted grammar as a secondary focus. Fifty percent, however, had writing about literature as a primary focus and another 40.3% as secondary. (In the other states in which interviews were
conducted, under 4 percent focused primarily on writing about literature.)
In New York, this difference suggests that the writing program is focused
on the kinds of essays that the Regents Comprehensives include, a somewhat narrow focus, but one that allows in some prompts for the kinds of
thinking that the Regents' standards wish to promote.

New York interviewees talked about certain aspects of current traditional
rhetoric: 47% talk about using models of writing; 58%, descriptions of structure; 11%, schematic diagrams for students to fill in; but only 5%, the five-
paragraph theme, the lowest proportion in any of the five states. The low
percentages on the two latter aspects suggest that New York's examinations
do not encourage formulaic writing. Indeed, the five-paragraph theme would
be of little use in responding to the prompts which require more than the
kind of thinking that suffices for five paragraphs of blether.

Mode of Instruction

The most common mode of instruction, here, as in other states is the presentational, the pattern that most teachers would have encountered in
college: lectures, recitation, and very infrequent discussions. Although
teachers interviewed often use the word *discussion*, other expressions such
as "I tell them over and over again" indicate that the "discussions" are
lopsided. Only 13% made use of workshop approaches, and none used
what I have called the environmental mode, the kind of teaching in Ms.
Levine's class (see Chapter 2).

The research evidence about effective teaching of writing and literature appears to have made little penetration into the state of New York,
the more amazing because the evidence strongly indicates that, given some
of the prompts in New York, students would be far better served by quite
different teaching. But then, the state makes little or no provision for professional development apart from training in scoring.

Writing Process

Overall, among the teachers interviewed, New York displays the least attention to the writing process: the second smallest proportion allowing
students to choose their own topics for writing (34%; only Texas is lower);
the second smallest proportion engaging students in peer response to
writing (61%; only Illinois is lower); but the smallest proportion engaging students in prewriting (63%); and the smallest proportion in revising
(32%). These results on the writing process go hand in hand with the
presentational mode of teaching and its objectivist rhetorical stance. Our
interviewees deal with bits and pieces of writing process, but not with the
process as a whole.

Teachers' Opinions of the Assessment

Finally, New York teachers interviewed did not have a high level of familiarity with the new exams. They knew about the old Regents high school
exams and regarded them as the province of the high school teachers of
literature. They knew about the old competency tests and did not think of
them as very important or challenging. Many seemed unfamiliar with the
scoring rubrics, especially those in large urban systems, who also had no
idea that the examinations were about to change. The impression of our
interviewers in New York was that teachers interviewed were unconcerned
about the new tests or did not know about them.

In certain suburban systems, the teachers who knew about the change
from competency exams to the Regents were in a panic even though the
actual change was 5 years in the future. In one suburb with high levels of
poverty (44%) and speakers of languages other than English, only 24%
had passed the Regents exams in the past. The thought of the Regents as
the measure for a high school diploma was a fearful prospect. Teachers
did not know what they were going to do. They hoped to organize enough
support to somehow influence the Board of Regents to change the requirements. Such a change has not come to pass.

Despite the relative lack of knowledge on the part of many teachers,
others had opinions about the testing program. About 45% of those in-

terviewed believed that the assessment supported a desirable writing program, and only 24% disagreed. Only 24% approved of the state scoring rubric, and only 18% disapproved. Finally, only 31% (the lowest proportion of any state) felt that the assessment served to improve the teaching of writing in the state, while only 16% felt it had not. No doubt these proportions will change as the new examinations are fully implemented.

CHAPTER 10

Portfolio Assessment in Kentucky and Oregon

Writing assessments in Kentucky and Oregon differ from those in other states in one important respect: A significant portion of the writing assessed is produced outside conventional testing situations. While both states administer and score a writing-on-demand assessment, other writing required is produced during the school year. In Oregon, 10th graders must develop a collection of three pieces, each in a different mode: narrative, expository, persuasive, or imaginative. In addition, the state assessment asks students to respond to one of four prompts, again, each in a different mode. The Kentucky portfolio is more elaborate, requiring several pieces of writing with distribution requirements to insure attention to different kinds of writing. There are other differences as well that may influence the nature of instruction in both states.

THE OREGON ASSESSMENT

On-demand writing assessments in Oregon are given in Grades 3, 5, 8, and 10, all of which cover four modes: narrative, imaginative, expository, and persuasive. Students receive three prompts, each in a different mode, and choose one for response. In each grade, the state recommends that students have three 45-minute periods on 3 consecutive days to do the writing. However, students may have more time if they need it. The state recommends that they use the time to enable the full writing process, from brainstorming to final revisions and drafting.

In addition, the state requires, but does not monitor, a "collection of work samples." In Grades 3, 5, and 8 the work sample is only one piece of writing in any of the four modes stated above. In 10th grade, the work sample must include three pieces of writing including expository and persuasive pieces and either a narrative or an imaginative piece. To reach what the state calls the Benchmark 1 standard in Grade 3, both the on-demand and the classroom pieces must receive minimal scores of 3 on four analytic scales (Ideas and Content, Organization, Sentence Fluency, and Conventions). In Grades 5 and 8, to reach the Benchmark 2 and 3 standards, and the Certificate of Initial Mastery standards, the minimal score on all four scales is 4 for each piece of writing, including the on-demand writing.

All of these compositions are also scored on scales for Voice and Word Choice, but those scores are not included in determining the level of the student's writing. While people designing the writing assessment believed that voice was an important dimension in thinking about the quality of writing, lawyers feared that the scale would be seen as too subjective and would induce law suits. Nonetheless, the inclusion of voice marks a difference from the scoring in Illinois, Texas, New York, and most other states.

All on-demand essays are scored within the state by Oregon teachers at 17 different sites using a six-trait analytic rubric. The work samples are scored by classroom teachers and the scores reported to their administration who, in turn, must report numbers of students attaining each benchmark level in several subjects to the Oregon Department of Education.

Oregon Prompts

The prompts used in Oregon for on-demand writing are similar to those in both Illinois and Texas. They are relatively brief and, unlike the New York prompts, usually provide no data or texts for response. While they specify the discourse mode, the audience, and the topic, they usually do not specify the subject matter. Here are two examples of persuasive prompts from Oregon.

1. People are always looking for ways to improve schools, and some of the best ideas come from students. Think of ONE change you could propose that would make your school better. Write a letter to the editor or an essay that would CONVINCE other students and teachers in your school to agree with you.
2. Almost everybody would like to change someone's mind about something. Perhaps there is something you would like a friend, parent, teacher, principal, public official, or someone else to feel differently about. Write to the person PERSUADING him or her to change that particular position or attitude. Use specific reasons and examples to make your argument convincing. (ODE, 2000, p. 5)

These prompts specify mode of discourse, audience, and topic, but not subject matter, allowing students a wide range of choice in what to write about. In contrast, the prompts in Illinois and Texas tend to specify the subject matter. For example, Texas students were required to deal with the specific subject matter of censorship of musical lyrics and the imposition of mandatory community or military service.

Oregon Scoring Criteria and Benchmark Papers

As already noted, Oregon uses four scales for rating that count and two for feedback only. The first scale listed is for Ideas and Content, the scoring category that includes what Texas and Illinois call support or elaboration. It describes a passing score of 4 as follows:

The writing is clear and focused. The reader can easily understand the main ideas. Support is present, although it may be limited or rather general. The writing is characterized by
—an easily identifiable purpose.
—clear main idea(s).
—supporting details that are relevant, but may be overly general or limited in places; when appropriate, resources are used to provide accurate support.
—a topic that is explored/explained, although developmental details may occasionally be out of balance with the main idea(s); some connections and insights may be present.
—content and selected details that are relevant, but perhaps not consistently well-chosen for audience and purpose. (ODE, 1997d, p. A1)

As in the case of criteria from other states, this criterion is not clear. We need to know what counts as relevant "supporting details" that, at the same time, "may be overly general or limited" or "not consistently well-chosen for audience and purpose." What counts for explanation/exploration "although developmental details may occasionally be out of balance with the main idea(s)"? We need to see a composition that Oregon scores as passing to determine what counts for support that is relevant and adequate, even if "overly general or limited" or "not consistently well-chosen for audience and purpose." Figure 10.1 displays a passing composition from Oregon.

The piece of writing in Figure 10.1 is clearly not an Illinois type five-paragraph theme. It does more than present reasons for instituting a new middle school. It explores the problem by examining some of the arguments that might oppose the creation of such a school. The writer begins by stating the need for a new middle school that would solve the problems of crowded halls and "class arrangements" but presents only one statement that passes as evidence of crowding in the halls between classes: "a 'bumper-to-bumper pile-up' in the halls getting to each class." The writer says nothing about "class arrangements" or why they are a problem. The fact that there is a problem is not clearly established.

Instead, the essay turns to the arguments against a middle school and devotes three paragraphs to minimizing them: the problems of younger students losing role models, providing money, and making younger stu-

FIGURE 10.1. Oregon: Grade 10, Score 4 on Content and Ideas Passing Persuasive Essay

Having a Separate Middle School

Each day students in grades seven through twelve roam the halls of High School together. They function as a large group, and sometimes that isn't always easy for either upper- or underclassmen, because of crowding and class arrangements. What can solve this predicament? Grades five through eight should be combined and made separate from the high schoolers so _____'s first middle school should begin.

Some people may feel that these students in grades five through eighth would miss a chance to be around older people to see as models and learn from. This is a definite loss, but they would make up for this by having the advantage of being able to control what rules and policies would affect them and they would have a smaller group to work with.

Anyone who has walked the halls of _____ High School will agree that after the bell there is a "bumper-to-bumper pile-up" in the halls getting to each class. Providing a middle school would enable both the older and younger students to have their own class, lunch, and break times. Undoubtedly cutting down on the "traffic jam" and making these breaks and class times more enjoyable for students during the school day.

The question now may be where the money would come from to expand, pay new teachers, and get new resources? _____ has already been talking about expanding, and making a middle school would be a great start. The money required to pay teachers and get new resources would be less, due to the fact that we already have two teachers and most of the resources needed to teach these particular students. The money that would be spent is worth spending because it would give students an enjoyable learning environment.

Some people think that having a separate middle school may make the middle school students feel less involved with the whole school's activities. This would be a minor problem, because the middle school has already got it's own sports programs. The students could be building their own government and in doing this, they could feel even more independent. Having their own government, they could learn more about leadership and responsibility to others. This government would also produce middle school representatives who could get many more of the younger students ideas across to the older students in a more effective way. In turn the middle school students would have an advantage in leadership skills, while working their way to high school. Having these activities should improve learning abilities and the desire to work in their own units.

We should provide a new, separate learning time for grades five through eight. Having their own middle school environment would give them the time they need to gain the confidence and learning skills needed as-they progress through high school and on into the future. (ODE, 2000, pp. 18–19)

dents feel excluded. Of these the last is most fully supported. It begins with a concession that "having a separate middle school may make the middle school students feel that they are less involved with the whole school's activities." The writer immediately makes the claim that "this would be a minor problem." We can analyze the support as we did the support in persuasive papers from Texas and Illinois.

Claim:	Middle school students' feeling that they are "less involved with the whole school's activities . . . would be a minor problem."
Evidence 1:	"The middle school has already got it's own sports programs."
Evidence 2:	"The students could be building their own government."
Warrant 1:	"In doing this, they could feel even more independent."
Warrant 2:	"Having their own government, they could learn more about leadership and responsibility to others."
Evidence 3:	"This government would also produce middle school representatives"
Subclaim:	"Who could get many more of the younger students ideas across to the older students in a more effective way."
Warrant 3:	"In turn the middle school students would have an advantage in leadership skills, while working their way to high school."
Warrant 4:	"Having these activities should improve learning abilities and the desire to work in their own units."

This part of the argument presents three pieces of concrete evidence that, in the school context, are probably readily verifiable. The subclaim is probably intended as evidence, but the effectiveness of representatives in getting ideas across to older students is open to question. Warrants 1 and 2 are generally accepted reasons for having student government in schools. Warrant 3 is an expansion of Warrant 2. The first part of the fourth warrant is certainly open to question. It is doubtful that such activities would improve learning abilities. But most of us would accept the second part, that such activities would improve "the desire to work in their own units." In short, this part of the paper turns out to be a fairly strong argument. The analysis above demonstrates that this passing paper in Oregon presents a fairly strong case, stronger than even the best examined from Texas and Illinois.

The scoring guide commentary on this piece of writing (and on others) points out the shortcomings of the piece. There is no pretense about its being strong, although it has strengths. Here is the Oregon commentary:

Supporting details are relevant, but overly general or limited in places: . . . The topic is explored; however, developmental details are out of balance. Much emphasis is placed on educational and social benefits; little in-depth attention is placed on practical issues of facilities and fiscal impact. (ODE, 2000, p. 20)

If this paper is passing, it will be instructive to examine a composition of the same type that is above the level of passing. The criteria for 6, the top score in "Content and Ideas," are more demanding, calling for the writing to be "exceptionally clear, focused, and interesting," to hold "the reader's attention throughout," to develop main ideas with "strong support and rich details suitable to audience and purpose." It calls for writing "characterized by clarity, focus, and control"; "supporting relevant, carefully selected details"; "a thorough, balanced, in-depth explanation/exploration of the topic"; and "content and selected details that are well-suited to audience and purpose" (ODE, 1997d. p. A1).

Figure 10.2 presents a composition that has received a rating of 5 on content and ideas. This paper goes far beyond the formulas of Texas and Illinois, considering the opposing arguments in some detail and presenting evidence of the problems involved in teaching foreign languages by satellite. The writer sets out the problem efficiently in the opening paragraph, briefly outlining how the satellite program works and adumbrating the problems, making a claim about the program and a recommendation: "The arrangement is not practical or effective. Foreign languages should be taught by a certified teacher who knows the language, not by satellite." The writer next addresses the propositions that teaching by satellite is less expensive than hiring teachers and that "students learn to be self-directed learners and are forced to become organized and responsible for their own learning in order to do well in the class." The writer offers appropriate counter claims for both of these assertions. The detailed arguments that follow support the claims made against those of expense and developing student independence. Nearly all of the evidentiary statements made in the following paragraphs are quite specific.

We might like to see more specific evidence "of the coordinator not knowing how to pronounce words or mispronouncing them." We might like to know what the mispronunciations are, how often they occur, and so forth. But there is no question that the writer describes serious learning problems that support the contention that a certified teacher should be in the classroom. It seems to me that this paper is far stronger than compositions receiving the highest scores in Texas and Illinois. Yet it receives only a 5.

Unfortunately, the Oregon *Writing Work Samples* does not explain why this piece is inferior to a 6. In the statements of criteria, only a few words

FIGURE 10.2. Oregon: Grade 10, Score 5 on Content and Ideas Passing Persuasive Essay

Foreign Languages by Satellite

At the present time _____ School is offering Spanish I and II and German I and II by satellite. For students who are involved in the program, this means watching a taped broadcast monitored by a coordinator during their language class. A hotline with a 1-800 number is available for students to ask questions, practice speaking, and get help on assignments. However, class time cannot be used to call, and the coordinator is not required to know either language herself. The arrangement is not practical or effective. Foreign languages should be taught by a certified teacher who knows the language, not by satellite.

The foremost argument in favor of the satellite program is that it is significantly cheaper than hiring a certified teacher to teach foreign languages. With a limited budget, this may seem like a good answer, but in reality the amount of learning is decreased so much that it would be worth it to spend the extra money to hire a teacher instead. The quality of education is lowered by offering satellite courses instead of foreign languages taught by a classroom teacher.

According to supporters of foreign language instruction by satellite, students learn to be self-directed learners and are forced to become organized and responsible for their own learning in order to do well in the class. This is true, but people learn in different ways, and the satellite program is not best for most people. What happens for many students is that they become frustrated and fall behind, after which it is very bard to get caught up.

Too much is lost by taking a foreign language course by satellite. No speaking of the language takes place in class, so students don't learn how to pronounce words or speak fluently. Advances in reading and writing of the language occur, but not verbally. Words are spoken on the broadcasts, but not often enough for students to really catch on, and if students aren't practicing speaking, they soon forget. Calling in on their own time is also difficult for some students to do. Besides, it is hard to understand pronunciation over the phone, especially when most of the people who answer the hotline speak quickly with thick accents. Pronunciation tests are part of the grading, which most students do poorly on because of lack of practice and knowledge. Then, there is the problem of the coordinator not knowing how to pronounce words or mispronouncing them, which can lead to confusion.

The university that makes the broadcasts began broadcasting in the fall before school started at _____ School. As a result of this, _____ is behind on the broadcasts. Missed school days because of weather, power outages and other variables have caused the school to fall further behind. An example of what this can mean for students is that they may be watching a tape talking about The Day of the Dead (the Spanish equivalent of Halloween) in December, or a tape during which they get to make Christmas decorations in January. Another problem with the timing is that a pace is set without the needs of specific classes in mind. Sometimes students need more work in an area before proceeding, but don't get it and become frustrated as they are forced to move on. Other times students need less time on the broadcasts taken up with a certain subject and become bored.

Considering the points on both sides, it is clear that having a certified classroom teacher for foreign language classes is much more productive, effective, and worth the money than offering the courses by satellite. Therefore, _____ School should hire a qualified classroom teacher to teach foreign language classes in the future. (ODE, 2000, pp. 27–29) mark the difference between ratings of 5 and 6 on ideas and content: For a 5, the writing is clear, but for a 6, it is *exceptionally* clear; for a rating of 5, the writing holds the reader's attention, but for a 6, it holds the reader's attention throughout; for a 5, main ideas are developed by supporting details, but for a 6 they are developed by strong support and rich details.

The generality of these distinctions makes them almost unuseable. My guess is that agreement among raters at the high end of the scale is low. States generally have had difficulty explaining the distinctions among the various levels of support, elaboration, or simply idea development. The lack of clarity concerning these distinctions is likely to cause difficulty not only in scoring, but in teaching. That is not to say, however, that the criteria offered by Oregon are not useful. They are more demanding than those in other states, as our analysis demonstrates.

There is another scale for judging writing in Oregon that deserves attention simply because it is rare in state rubrics: voice. Voice is a slippery concept to begin with. What does it mean for a piece of writing to display *voice*, the qualities that enable readers to think that a human being with a personality has written it? There is no mistaking that voice is present in fiction like *Huckleberry Finn* and *Catcher in the Rye*. However, the concept is complicated when we consider that in many kinds of writing readers expect the voice to be one of reason and logic, and inklings of a writer's personality are supposed to be subordinate to the message. Nevertheless, a few states include voice as a scale for judgment.

Oregon includes a criterion statement for each level, 1–6. At the highest level, the criterion states that "the writer has chosen a voice appropriate for the topic, purpose, and audience. The writer seems deeply committed to the topic, and there is an exceptional sense of "writing to be read." The writing is expressive, engaging, or sincere." Such writing is characterized by "an effective level of closeness to or distance from the audience," "an exceptionally strong sense of audience," and a sense that "the topic has come to life" and, "when appropriate, the writing may show originality, liveliness, honesty, conviction, excitement, humor, or suspense" (ODE, 1997d, p. A3).

Although this quality is difficult to judge reliably, we all know what it is. And although the quality does not officially count in Oregon's assessment, it seems to me to show up more in the samples of Oregon writing that are available than those from other states. Both pieces in Figures 10.1 and 10.2 have voice, in a degree greater than we have seen in the writings from other states. I suspect that the inclusion of such a criterion works against the tendency to treat writing in formulaic ways in classrooms.

What we see in Oregon are criteria that, in combination with the benchmark papers, are more demanding than those in Illinois and Texas.

In addition, the writing program, as exemplified in state testing, is richer than in any of the states examined so far. From the persuasive samples alone, we can assume that Oregon teachers cannot afford to make the five-paragraph theme the object of their teaching. The papers examined show evidence that teaching has not dwelt simply on three reasons to support a position. Rather, even the passing paper attends to the positions that are in disagreement, a sign that the curricula and its attendant classroom experiences are likely to be more conducive to the kinds of thinking necessary for the education of future citizens of a democracy.

THE KENTUCKY ASSESSMENT

As already noted, there are two parts to the writing assessment in Kentucky: a writing-on-demand sample and the writing portfolio, a collection of writings that students develop over several months or even years. The latter is intended as an opportunity for students to show their best work developed over a series of drafts, replete with feedback, revision, editing, and time to think carefully. It is writing as real writers do it. In that sense it is more elaborate that the "work collection" in Oregon and the antithesis of writing-on-demand in Texas and Illinois. In Kentucky, however, both the writing-on-demand and the portfolio scores are entered into a formula for computing the Accountability Index, a means of evaluating the performance of schools and districts. Writing portfolio scores are weighted at 14 percent of the Index, writing-on-demand scores at 3 percent.[1] For that reason, this chapter will focus on the portfolio.

A publication of the Kentucky Department of Education, the *Kentucky Writing Portfolio Development, Teacher's Handbook* (1999b) defines a portfolio as a "purposeful selection of student work that exhibits a student's efforts and achievement" (p. 2). The *Portfolio Development* lists the goals of writing portfolio assessment:

- Provide students with skills, knowledge, and confidence necessary to become independent thinkers and writers.
- Promote each student's ability to communicate to a variety of audiences for a variety of purposes.
- Document student performance on various kinds of writing which have been developed over time.
- Integrate performance with classroom instruction.
- Provide information upon which to base ongoing development of a curriculum that is responsive to student needs. (p. 2)

Portfolio Development stipulates the teachers' roles as those of "colleagues, coaches, mentors, and critics" (p. 2). It proposes that "quality writing instruction is anchored in the writing process" and includes process categories generally parallel to those in Chapter 2, explaining how teachers go about implementing the writing process: prewriting, drafting, conferencing, revision, editing, and publishing (pp. 2–5).

The Kentucky Writing Portfolio Assessment regards the students as the "sole creators, authors, and owners of their work" (KDE, 1999b, p. 2), and, therefore, the writing process guidelines indicate that teachers must provide "some choice" in what students write and must "respect the writer's ability to make choices about purpose, audience, form, content, and length and refrain from setting artificial limits or constraints upon these areas." In conferencing, teachers "may ask questions and offer suggestions." However, "the writer will decide what to incorporate and what to reject" (p. 3). In making revisions, "teachers and students should ensure that authors have the final say in the revisions they make in their writing" (p. 4). Finally, in editing, teachers are forbidden to make changes. "Teachers will not at any time actually do the writing or make direct corrections for the student on student work" (p. 4).

We find no such injunctions in other states. As we have seen, teachers in Illinois and Texas frequently require specific forms for student writing, and the topics of writing are usually assigned. In Kentucky, personal ownership becomes a very important part of the theory of writing. In other states, ownership is assumed to be something to worry about after students have learned "the basics."

The Portfolio

The Kentucky writing assessment embraces a wider universe of discourse than any of the assessments we have examined in detail. Each portfolio must contain several types of writing. And since the writings are not prompt dependent, the student writer may select from a wide range of possibilities within each general type. When the Kentucky portfolio system began, portfolios were assessed at 4th, 8th, and 12th grades. Since then, portfolio assessment has been moved to 7th grade, rather than 8th. In 1998, because of complaints about time taken in preparing them, portfolios were reduced by one piece of writing. Otherwise the structure is essentially the same. Table 10.1 outlines the kinds of writing required. Note that some pieces of writing must originate in content areas other than English.

The reduction in number of pieces in 1998 appears to be a significant reduction, especially at the middle and high school levels. At those levels two of the pieces that supposedly can be in any category except reflective,

TABLE 10.1. Distribution of Writing in Kentucky's Student Portfolios

Categories	Grade 4	Grade 7	Grade 12
Reflective piece to the reviewer	1	1	1
Personal expressive	1	1 or 2	1 or 2
Literary	1	1 or 2	1 or 2
Transactive	1	1 or 2	1 or 2
Pieces originating in subject other than English	1	1	2
Total	4	5	5

must come from areas other than English. The *Handbook* says, in fact, that the non-English pieces must originate and be developed in non-English areas. Since it is very unlikely for non-English teachers to work with students on imaginative (literary) or expressive writing, we can guess that 90 percent of the transactive pieces come from subjects other than English. It is not at all clear that non-English teachers will receive training in the teaching of writing. But it does seem clear, that in practice, English teachers will still take the blame for weak transactive writings that pull down portfolio scores. It seems predictable that if the requirement remains in place that two pieces must originate and be developed in non-English classes, that change will be a source of consternation. It is also worth noting that English teachers will have less encouragement to teach their students how to make a case regarding humanistic ideas such as human understanding, equality, and justice that are frequently the focus of literary texts.

Scoring Portfolios and Criteria

The Kentucky portfolios are scored in the schools by teams of teachers. Sometimes administrators work with them. The KDE has set up procedures to follow. Anyone scoring must have had training in the year of the scoring. KDE recommends that scoring be done in groups; that time be set aside for scoring; that scoring use variations of blind scoring (so that raters do not know authors of the portfolios and teachers do not score their own students' portfolios); and that two readers score each portfolio and either discuss disagreements to reach agreement or submit the portfolio to a third reader.

The practice is to score the portfolio as a unit, rather than to score the individual pieces. A speaker in a video produced by the KDE, entitled *Writing Portfolio Scoring Training, Grade 12* (1996), indicates that the point of scoring is not to "weigh and gauge how well individual pieces lump together to give us a performance, but [to] look across the body of work in order to determine the sustained performance of the student across the evidence in the portfolio." That is, individual pieces are not scored as in other states.

Raters must bear in mind the qualities of writing listed in the "Kentucky Holistic Scoring Guide" (See Figure 10.3) as they examine the collection of writings as a performance that will be rated as Novice, Apprentice, Proficient, or Distinguished. These abstract qualities must be used in conjunction with a knowledge of the benchmark papers, the exemplary portfolios, and the high-end portfolios in the *Scoring Handbook* (KDE, 1999c, d, e). High-end papers are those at the high end of portfolios scored as novice, apprentice, and proficient. The idea is that if a scorer is having trouble deciding between two adjacent ratings, the scorer may refer to the high-end portfolio for the lower rating. If the portfolio is stronger than the high-end portfolio, it receives the next higher rating. The high-end portfolios define the rating boundaries.

The qualities listed under each level (Novice, Apprentice, Proficient, and Distinguished) are arranged by importance, with the first three carrying greater weight than the second three. The most important includes, at the Distinguished level, what are often considered three separate criteria: an established purpose and clear focus; a "strong awareness of audience"; and "evidence of distinctive voice and/or appropriate tone."

The second criterion, regarding idea development and support, is demanding: "Depth and complexity of ideas supported by rich, engaging, and/or pertinent details; evidence of analysis, reflection, insight." A comment states that this criterion has to do with the "degree to which the writer develops and supports main ideas and deepens the audience's understanding by using," among other things, "logical, justified and suitable explanation" and "relevant elaboration." This language reflects a call for thinking of even greater complexity than does the language of the Oregon criteria. But as in the case of the Oregon criteria, each term in the Kentucky statement must be interpreted as to how it applies to an even wider variety of kinds of writing: poetry, fiction, drama, and the varieties of expressive and transactive writing. The training video (KDE, 1996) makes the point that the support and elaboration criteria are indeed applicable to poetry in the sense that figurative language supports a major motif or

FIGURE 10.3. Kentucky Holistic Scoring Guide

Novice	Apprentice
• Limited awareness of audience and/or purpose • Minimal idea development; limited and/or unrelated details • Random and/or weak organization • Incorrect and/or ineffective sentence structure • Incorrect and/or ineffective language • Errors in spelling, punctuation, and capitalization are disproportionate to length and complexity	• Some evidence of communicating with an audience for a specific purpose; some lapses in focus • Unelaborated idea development; unelaborated and/or repetitious details • Lapses in organization and/or coherence • Simplistic and/or awkward sentence structure • Simplistic and/or imprecise language • Some errors in spelling, punctuation, and capitalization that do not interfere with communication

Proficient	Distinguished
• Focused on a purpose; communicates with an audience; evidence of voice and/or suitable tone • Depth of idea development supported by elaborated, relevant details • Logical, coherent organization • Controlled and varied sentence structure • Acceptable, effective language • Few errors in spelling, punctuation, and capitalization relative to length and complexity	• Establishes a purpose and maintains clear focus; strong awareness of audience; evidence of distinctive voice and/or appropriate tone • Depth and complexity of ideas supported by rich, engaging, and/or pertinent details; evidence of analysis, reflection, insight • Careful and/or subtle organization • Variety in sentence structure and length enhances effect • Precise and/or rich language • Control of spelling, punctuation, and capitalization

theme of the poem. The problem is that evidentiary support is quite different in character from thematic support, and the two remain undifferentiated in Kentucky and most other states.

The *Scoring Handbook* (KDE, 1999c, d, e) includes one complete portfolio at each rating level. The 12th grade exemplar portfolio contains two transactive pieces, one from journalism and one from American studies. The piece from journalism is entitled "Choking Smoking: A Proposal." It is a well-written proposal to install a smoke detector system in the bathrooms of Shelby County High School "in order to eliminate the smoking problem," which becomes more narrowly defined as a problem of smoking in the lavatories. The author addresses the proposal to a very specific audience, the Shelby County High School Management Council and begins by quoting the rule prohibiting possession and use of smoking materials on school grounds.

In length, thoughtfulness about reasons, and support of claims, the paper is superior to the highest score exemplars of Texas and Illinois and comparable to "Foreign Languages by Satellite" from Oregon. The writer makes the case for smoke detectors, first, by claiming that there is a problem of smoking in the lavatories and, second, by discrediting other plans to control that behavior. The evidence that a problem exists consists of three pieces of testimony from three students who claim to have witnessed smoking in the lavatories. The claims by these witnesses appear to be exaggerated and one must question their veracity. One witness says, for example, that "the smokers are claiming all the territories for their own satisfaction while I have to hold it until 3:00." Another claims that "In every bathroom there's about fifteen people and a huge smog of smoke. No one can ever get to use the bathrooms." A third claims that when she can manage to use a lavatory, she "leaves with her hair and clothes completely saturated with smoke, as if *she* were the one with the cigarette." The problem might have been examined more systematically to obtain more complete and reliable information. The question is whether the testimony of three students is sufficient to demonstrate the existence of a problem.

The writer's second tactic is to argue against other proposals, both of which have been used in the school. One of these requires that teachers visit the lavatories between classes. The writer claims that "Not only is this job disliked by the faculty, but it is disruptive of their daily schedules." Further, she claims that "some" teachers "ignore the smokers to avoid an unpleasant confrontation, proving the system to be totally inefficient." The second solution apparently has been to lock the "bathroom doors." This system, the writer claims, "simultaneously punishes" smokers and nonsmokers alike.

The second of these arguments can stand on its own, if it is not illegal to keep students from using the lavatories. But the first presents no evidence that teachers dislike the job (although I believe they would indeed hate it) and no evidence that "some" ignore the smoking. Even, if there were evidence that some teachers ignore smoking by students, that evidence would not prove that the system was "totally inefficient" (KDE, 1999e, pp. 89–90).

Finally, the writer can only speculate that smoke detectors would be sensitive enough to react to cigarette smoke, even if the school were to purchase unusually sensitive detectors. Why would a proposal to buy and install smoke detectors (under a grating) for every lavatory in a school be persuasive without some evidence of their sensitivity to cigarette smoke? It is hard to believe that the real audience for this proposal, the Shelby County High School Management Council, would find it convincing.

The second piece is a letter to an editor of an anthology of contemporary and near-contemporary literature of the American Civil War. The writer wishes to recommend three pieces for inclusion in the anthology. The letter consists of brief synopses of the nominated pieces along with encomiums for each. For example, of a selection from Lincoln, the writer makes the following statement:

> In your compilation, it is certain that you will not forget who refused to let America die in the years of wrenching warfare: Abraham Lincoln. Unlike most great captains of our country, Lincoln's leadership was matched by his sincerity, kindness, and truth. In his "Letter to Mrs. Bixby" Lincoln's genuineness is clear. Simple and short as Lincoln's points often were, the letter displays his respect for her "sacrifice on the altar of freedom"; her five sons all died on the Civil War battlefields. Although it was written upon a grievous misfortune, the letter retains a firmness in reverence and patriotism that was a critical part in supporting the cause of the war: to keep the union together.

Does this piece of writing reveal "Depth and complexity of ideas supported by rich, engaging, and/or pertinent details; evidence of analysis, reflection, insight?" Does it make use of "logical, justified and suitable explanation" and "relevant elaboration?" Where are the rich, engaging, and relevant details?

The letter to the editor provides a set of generalizations that remain unsupported. What does it mean for the letter to retain a "firmness in reverence and patriotism?" This claim might be supported with quotations from the letter, but the writer expects us to accept the judgment without support. In what sense are reverence and patriotism "a critical part in supporting the cause of the war." Certainly this is a defensible claim, but it remains unexplained and unsupported.

A more important problem is why the selection should be included at all. Because it supports "the cause of the war," by which this writer means one goal of the war, to preserve the Union? If a piece of writing supports "the cause of the war," is that sufficient warrant for inclusion in the anthology? Probably not. The writer has not thought through what warrants inclusion in the anthology. Perhaps this piece could accomplish its purpose "in the real world," as *Portfolio Development* (KDE, 1999b) suggests student writing should try to do, with an editor already sympathetic to the selections. But it is doubtful that the letter would convince an editor who already thought she had enough material.

These exemplary pieces from a top-rated portfolio help to define what is meant by "Depth and complexity of ideas supported by rich, engaging, and/or pertinent details; evidence of analysis, reflection, insight." And for Kentucky, as for Illinois and Texas, that definition does not necessarily include concrete evidence to support claims.

Materials for Preparing Students for Portfolio Writing

Commercial materials for the teaching of writing designed specifically for Kentucky appear to be nonexistent. Teachers do not mention any, and I have found none. Why? I suspect there are two possible answers. First, Kentucky may be too small for commercial publishers to bother with. Second, the Kentucky portfolio assessment is simply not conducive to workbook material like *The IGAP Coach* in Illinois or the *Step up to TAAS* and *TAAS Master* series in Texas.

The Kentucky Department of Education does provide guidance for teachers, guidance that adheres closely to the intentions of the assessment. *Portfolio Development* provides a sequence of ten steps for "teaching any genre" (KDE, 1999b, p. 46). The sequence begins with reading "examples of the kind of writing [students] will be producing" and lists a series of questions about typical beginnings, endings, supporting details, tone, sentences, and language. Because they are intended for any genre, the questions must be broad. Step 2 involves deciding on a topic; 3, narrowing the focus; 4, analyzing the audience; 5, defining the writing task, including the writer's role, the audience, and the purpose; 6, planning and doing supporting research; 7, organizing the details; and finally, the steps of drafting, revising, and editing.

This sequence of steps has much in common with the college textbooks and programs that call for students to write a particular kind of essay and proceed by first studying the characteristics of the form, choosing a topic from their own experience, narrowing it, and then doing the necessary research, organizing (frequently outlining), drafting, revising after feedback, and editing. This is the essential sequence (often with the exception of separate drafts for revisions) used by the 17 of 19 college instructors in a study of community college teachers (Hillocks, 1999), the very definition of current traditional rhetoric. It is also the sequence, with variations, that we see in Illinois, Oregon, and Texas.

There are a number of theoretical and pedagogical problems with this sequence, which I will examine in some detail in the final chapter of this book. Kentucky teachers have begun to overcome one of the most important. This standard sequence, perhaps because it puts form first as the target of learning, neglects teaching the students the processes necessary to developing the kinds of support required by different genres, how to process data from which the support or elaboration is to be drawn. Support, elaboration, "rich, engaging, and/or pertinent details; evidence of analysis, reflection, insight," all of these do not appear by magic. They have a source in the data or body of content surrounding an issue or idea. They hardly ever pop out cheerfully to befriend a writer. On the contrary, they are reclusive and frequently reluctant and often must be wrested from hiding.

Some Kentucky teachers are working on the strategies required by different genres. In *The Jefferson County Public Schools Curriculum Handbook/Content Guidelines* [JCH] (n.d.), Jefferson County Public Schools have published the Kentucky writing standards along with a set of descriptions of kinds of writing but, most importantly, accompanied by a set of "skills and prior learnings" required by each type. For example, the guide states the general writing objective, that "students write using appropriate forms, conventions, and styles to communicate ideas and information to different audiences for different purposes" (p. 19). It then focuses on each kind of writing assessed. Under Personal/Expressive Writing, *JCH* states the following more specific objective:

Compose one or more forms of Personal/Expressive Writing that focus on the life experiences of the writer and use the appropriate elements—personal experience, first-person narrative, relevant and significant details, natural and informal style. (p. 19)

It then provides a stipulation or definition: "A Personal Narrative focuses on developing the significance of a single incident in the writer's life." It presents a performance standard, which is more or less a rephrasing of the criterion statements above. To this point, Jefferson County has not moved much beyond the KDE. Then, however, *JCH* presents an analysis of the necessary "supporting skills and prior learning," what the student should be able to do in order to write "any proficient piece of Personal/Expressive Writing" (p. 20). It presents skills that cut across many writing tasks and then becomes more genre specific, presenting a list of "additional supporting skills and prior learning for personal narrative." I include the list here because it is the first that I have seen among materials intended to prepare for a writing assessment in any of the five states studied:

narrow topic and focus on one event.
communicate the significance of the event so that it is clear to the reader.
describe emotions, thoughts, and actions to relate the event.

include dialogue when and where appropriate.
create a mood by developing characters and setting and by using effective
   language.
sequence events/develop plot. (p. 21)

The Kentucky Supreme Court decision (Rose vs. Council for Better Education, 1989) calls for the educational system to develop student capacities, which includes knowledge of things and the "ability to do" things. The task analyses that the Jefferson County Schools has developed is a helpful move in that direction.

In addition, school districts have begun to develop specific lessons designed to help students develop their capacities. Ellen Lewis, writing specialist for Jefferson County, has developed a set of inquiry-based lessons for working on writing short stories. The sequence is based on a task analysis of what middle school students will have to know and be able to do in order to write a "proficient" short story. (Remember that "Proficient" is a quality level in the Kentucky system.) The set of lessons takes students through finding story ideas, "mapping" them, "getting to know your character, dividing the story into scenes, drafting the story, writing an effective lead . . . showing action, using dialogue to advance the plot, punctuating dialogue" (Jefferson County Public Schools, 2000, p. 20). Because the sequence begins with finding story ideas, all subsequent lessons can be tied to the writing of a short story. In fact, many lessons call for use of materials that the students have created as they are progressing toward that goal. The important point is that the lessons engage students in the microprocesses of creating the details, dialogue, openings, and so forth that they will need to develop an effective story. These lessons do not simply employ general writing processes; they recognize the need to provide much more detailed help by teaching students strategies that enable them to wrest appropriate support and elaboration from their content. One would hope that all writing teachers would begin to use this sort of thoughtful analysis of the writing tasks they teach.

NOTE

1. The Index is computed with and without the use of scores of a nationally normed test. When that test is included at 5% weighting, writing portfolio scores count as 11.4% and the writing-on-demand scores as 2.85% (KDE, 2000, p. 12).

CHAPTER 11

Response to Portfolio Assessments: Oregon and Kentucky

How do teachers respond to the demands of the writing portfolio assessments in Oregon and Kentucky? This chapter will examine how teachers prepare students for the assessments, how they react to the underlying theories of writing, teachers' attitudes toward the assessment, the state's role in helping teachers learn to teach writing, and various other research findings. We will turn first to Oregon, since its assessment was less well established than Kentucky's.

RESPONSE TO THE OREGON ASSESSMENT

Even though a large part of the Oregon assessment is not monitored, it seems to insure that the writing curriculum will not be restricted as it has been in Texas, Illinois, and New York. The inclusion of imaginative writing signals a richer, more diverse writing program, which should remain a safeguard against the stagnation of formulaic writing. Oregon began assessing student writing in 1978 when the ODE collected writing samples from a representative sample of students in Grades 4, 7, and 11. In 1982, the state collected another sample. In 1985, 1987, and 1989 the ODE collected writing from random samples of eighth graders and used an analytic scale for scoring. Through 1995, the state assessed "two sets of grade levels in alternating years" (ODE, 1998, p. 1-1). Beginning in 1996, all 10th graders were assessed, but not until 1999 were they held to passing scores of 4 (on a 6-point scale). From that year on, the state expected all 10th graders to pass at that level to achieve the Certificate of Initial Mastery (CIM).

We undertook interviews in 1997 and 1998, when assessments were regularly made in Grades 3, 5, 8, and 10, but before the CIM was in effect. Many teachers interviewed seemed unaware of the full implications of the assessment, and, despite talk about the scoring criteria, seemed oblivious to them. In 1998, for example, 9th and 10th grade teachers at one high school explained that the 9th grade curriculum called for work on "the paragraph." They talked of students' writing narrative, expository, descriptive, and persuasive paragraphs. In the 10th grade, they said they worked on "the five-paragraph theme." One teacher said that in ninth grade with persuasive paragraphs,

> we'll brainstorm a list of semicontroversial topics and they have to be able to try to persuade through facts or statistics. . . . We'll do a little research in the libraries, very brief, because . . . trying to fit that in a paragraph is almost impossible.

He explains that the persuasive paragraph is the last one he works on

> because that's the next big jump for them is to go to the sophomore level and be able to write a persuasive essay with some factual documentation in it. They go from the end of their first semester [of 9th grade] and they don't get that major piece of writing again until the beginning of their sophomore year. So, they go almost 18 weeks of school and then 3 months in the summer with really without any type of major writing.

When asked the reason for focusing on the paragraph, he says that "if I'm not mistaken, it's what the state has told us." I have been able to find nothing from the state about such a focus.

In 10th grade he focuses on the five-paragraph theme, but only the persuasive. When questioned about prompts for other modes of writing, he is not sure of what is tested, but later claims that he is teaching five modes, "giving them to write a paragraph in each." When asked if he thought focusing on single paragraphs would enable students to pass the test, he says "yes" confidently. However, at least 15 months prior to this interview, documents from the state that included the scoring guides and sample pieces of writing clearly indicate that this kind of writing is unlikely to pass the state test (e.g., ODE, 1996a).

This teacher claims that he gives the students a "watered-down version" of the state scoring guide. He admits that "Whether it's used religiously, I'm not sure; it probably isn't, but I think it helps." He tells students that "this is where you need to be in order to meet the standards set for you by the school and by the state." He goes on to say, "In the past I've given them the state scoring guide," but, "because it's so complex and so detailed, they don't want to do that. I would imagine probably a good portion of the teachers haven't read it thoroughly, unless they've sat down and done their own smaller version of it." This teacher's talk about the scoring guide is very ambivalent. He says that he gives students a "watered-down version" because they will not use the "complex" state rubric. But he is not sure that students use it. He apparently does not engage them in its use regularly.

Just as clearly, at that point, the department had not addressed the rubric as a whole or had much discussion of how to teach writing process. The department has a curriculum that calls for paragraphs in the 9th grade, "one every couple of weeks in the first semester" and the persuasive five-paragraph theme in the 10th. In the second semester of ninth grade the curriculum turns to traditional grammar and literature. The main focus is on grammar, teaching "nouns, and verbs, and clauses, and prepositions."

The teacher claims that he has not taught sophomores for a year and is "still in the learning process." Because he was removed from teaching sophomores for a year, he says, "I have to refresh my mind." It appears that the whole department should refresh collective minds. Teachers report that at the 10th-grade level the year before, only 40% passed the state assessment. That should not be surprising if all ninth graders write only nine paragraphs during the first semester and then nothing until the following year when they undertake the five-paragraph theme. Given the criteria Oregon uses, it is surprising that so many pass.

Meanwhile down the street in the same district, a seventh and eighth grade teacher requests three paragraphs from his students. He is familiar with and understands the scoring rubric and distributes a version to his seventh graders to help get them ready for eighth grade. He understands the need for evidence in certain kinds of writing, tries to explain voice, and helps students enter the "five steps" of the composing process. He understands that the state scores students on sentence fluency and conventions. At the same time he tends to underconceptualize all of these concepts. He assumes that we find evidence by going to the library and searching, which is appropriate for certain kinds of problems. He believes that the writing process has five steps that are linear rather than recursive. He works on sentence fluency by integrating traditional grammar with other parts of the English curriculum. He does not know about the possibilities of sentence combining, even though the research showing its effects on the quality of writing has been available since the 1970s. At the same time he has moved far beyond the limited teaching of writing in the high school to which his students will move. But he is unaware that 9th-grade teachers at the high school ask only for single paragraphs and, in effect, are regressive in their teaching.

At the time of the interviews, I have to assume that the Oregon assessment had not had time to become established in the schools in the sense that teachers understood the criteria for judging student writing. It was clear that many teachers did not know the criteria or how the assessment worked. Oregon had not established an educational program for helping teachers learn more about the teaching of writing. The main educational effort was distributing the state documents with the scoring guides and sample papers and enlisting teachers from around Oregon to score the writing, thereby teaching them about the scoring procedures. For whatever reasons, Oregon teachers had not been fully informed about the assessment.

At the same time, nearly all teachers interviewed in Oregon knew about the modes of writing. Of teachers interviewed, 86.79 percent had adopted current traditional rhetoric as their main rhetorical focus, a higher percentage than in any other state, including Texas and Illinois. That leaves very few teachers with alternative approaches. While only 2% of teachers we encountered used expressivist and none used epistemic rhetoric as a major focus, nearly 10% made some use of expressivist rhetoric and 10% some use of epistemic rhetoric, more than in most other states studied.

As might be expected with the current traditional rhetorical focus, the teaching described by those interviewed is presentational in 79.3% of our cases. However, there is some use of workshop and environmental approaches (9% and 4% respectively). Most of the Oregon teachers interviewed see their role as providing information to students.

Despite that, relatively few Oregon teachers interviewed use formulaic approaches to teaching writing. While 77% of our interviewees said they described the structure of the kinds of writing taught, only 28% defined that structure as the five-paragraph theme and only 13% used diagrams of structures for students to fill in. These percentages are quite low compared to those in Texas and Illinois. In addition, quite high proportions of teachers tell us they make use of aspects of the writing process: prewriting (72%), peer response (77%), revising (84%), and editing (83%). These are higher percentages than in most other states.

It seems apparent that the Oregon assessment is not likely to engender formulaic writing. Whereas in Illinois, the criteria for organization and focus seem to call for formulaic writing, the Oregon criteria for organization are designed to fend off the formulaic, inasmuch as they call for organization that is organically related to the subject. *Oregon's Test Specifications, Grade 10*, state that, for a rating of 6, the writing is characterized by

—effective, perhaps creative, sequencing; the organizational structure fits the topic, and the writing is easy to follow.
—a strong, inviting beginning that draws the reader in and a strong, satisfying sense of resolution or closure. (ODE, 1997d, p. A2)

The five-paragraph theme structure is one that is devised to fit any subject if one is willing to treat any subject superficially. The Oregon criteria for the organization to fit the subject stand in sharp contrast, strongly suggesting that a subject must be understood in enough depth to decide how to develop an appropriate organization.

It is also apparent that when teachers and school systems ignore the criteria and focus on blethering through five-paragraph themes, their students will fail the assessment. At the same time, it seems also apparent that the state needs to do more than formulate a test and inform teachers about it. If our interviews are any indication, teachers will need support in learning how to teach so that their students can meet Oregon's relatively sophisticated standards.

THEORY AND KINDS OF WRITING IN KENTUCKY

As I have shown, the spectrum of writing used in the assessment in Kentucky is far broader than in any other of the states examined in this study and also in most other states that conduct writing assessments. Almost all Kentucky teachers interviewed talk about many kinds of writing from personal narrative, memoir, and essay to fiction, poetry, and drama. In addition, they talk about teaching many different kinds of transactive writing including editorials, surveys, interviews for feature stories, laboratory reports, reports about school and public problems, reviews, and so forth. In addition, teachers in Kentucky attend to the ideas of audience and purpose more than teachers in other states studied. In Kentucky, 52.3% of those interviewed talk about teaching students the concept of audience and demonstrate by talking about different audiences, the school principal, the mayor, the newspaper readers in the community, and so forth. In Texas, on the other hand, only about 33% mention audiences, but it is in passing, not in the kind of depth that we find in Kentucky. One Kentucky teacher admits that a "sense of audience has never been a big thing in teaching composition before. The *purpose* was the big thing. You know, you were writing to *persuade*. But I would think that . . . I know in my experience, 23 years' worth, I had never emphasized 'This is going to go to . . . the chairman of the board,' or 'This is going to go to the newspaper.' So that sense of audience has been really . . . hard for us to adjust to." Nevertheless, in Kentucky the change is being made to thinking far more seriously about an audience.

With the emphasis from the advocates of writing process, such as Calkins (1994), Graves (1983), and Atwell (1987), on the writing process and with the emphasis on process in *Portfolio Development* (KDE, 1999b), one might expect an expressivist rhetoric to be widespread in Kentucky. But, in fact, only 6% of teachers we interviewed seemed to use such an approach. Far more, 75%, were categorized as using CTR as their major rhetorical stance. That is, most teachers focused primarily on the structure of the writing. Many (78%) said they taught the characteristics of the kinds of writing to be produced for portfolios through the reading and examination of model pieces of writing. Only 9% talked about using schematics of various kinds to reinforce the characteristics. Some (8%) taught the five-paragraph theme, despite its derogation in the *Portfolio Development*.

At the same time, Kentucky teachers are far more likely to make thorough use of the writing process in one way or another. Table 11.1 indicates that very high percentages of teachers talk about using most parts of the writing process with their classes. Most teachers believe that most elements have to be engaged for the process to work. For many, the process seems to have become standard.

A major idea in the writing process theory is that for students to become writers, they must have some choice in what they write about. Kentucky specifically provides that writing may be for learning or for showing what has been learned. Twenty years ago such writing was the rule in classrooms (Applebee, 1981; Britton et al., 1973). However, the Kentucky writing assessment insists that students choose their own topics, for their own purposes. In our interviews, 67% indicated that they gave students choice at or near the beginning of each writing unit, not simply on the pieces for the portfolio.

In this regard, there is an important difference in the kind of brainstorming practiced in states with different kinds of assessments. In Texas and Illinois, brainstorming was conducted to give students practice in responding to topics in the state prompts. In Kentucky, brainstorming was used to help students think of and develop their own topics.

TABLE 11.1. Percentages of Kentucky Teachers Interviewed Who Indicate Using Parts of the Writing Process

Choosing own topics	67.2%
Prewriting	76.6%
Drafting	100.0%
Peer Feedback	76.6%
Conferencing	46.9%
Revising	82.8%
Editing	73.4%
Publishing	25.0%

The widespread emphasis on choosing topics for writing and on emphasizing the development of writing through process suggests that Kentucky students are learning more about writing than simple forms and formulas. While a few teachers in our Kentucky sample teach the five-paragraph theme and other formulas, the vast majority appear not to teach such formulas.

What appears, however, is a standard pattern of teaching, the pattern or sequence described in the *Portfolio Development*. It begins with reading models of a special kind of writing (e.g., editorials), brainstorming for topics meaningful to the students, then using the stages of the composing process, including conferencing, a major means, in Kentucky, of helping students learn the type of writing and produce their own pieces successfully.

Frequently, teachers provide students with information in addition to the models and their characteristics. One teacher talks about eleven "things" that students must have in their notebooks for a unit on persuasion. These include handouts on persuasion in advertisements, a sheet containing 300 ways to say "said," a sheet with expressions for naming feelings (e.g., "ways to say you are sad"), and sheets designed to help with thinking about audience and purpose, as well as the student's role as a writer. This sheet, developed by Dr. Charles Whitaker of Eastern Kentucky University, is accompanied by "examples of students' roles: student, consumer, son, daughter, peer, concerned person, reviewer."

Many who talk about this instructional sequence frequently say that students must practice until they learn how to produce the kinds of writing desired. One says, "You need to infuse your instruction with the types of writing that are involved in these assessments. As far as specifics like 'how to'—essentially how to raise your scores—practice, practice, practice."

The major instructional parts of this sequence are the reading and discussion of the models of writing, the handouts for reference, and the conferences with other students or teachers. According to teachers interviewed, the conferences afford opportunities to deal with a youngster's specific problems in writing, to make suggestions about content, organization, mechanics, all without actually making corrections. Here, for example is one fourth-grade teacher's description of the sequence:

> I do several minilessons on each type of writing, and I share examples with them, and talk about why this is a personal narrative, why this is supporting a position, or problem solution, or whatever. And why this is fiction. . . . As far as the writing process goes, I'd say my class has a good understanding that they need to make a plan. We usually do some kind of a web . . . first. They understand there's

a rough draft, which they've gotten to the point they don't care how it looks or what's spelled right. Then they know that that needs to be taken to the next level. Then they want to conference with me after that, and see what suggestions I have, or what we can work out together, or with another student.

One thing I do that's real effective is I take about 15 minutes each day to let the kids—not all of them, but certain kids each day—share with the group. And we usually do this at the beginning of writing [class]. Then I'll let the students make comments: positive or constructive criticism. That way, they've got this right in their mind, writing just starting, everybody's heard what so-and-so needed to do to make the story better, and what so-and-so did that I liked and they liked. Then they're going off with those ideas when they start writing. That probably helps them as much or more than when I'm commenting to them. Because sometimes I'll tell them something, and in the other corner, one of the other students thinks, "you need to do this, and that would be really good."

A 12th-grade teacher echoes the same process, stressing that at the 12th-grade level he does not need to work on "the basics." He says, "We practice writing, we critique other writing, and we work on revision, primarily. I'm not teaching a lot of the basic skills that they've learned in previous grades, and especially not . . . the writing process and the elaboration of thoughts." According to this teacher, students have already learned about those. Now they must simply practice what they know. About 64% of teachers interviewed in Kentucky talk about teaching writing in this way, considerably fewer than in other states.

Over 35% of the teachers in our Kentucky sample say that they engage their students in activities that help them learn about writing, activities other than simply listening to the teacher. For example, one very enthusiastic second-grade teacher, Ms. Weaver, provides a fairly extended statement of how her teaching works. She explains that good "lessons stem from teaching what every piece should have, every element." She explains that as a second-grade teacher, "I have to . . . decide which parts I'm going to introduce to my kids." She talks of the importance of showing her students samples. "I've found literature is so important with the children," she says. She tells of bringing in papers that her own children have written for school and reading them to her students. She concentrates on short stories:

There's a great book that's called *Dear Isabelle, Tell Me A Story*. And it's about this woman, a little character comes up to her grandmother and says "tell me a story" and the whole book talks about "Well, if you're going to tell a story, you need to have characters. What kind of characters do you want?" And so she develops this whole story. And that's kind of like I do with the children. Then I'll say, "Okay, now, as a group, we're going to work together to make a big group story. And we're going to choose our characters." so they choose characters, and then we talk about problems and we talk abut solutions. . . . And I usually do a group story. . . . "Okay, we've got all of these characters here. We've got a knight, we've got an alien, and we've got a mouse. Let's vote as a group, because I think they're all good characters." Then we take our characters, and then we . . . web our characters.

I'll say, "Okay, if we're going to write about our alien, we have to come up with ideas. What's our alien going to look like? What's it going to act like?" So from there, I do a simple spider web, which is a circle, and I stem off. Okay, he's green—they're just describing the alien. . . . They're giving it to me and I'm recording it on a big chart. They do this as a group first, and we got through all this. So we've got our alien. Then I show them how we could put these ideas together as sentences and make a good description of our alien. And then we take the alien and we say, "Now what world is this alien in? Where's our setting?" And we talk about setting.

Ms. Weaver develops these story ideas over a long period of time, perhaps a month or more. She records student ideas on a very large piece of butcher paper that extends across her chalk board. She refers to idea sessions such as these as "focused writing." For each of four kinds of writing in the second grade, Ms. Weaver spends 2 weeks to a month on the focused writing, usually 10 to as much as 30 minutes per day, depending on student response. Following such sessions, she helps students take ideas they have generated and write them into sentences. After each minilesson, she asks the students to write at their desks:

It can be either on what we've been talking about, or, if I don't feel like they're ready, I'll say this is a free-choice write. . . . I've been very fortunate, and my kids love to write. And they'll be creating plays, or writing stories or poems with partners. And I encourage that a lot, instead of just writing independently all the time. Because I think they learn so much from each other.

Sometimes, Mrs. Weaver does this writing differently. If students know what webs are,

I'll say, "This is our alien, and we've done a character sketch. That's all we've done." And I say . . . "Take these: green alien, pointy ears; long, sharp nose, purple." I'll show them how to write that in sentences. At that point, if I've found that the kids are ready, and it depends on your group, I'll say, "I'll get you into small groups, and I want you to write the sentences that you find from this big web here." Then we come back together, and then we record [their sentences].

At some points, she asks students to work in groups on the ideas developed in their class webs. The group takes a section of the web and writes it as a paragraph. When they have developed all the parts of the story, she helps the class put them all together.

It is then time for them to work on a story individually. As they work, Ms. Weaver says, "[I] walk around and help, help, help! There's some kids that still need my hand-holding." She coaches them on developing ideas and on putting them into sentences, a key effort in second grade.

A few teachers at higher grade levels, particularly fourth and seventh or eighth, use the method called inquiry (see Hillocks, 1995, for an extended definition). In this method, teachers provide sets of material, pictures, objects, texts, in short, observable data for students to examine and analyze. While students are learning how to be specific in their writing, it is easier for them to focus on something present to the senses than to recall something from experience and hold it in mind so that it may be described.

Ms. Glaser, a fourth-grade teacher, uses this procedure frequently with actual objects and pictures.

We talk about digging for details. . . . It's really showing the kids how to make an object come alive, really looking for details. You find a funny hat and you pass it around, and when they pass it, they describe it, they give an adjective about it and you make this list as you're going along, on the chart. I usually use chart paper and write on the chart and then when they get finished, you say, "Okay, now I want you to really describe this hat, not just fluffy, soft, black. I want you to make this hat come alive. I want you to think of what this hat reminds you of, or what it looks like. I want you to just make it come alive." And you wouldn't believe the things they come up with. We've got all kinds of good things . . . all these different things that it looked like to them and it could be anything. It just kind of got them motivated that there is no wrong answer, you know, it's what they think that makes sense. So, we really worked on that and they really get into that.

And then we talk about snapshots and thought-shots. [Snap-shots involve] basically taking a photograph of something and describing something so you can see it and use it as details. "I want to see what you're seeing [in your mind]. I want to see that picture that you're seeing."

One activity . . . is giving postcards to kids, to have them describe it as well as they can, and then they give that description to another player and they have to try to draw it from what they've said. . . . This year, we looked . . . at snapshots in two books. . . . I just flipped through [them], found snapshots, made copies for all my students. We looked at it, then they drew a picture of that snapshot.

Following the drawing, students wrote about their snapshots. Then other students read the descriptions to see if they could match it to one of the pictures. A thought-shot, Ms. Weaver explains, is about "thoughts and feelings" at a particular moment.

I do encourage my kids to really get into it, feel, and think, especially in the personal narratives. I want to know what you were thinking at the time that that happened. I want to know how you were feeling. You know, explain it to me. I want to be there. . . . I pick something that most of them have been to. So, a lot of them have been to Kings Island. That's a big amusement park and most of them have been to it. So, I usually use that. I say okay, how about the roller coaster. "When you ride on the roller coaster, what are you feeling?" Then they talk about butterflies in their stomach, I'm nervous, I'm shaking, and they talk about all these feelings that they're having. Then I say okay, what are you thinking? And they'll say, "I think I'm gonna die; what if the seat belt comes undone?" And they talk about all these thoughts that they have. Then a lot of times I'll just give them about 10 min-utes. "I just want you to write down any thoughts and feelings you have right now." And they just write down anything. "I wish Miss Glaser would be quiet. You can write that. . . . I just want you to write down all the thoughts you have." Those are thought-shots, you know. I really, really ask for those in their writing. You know, what were you thinking at that time? That makes it so much better. When people read that they want to know, they want to be there, they want to see what you saw, they want to feel, they want to know what you were thinking. So, we really focus on that.

Ms. Glaser's teaching, like Ms. Weaver's, is aimed at helping students learn the strategies they will need to produce specific detail in their writing. Research suggests that the target of instruction, the strategies of production, are generalizable to other comparable tasks (Hillocks, 1979). When instruction is aimed at developing a particular narrative, students may not learn those strategies of production for use independently.

While not many teachers focus on the microstrategies by engaging students in their use so that teachers can coach as they begin to use them, more do so in our Kentucky sample than in our samples in other states. In the Kentucky sample, 13% use such activities consistently, as do Mrs. Weaver and Ms. Glaser, while in our Texas sample only 4% do.

Writing Across the Curriculum

An unusual but explicit goal of the Kentucky portfolio assessment is that writing be treated across the curriculum in all subject matters and by all teachers. For that purpose, the requirement remains that at each tested grade level, one or more papers must originate in a content area other than English. One of the problems with this arrangement is that teachers in subjects other than English are not disposed to teach writing, many believing that teaching writing is not part of their academic assignment. Our interviews indicate that involving teachers in content areas has not been easy. Callahan (1997; 1999) writes of her observation of an English faculty struggling to meet the demands of the Kentucky assessment without the support of the school principal. Few if any faculty outside English were willing even to make writing assignments, let alone teach writing. As a result, the English department were very frustrated in their attempts to meet portfolio requirements.

In our interviews, we seldom encountered such entrenched recalcitrance, perhaps because our visits and interviews did not begin until 1996, several years after the assessment had been in effect. What we have found is a number of stories of interdepartmental cooperation on writing papers for possible use in portfolios. Usually, this means that content teachers assign appropriate papers in their classes but without teaching how to write the essays. Significantly, in most of these cases, the cooperative effort had the support or even the instigation of the school principal.

One such story came very late in our interviews (2000). Ms. Flowers, an 11th- and 12th-grade teacher at a high school in a large urban area of Kentucky, explains that portfolios are developed at every grade level in her high school. She thought that if "the junior teachers' . . . responsibility is specifically to teach the editorial, then some of the junior content teachers should be offering that as their content piece. Then we could work hand in hand!

And it doesn't have to be such a struggle for either the content teachers or for the English teachers." It occurred to her that since nearly all the students in 11th grade took chemistry, she could approach the chemistry department about the possibility of helping with such an assignment. She explains:

> The junior English teacher would teach the basic editorial and actually have the students produce one. The problem with the English teachers only doing the editorial, for example, and not sharing it with the content teachers is that the students have to have two pieces in their portfolio that are from other areas. . . . The letter to the reviewer has to be from the English class. The literary piece, which is the poem, short story, play, and so forth, rarely comes from another class. There's no reason why it couldn't, but let's face it. It rarely does! And the personal expressive piece, same thing. It could come [from another class], but actually I'd say the personal expressive piece is the one that is really less likely. Because there are some few classes, some of the foreign language classes, for example, humanities, that might get into the literary piece. Or even, some of the social studies kids have written poems. . . . So . . . we would teach the editorial, and . . . the editorial they write for us is practice, and we would have it as a grade in our class. But they're not going to use that for their portfolio; they're not going to have an opportunity to. So, I don't have the feeling that it's wasted time; it's not. They've learned those skills. But the kids feel . . . "Well, this is all well and good, but my portfolio is full of pieces now that I can't use! Here's this that I've written in 9th grade English, this that I've written in 10th grade, and this I've written in 11th grade." But very few pieces that are actually of the quality and caliber or even will fit . . . the portfolio, are coming from the content area. But by working together with the chemistry teachers, then, after we have taught [the editorial], then . . . several of the chemistry teachers actually took . . . the same [materials] that I was using to teach it, and followed through with it.

Students writing such an editorial for chemistry in this school wrote about a variety of topics including the irradiation of foods, "nuclear power plants or nuclear waste," and issues in ecology. Some of the chemistry teachers followed Ms. Flowers's guidelines about drafting, revising, and editing, and read the resulting papers mainly for substantive concerns but also for expression, organization, and support.

Ms. Flowers understands that often teachers are unwilling to undertake such a project because of the extra work it entails. In this case, however, she claims that "teachers were not only interested, but very helpful." She goes on to make a comment about the principal's support:

> The principal here is really instrumental in this. Because when I approached . . . Mr. Burke . . . as an administrator, not only did he think this was a great idea, but he was willing to say something about it, to actually go to the chemistry teachers and say something. And then to talk to the whole faculty about it. And we called it kind of like a pilot program, to see if it turned out well, then we would try it with other things. Then we talked about what other things, maybe, could be done. Another [possibility] with juniors is social studies, because every single junior does take American history.

What we see generally in the schools visited is faculty cooperation on writing across the curriculum. It takes other forms than that described above, usually with content area teachers requiring writing which English teachers subsequently help students shape. It appears that writing across the curriculum is working fairly well in Kentucky despite apparent failure in the school observed by Callahan (1997). In Kentucky, 73% of teachers interviewed talk about writing across the curriculum as opposed to 19% in Texas. Nor did we encounter any cases in Kentucky in which teachers at the elementary level had been asked to align the curriculum, to avoid teaching science, as in Dr. Jayne's Texas school, until the writing test had been administered. On the contrary, elementary teachers talk about integrating writing into their science, social studies, and even math lessons.

Responses of Students and College Faculty

Some studies have examined the responses of students to the portfolio assessment. One of these, Coe et al. (1994), examined the attitudes of 100 junior high and high school students. Most indicated that the portfolio had helped to increase their writing ability and felt generally positive about the effects of the Kentucky Educational Reform Act. Mincey (1996) studying the attitudes of students at a regional Kentucky university, concluded that college "freshman portfolio writers tell us, 'We wrote more in high school than non-portfolio writers, and that has paid off in helping us to learn, become more comfortable with writing, become better writers, and prepare us for college'" (p. 3). Further, Mincey surveyed faculty teaching first-year writing courses. She develops the following generalization from faculty responses: "When it comes to being writers, first year writers are demonstrating significant improvement in understanding the writing process and showing more comfort with writing" (p. 3).

However, Spalding and Cummins (1998) find almost the opposite in a study of the attitudes of 450 University of Kentucky freshman. "Two thirds of the students expressed the view that the portfolio was not helpful" (p. 182). On the other hand, Spalding and Cummins report that the "majority of responses . . . named some positive outcome from high school writing" (p. 184). Further, 91.4% rank themselves as average, above average, or excellent as writers (p. 185).

One clue to this disparity in responses is that many students who find the portfolio not helpful also believe that it did not prepare them for college writing, with 26.2% indicating that "college writing is not like high school writing" (p. 184). Spalding and Cummins note that "many students bitterly noted the gulf between genre requirements and performance standards of the [Kentucky] portfolio and those of the University" (p. 186).

Spalding and Cummins indicate that the University of Kentucky freshman English program focuses on argumentative writing. Indeed, Peter Mortensen, former director of the writing program at the University informs me that from 1992 to 1998, the writing program had adopted Ramage and Bean's text, *Writing Arguments* (1992), which is based on Toulmin's (1958) theory of argument. Undoubtedly, the disparity between the idea of support in a piece of writing in high school and in freshman English is considerable. This disparity is the same difference in support that I have considered in earlier chapters, the difference between blether and warranted evidence. If teachers followed only the suggestions for preparing students for the portfolio that appear in the *Portfolio Development* (KDE, 1999b), it is certain that they did not prepare students for the kind of thinking and writing involved in Ramage and Bean's text. If high school teachers accept the kind of support for claims offered in newspaper editorials and feature stories, as they well might because they may teach those forms, and if their students use comparable support in their college writing, the students might well complain that high school writing did not prepare them for college.

At the same time, while the *Portfolio Development* recommends that all pieces of writing come from ongoing instruction, it also warns against using any piece intended for the teacher only. Units of instruction in English might readily include personal and imaginative writing as well as literary criticism or writing that would be appropriate as reviews or academic articles. Despite the fact that the *Portfolio Development* warns against writing that is only intended for the teacher, such writing qualifies for inclusion in a portfolio unless it is canned coverage of a topic taken from teacher lectures or books. In fact, *Portfolio Development* indicates that book reviews and academic journal articles are eligible. Such writing may be written for the teacher to demonstrate learning, but it may easily pass as intended for a more general audience. And it ought to use rigorous arguments.

The best high school academic writing I have seen in English is often appropriate for a broader audience. It frequently involves students taking concepts studied in class and applying them independently to works read outside class. For example, a ninth grader of mine read *Lord of the Flies* independently as his final project in a unit focused on the interpretation of symbolism. He saw parallels between the novel and ideas he had read in chapters of *The Prince* during the eighth grade. Part of his point was that the novel is a fable for our time and that Machiavelli's cynical view of mankind is echoed in the novel. The piece was extraordinarily well written for a high school student. It demonstrates skill in argument, powerful insight into the novel, and originality in bringing Machiavelli to bear. While the purpose of the assignment from my point of view had to do with evaluating the success of my instruction over the unit, the piece clearly meets the portfolio requirements.

Many teachers interviewed in Kentucky believe that such writing is not eligible. It is. One problem with including it is that two pieces of writing in the portfolio must originate in subject matter areas other than English. If ordinarily, as many teachers report, those pieces are the transactional entries in the portfolios, then distribution requirements prohibit inclusion of a piece of literary criticism, which is also classified as transactional. However, because legitimate academic writing is eligible, its inclusion in the portfolio should help to insure that teachers integrate the writing of portfolio pieces in the regular curriculum and encourage the kind of writing that students can be expected to need in college, a change that might contribute to students seeing the portfolio as more valuable.

Despite certain minor problems, the Kentucky portfolio venture is a model for imitation. It avoids the formulaic, treats writing as a meaningful and serious pursuit for students, engenders a rich writing program, and provides for the professional development of teachers who must do far more than teach students to fill out schematic diagrams. Every state has much to learn from what Kentucky has accomplished.

CHAPTER 12

Testing, Thinking, and Needed Change

Researchers have known for a long time that testing drives the school curriculum (Madaus, 1988). One would expect that if students are to be tested on persuasive writing, teachers will teach it. If narrative is tested, teachers will teach that. The question for this study is whether assessments influence more than the general content of the curriculum. To answer that, I have looked closely at the features of writing assessments in five states. Now some comparisons are in order. Next, I will turn to the question of the impact these different assessments have on the teaching of writing. Further, because writing cannot be divorced from thinking about the content of the writing, I will examine the impact of assessments on the kinds of thinking students are encouraged to do in classrooms. This chapter will focus on these three questions before turning to recommendations.

THE NATURE OF WRITING ASSESSMENTS

It should be clear by now that writing assessments differ enormously, from the 40-minute assessments in Illinois to the portfolio assessments in Kentucky. Statements of standards lead people to believe that the stories of assessments are obvious in the standards, but they are not. As I have shown, it is imperative to examine the prompts, the criteria, and the benchmark papers to understand what the standards mean. Only upon such analysis can we discover the banal writing that assessments in Texas and Illinois not only encourage but hold up for admiration. Only then do we see that the Illinois criteria encourage the five-paragraph theme. Only then do we see that Texas and Illinois ignore the need for real evidence in making a case. Only then do we see that in Illinois narrative turns into the exposition. Only then do we see that "in-depth analysis" in New York actually means relatively simple analysis. But at least it involves some analysis and requires actual evidence in some responses to the assessment.

Analysis of the prompts, criteria, and benchmark papers across states reveal some remarkable differences. Why are the top-rated papers in Texas and Illinois filled with banality while the top-rated papers in Oregon and New York are not? There seem to be two reasons: the criteria and the testing format. In both Oregon and New York, criteria call for evidence and the top-rated benchmark papers display it. In New York, students receive material about which to write. The students have potential evidence at hand. In Oregon, students write their papers over a period of three class periods. They have opportunities to develop or find evidence.

In Kentucky, criteria apply to the portfolio as a whole and do not call for evidence in transactive writing. Yet because students have time, they can find the kinds of information to make a strong case. However, as we have seen, specific criteria and models of effective use of evidence would probably be helpful in Kentucky.

THE IMPACT OF ASSESSMENT ON TEACHING

When we examine what teachers say happens in classrooms, the impact of the assessments is brought into even stronger relief in all major categories: rhetorical stance, instructional mode, and writing process. It will be useful to compare these patterns of instruction to the results of experimental studies for similar patterns of teaching.

Rhetorical Stance

The rhetorical stance of the teacher represents a typical approach to teaching writing and strongly suggests how teachers understand knowledge, teaching, and learning. In our sample, the preponderance of teachers are closely tied to current traditional rhetoric (CTR), as Table 12.1 indicates—over 80% of teachers in Illinois, Oregon, and Texas. They see their task as teaching knowledge about standard forms of writing that have been in the American curriculum for a hundred years. They focus on the structure of texts in the sense of what comes first, next, and last in a piece of writing, what its characteristics should be, and the kinds of expression appropriate in each. They tend not to deal with strategies for generating content beyond relatively simple prewriting. They do not teach strategies for generating the specifics.

The percentages of teachers engaged in expressivist or epistemic rhetoric are indeed low, well under 10% in every state studied. Only Kentucky has more than five percent. In New York and Oregon we did not find a single example of epistemic rhetoric.

TABLE 12.1. Main Rhetorical Focus

	Illinois	Kentucky	New York	Oregon	Texas
Current traditional rhetoric	83	75	29	87	84
Expressivist	2	6	3	2	2
Epistemic	2	9	0	0	2
Grammar	4	0	10	6	6
Writing about literature	4	8	50	2	4
Not identifiable	6	3	8	3	4

In New York, however, there is a far smaller percentage of teachers engaged in CTR. Instead, they focus on writing about literature. That is what the assessment examines in the high school. In addition, the tradition in teaching writing for many years in high school was writing about literature. When I began teaching, few teachers taught anything in writing except grammar, mechanics, and writing about literature. That is what Applebee found in his 1981 study of writing in American high schools. New York has remained close to that tradition. In New York, we found only 29% who focused on CTR. Most of these are at the elementary and middle school levels or focused on the old competency exams which do not require writing about literature. Clearly, however, the assessment controls what is taught and what students learn.

In Kentucky, the percentage of teachers interviewed who adopt CTR is lower than in Texas and Illinois, 75%, but still quite high. The assessment indicates the types of writing students must produce for a portfolio, and *Portfolio Development* (KDE, 1999b) recommends that teachers need to begin the process of teaching with study of the type of writing through reading and discussing many models. Still, in Kentucky, a higher proportion of teachers in our sample has taken either an expressivist or epistemic stance, a total of over 15%, several times the percentages in other states. The Kentucky portfolio assessment encourages teachers to move away from a strict adherence to simply telling students the formal characteristics of the kinds of writing.

In Texas and Illinois, teachers believe that the best way to help students pass the test is to explicate the features of the types of writing and give students practice in producing them until they can replicate them on demand. Because the tests provide only a prompt and no data set to examine, there is no obvious point to helping students learn how to examine problems and analyze data. The Texas and Illinois tests separate such thinking from writing. While Oregon teachers adopt a comparable approach, the criteria demand thinking, and the testing format allows it. In New York, on the other hand, teachers and the tests hold students responsible for thinking through problems in the texts presented.

While teachers exhibit a major rhetorical stance, they also talk about activities that indicate some other occasional stance. For example, on occasion, a teacher who ordinarily teaches the formal characteristics of writing may focus on the analysis of some problem or some other aspect of writing. Large proportions of teachers also teach grammar and mechanics, most as mechanical problems appear in writing. Therefore, we also coded evidence of secondary stances as they appear in our interviews. Table 12.2 presents a summary of these findings.

The most frequent secondary foci are grammar (and mechanics) and writing about literature. The data also reveal, of course, that nearly all teachers focus some of their time on CTR, virtually shutting out other more powerful approaches. Even at the level of secondary focus, few teachers in our sample use expressivist or epistemic rhetoric. In Kentucky, however, over a third of the teachers in our sample adopt an expressivist or epistemic stance at least in some of their teaching.

Judgments about focus were made on the basis of a global view of a teacher's description of teaching. We also coded specific activities that teachers mentioned.

Table 12.3 provides percentages of teachers in our sample who mentioned activities related to CTR. Most teachers use model compositions to show students what they are expected to write. Many use models of stu-

TABLE 12.2. Secondary Rhetorical Focus

	Illinois	Kentucky	New York	Oregon	Texas
Current traditional rhetoric	15	20	37	8	16
Expressivist	4	13	8	9	7
Epistemic	4	6	5	9	11
Grammar	64	69	58	77	84
Writing about literature	47	52	40	51	45
Not identifiable	11	8	11	2	7

TABLE 12.3. Aspects of Current Traditional Rhetoric

Emphases	Illinois	Kentucky	New York	Oregon	Texas
Models	58	78	47	75	76
Description of structure	89	78	58	77	98
Schematics	38	9	11	13	53
Five-paragraph theme	72	6	5	28	55

dent writing from the scoring manuals or from professional writers. When actual models of writing are not in use, teachers may use descriptions or sets of prescriptions about the structure of the required discourse. New York teachers use models less frequently. Rather, they talk to students about supporting a thesis statement using details from the text as evidence. It is not easy to find models of literary criticism that are accessible to elementary and secondary students. Thus, students write a kind of faintly imitative literary criticism in these programs that has neither the rigor nor the insight and development of real literary criticism.

It is rather surprising that models do not appear as frequently among the Illinois sample, especially with its emphasis on the five-paragraph theme. On the other hand, the formulas (five-paragraph theme) and the schematic diagrams so frequently mentioned by Illinois teachers are themselves virtual models that students must practice and follow. Over two thirds of teachers interviewed in Illinois use the five-paragraph model and over a third reduce it further to a simplified diagram that sometimes tells how many sentences must be included. As I have pointed out, students continue to use this form in college, to the dismay of their teachers there. It is also clear that, in contrast to other states, the assessments in Texas and Illinois encourage the use of this reductionist form of writing.

Mode of Instruction

Do assessments have any impact on the traditional ways of teaching? In 1984 Goodlad found that the great preponderance of the thousands of classes he visited at all grade levels were taught through what he called "frontal" teaching, essentially the same as this study's presentational teaching. Students listen to lectures and participate in recitations in which the teacher asks questions with set answers that require no critical thinking or even inference (Nystrand, 1997). As Table 12.4 indicates, writing as-

TABLE 12.4. Mode of Instruction

	Illinois	Kentucky	New York	Oregon	Texas
Presentational	81	64	74	79	82
Workshop	2	13	13	9	9
Environmental	4	13	0	4	4
Not identifiable	13	11	13	8	5

sessments have done little to change that. I suspect that, in many cases, assessments have actually reinforced this sort of teaching. In Illinois and Texas, in particular, the assessments suggest that writing is cut and dried and need not be taught with high levels of student participation, the kind appearing in Ms. Levine's class in Chapter 2. Only Kentucky shows much change from what Goodlad called frontal teaching. In Kentucky 25% percent of the teachers interviewed indicate that they use other methods, either the workshop approach or environmental teaching. No other state in our sample has as many teachers moving away from lecture and recitation as a staple of teaching.

Why is Kentucky different? In an interview, Starr Lewis, the director of writing assessment in Kentucky for several years, reports that prior to 1990, "students did precious little writing in Kentucky schools" and that what they did was mostly the five-paragraph theme (personal communication, June 15, 2001). I believe that the difference in Kentucky lies in the nature of the assessment, the training afforded the teachers, and the guidelines set out by the state. Kentucky has more open criteria for good writing, more teacher education through eight Writing Project sites, strong guides to the teaching of writing in its various state and local handbooks, and an assessment that permits development of writing in a serious way. My guess is that the stronger, epistemic, methodologies for teaching will spread in Kentucky as the assessment continues, although the state may have to take a stronger leadership role in developing methods other than those in place.

WRITING PROCESS ELEMENTS

Since the 1970s, there has been a very strong push in the profession to employ what has come to be known as the writing process. Applebee's 1981 study suggests that teachers in the late 1970s and very early 1980s truncated their teaching of writing simply by making assignments and grading the results. As Table 12.5 indicates, teachers now are doing much more. In most states studied, fairly large percentages of teachers interviewed report using prewriting activities, peer response, revision, and editing. The largest percentages of these are in Kentucky and Oregon, both of which make use of collections of writing as a part of their evaluation.

It is interesting to note that prewriting is high in all states, including Illinois and Texas. However, in Illinois and Texas the reasons for teaching prewriting are quite different from the reasons for it in Kentucky. In Kentucky, prewriting is viewed as a means of helping students develop their own ideas about their own topics, In Illinois and Texas, it is viewed as a means of enabling students to deal with whatever topic appears on the exams.

In this regard, we should note that teachers in Kentucky indicate that students commonly choose their own topics for writing. Over two thirds of Kentucky teachers say they provide such choice, more than twice as many as in Texas. When Kentucky teachers talk about allowing such choice to students, they talk about it as a general rule. The state requires that students develop their own pieces for the portfolio. In Texas, Illinois, and New York, student choice is almost always occasional. In those states, teachers assign topics, subject matter, and even points of view because the assessments impose such restrictions. In Kentucky, on the other hand, freedom of choice in terms of topic, subject matter, and point-of-view is central to the portfolios.

The percentages for Kentucky teachers are consistently high in using all elements of the writing process. In other states, teachers tend to use some parts of the process but not others. For example, some teachers in

TABLE 12.5. Elements in the Writing Process Reported

Elements	Illinois	Kentucky	New York	Oregon	Texas
Students choose topics	45	66	34	55	27
Prewriting (e.g., brainstorming)	66	75	63	72	80
Drafting	100	100	100	100	100
Peer response	52	75	61	77	64
Revising	50	81	32	84	55
Editing	63	72	68	83	80
Publishing	30	25	26	40	38

Illinois, Texas, and New York attend only to editing. But editing is perhaps the least important part of the writing process. In real-world writing, careful editing of insipid ideas will be of little use. As we have seen, in Illinois' writing-on-demand, revision is not possible. There is too little time. Illinois has one of the lower percentages for revision. Once again, the success of the assessment in promoting better teaching of writing is dependent on the character of the assessment.

ATTITUDES ABOUT THE ASSESSMENTS

It is fairly common to ignore teacher opinion concerning assessments. However, what the teachers think of the assessment is likely to drive their efforts to meet its expectations. The interviews tried to get at teacher attitudes in several ways. We asked whether teachers felt the assessment supported the kind of writing program they would like to have in schools, whether they approved of the state scoring rubric, whether they approved teaching to the test, thought the test was valid, and whether the assessment had improved writing. These items appear in Table 12.6.

Frequently, however, teachers did not have opinions about validity (about whether the tests actually tested what they were thought to test). Sometimes, they knew the scoring rubrics only in a general way. In Illinois, for example, many teachers were asked direct questions about spe-

TABLE 12.6. Teacher Opinions of the Writing Assessments

		Illinois	Kentucky	New York	Oregon	Texas
Does assessment support desirable writing program?	Y	51	77	45	45	61
	N	32	13	24	11	24
Do you approve of state scoring rubric?	Y	57	67	24	60	58
	N	28	20	17	6	16
Do you approve teaching to the test?	Y	54	56	47	30	49
	N	30	16	34	15	33
Is test a valid measure of writing?	Y	17	34	18	19	23
	N	40	20	26	25	37
Has assessment improved writing?	Y	42	80	31	36	47
	N	8	6	16	17	20

cifics in the scoring rubric but appeared not to know about the criteria. They had not read the scoring manual in any detail and, if they had, had no means of evaluating the criteria. For these reasons, the percentages of responses to validity, the rubric, and other items in Table 12.6 fall short of 100%. Nonetheless, the comparative analysis of these responses reveals teacher support or opposition to the state-mandated assessment.

Kentucky teachers interviewed have much more positive opinions about their state assessment than do teachers in other states. Over three quarters (76.6%) believe that the state assessment supports the kind of writing program they would want in their schools. Over two thirds (67.2%) are positive about the scoring rubric. More teachers in the Kentucky sample than in other state samples see the assessment as valid and approve teaching to the test, preparing for the portfolio, in other words. But perhaps most impressive is that nearly 80% of the teachers interviewed feel that the portfolio assessment has helped improve writing in the state. No other state writing assessment studied comes close to having such a strong endorsement for its appropriateness and its power in bringing about change.

In other states, the teacher endorsement is far less positive. However, what is most disturbing about these findings is that in Illinois and Texas, states that have largely ignored the research of the last 30 years, so many teachers endorse the assessments, especially in Illinois where the scoring rubric encourages formulaic writing and the time limit seems to demand it. In Illinois and Texas, where we find the greatest devotion to formulaic writing, a majority of teachers approve the scoring rubric and believe that the assessments provide a strong basis for school writing programs, even though the assessments test only a narrow range of writing.

In Illinois, a fair proportion of teachers interviewed (40%) believe that the test itself is not a valid measure of a student's writing ability. That seems to be out of line with those who believe that the test supports the kind of writing program they would like to see in the schools (51%). The discrepancy indicates that while interviewees largely support the kinds of writing prescribed by the assessment, they do not feel that a forty-minute time period is adequate for the writing, that it is too short to permit students to do their best work.

In New York and Oregon, fewer teachers had strong opinions about the validity of the tests. Perhaps this is a result of general lack of familiarity with the testing programs. In both states the assessments were still in a process of implementation.

In our several hundred interviews with teachers and administrators, we found few vocal critics of the assessments and no one who made a systematic, articulate criticism of the state's writing assessment. Many teachers, particularly in Texas, complained about the incessant testing. Many complained about the extra work the tests imposed, as well they might. A percentage of teachers in all states were unhappy about the fact that school scores were published in papers or that their schools were judged on the basis of test scores when "We have very weak students in this district."

Teachers interviewed could certainly find fault with certain aspects of the assessment process, but, by and large, the actual parts of the assessments (prompts, types of writing, criteria, scoring guides, and so forth) were seldom subjected to analysis by teachers. Few teachers had special training in composition and rhetoric that might enable them to conduct a detailed critique of the assessments. Indeed, it is much more common for the state assessment to become the theory of writing upon which teachers base their teaching.

IMPACT ON THINKING IN CLASSROOMS

In the minds of some people, writing is one thing, but thinking is quite another. If they define writing as spelling, the production of sentences with random meanings, and punctuation, then they might have a case. But who would accept such a definition? Writing is the production of meaning. Writing *is* thinking.

When Socrates argues that writing is a mere mnemonic device in Plato's *Phaedrus*, he does so because writing lacks the dialectical forum of the spoken language that allows another speaker to question and prod until understanding is reached. Toward the end of the dialogue, it is apparent that Socrates is really challenging bad writing, writing that does not instill within it the kinds of dialectical processes that lead to understanding, writing that does not question its own assumptions, writing that does not consider any objections or alternatives to the propositions it proclaims.

Socrates does not give up on writing. After the initial condemnation, he asks Phaedrus, "Can we distinguish another kind of communication which is the legitimate brother of written speech?" A moment later when he names it, he uses the metaphor of writing to talk about it. "I mean the kind that is written on the soul of the hearer together with understanding; that knows how to defend itself" (Plato, trans. 1973, p. 98). We might say that the closer writing can come to revealing and explicating the complexities and ambiguities of its own meaning, the closer it comes to writing "on the soul of the hearer" and carrying the conditions for understanding. (See Derrida, 1972/1981, "Plato's Pharmacy," for an in-depth discussion of the slipperiness of meaning in language).

We have all encountered that kind of writing, the kind that writes on the soul, that changes forever the way we think about issues and people, that provides insight into human experience, institutions, and ways of thinking. Such writing is obviously the product of thinking. But the test of it is the extent to which it stimulates the reader's thinking. To do the latter successfully, it must re-create some of the thinking that went into it, not the twists and turns leading to dead ends, but the sets of related thinking that underlie main ideas and messages. The conditions for dialectic must be present. The reader needs enough detail to interact with the thinking of the writer. In an imaginative work of literature, that means enough detail not simply to generate intellectual understanding of a character's state of mind and situation, but to garner an emotional connection of some sort, often an empathic response. In writing focused on our perceptions of the real world, that means detail again. It means detail to clarify, differentiate, explain, extend, and support more abstract statements that are open to a wide range of interpretations. The detail makes a conversation with a text possible. Because the details are there, I can question a character's motives or morality and perhaps come to some decision or hold the question in abeyance. Because the details are there, I can more readily feel what the character feels and more adequately share her perspective.

To provide this level of specificity, the writer must know how to engage in his or her own dialectical process of composing, asking questions about the interpretation of the subject at hand, about what the reader will understand by certain words and phrases, about whether generalizations are clear and supported by the data available, about answers to the many questions arising from combinations of purpose, subject, data, and audience. At the same time, the writer must engage in a process of generating the specifics that will give the writing its foundation and its appeal. In a narrative, for example, a writer has to generate an array of detail from sensory details about sights, sounds, smells, and inner sensations of the body to details about attitudes, feelings, and emotions, and often dialogue that reveals feelings, thoughts, and motives.

In writing an argument, the writer is in touch with some situation or environment that comprises a set of data, notices and identifies a problem, explores the data in greater detail to find an explanation, develops a tentative hypothesis, checks or tests alternative explanations, arrives at a qualified conclusion, assembles evidence, explains why the evidence supports the conclusion, and so forth. This is a process of inquiry.

John Dewey (1938) argues that inquiry begins with doubt, an uncertainty or a question. Teachers who engage their classes in systematic inquiry, whether focusing on argument or imaginative writing, often present selected materials for students to examine that illustrate a problem, for example, articles from different perspectives on the Chicago gang loitering ordinance or perhaps an evocative story that illustrates a problem. After students have discussed this initial material and developed questions about the problem, teachers of inquiry introduce larger sets of data that may include stories and poems, statistical surveys, magazine and newspaper articles, any material that is relevant to the problem and is accessible to the students. In such classes, students will often have immediate explanations and solutions that are not based on a thoughtful examination of the material. A major task of the teacher is to help students identify and question the assumptions underlying their ideas, hold off on premature conclusions, and examine nuances and perspectives they have not considered.

Teachers of inquiry engage their students in using particular strategies: collecting and evaluating evidence, comparing and contrasting cases to develop inferences about the similarities and differences, creating hypothetical examples to clarify ideas, explaining how evidence supports or does not support a claim, imagining situations from perspectives other than one's own, "seeing" situations in the mind's eye, and so forth. These very strategies that are important to conducting inquiry are the same strategies that writers need in producing the content of writing. Thus, when students in inquiry classes come to writing, they have already practiced the strategies in discussions with peers that they will need in their writing.

A synthesis of research that compared the effects of different approaches to teaching writing indicates that teaching inquiry has effects several times more powerful than other approaches included (Hillocks, 1986a). All of the studies focused on inquiry exhibit the characteristics of epistemic rhetoric, interactive and deliberative thinking through problems and their relevant data with attention to different perspectives. The weakest effect resulted from the study of grammar, with no change. Studying model pieces of writing as illustrative of different types of writing, current traditional rhetoric, showed stronger gains (.22 standard deviations). However, the effects for treatments involving inquiry are two and a half times greater (in standard deviations), a very large gain indicating that, assuming a normal distribution, 71.2% of students taught through inquiry scored at or above the mean for those in control groups, while only 28.8% of students in control groups scored at the mean or above of the inquiry groups.

The change is due to the kinds of thinking in which students engage in inquiry-based (epistemic) classes. The vast majority of teachers in all states do not describe such teaching. Rather, they focus on the study of models and teaching the structure of various kinds of writing so that their students learn what goes where in a comparison-contrast paper or in a five-paragraph theme, but not on the production strategies necessary to thinking through problems.

As teachers describe their teaching, most never ask students to examine a set of data of some kind in order to identify a problem, develop hypotheses, consider and test alternative explanations, marshal evidence, explain why the evidence supports one or more possible conclusions, and so forth. Rather, they give students a problem, ask for opinions (usually to agree or disagree with the problem statement), and then ask students to suggest reasons why they think their opinion is justified. These reasons are to be developed by adding other relevant sentences, but not necessarily evidence to support the asserted reasons. In short, the classroom work emphasizes thinking by association, off the top of the head, with no checks for rigor. Writing assessments in Illinois and Texas endorse this truncated thinking as good writing.

Truncated thinking appears as a usual classroom process in Illinois and Texas for a variety of reasons. First, teachers imitate the state assessment prompts to prepare their students for the assessment. Second, the prompt is such that no evidence is available to the writers. Third, the criteria for judging the papers do not call for evidence (only support). Fourth, support is interpreted to include statements that reiterate or expand upon claims. Fifth, benchmark papers at the highest levels of approval incorporate little, if any, actual evidence. Sixth, students study benchmark papers as models, models that exemplify vacuous thinking.

If state assessments have the following characteristics for expository and persuasive writing, it is predictable that they will engender formulaic writing and the thinking that goes with it: (1) prompts providing a specific topic and subject matter with no or highly limited accompanying data, (2) one limited session for writing, and (3) criteria that call only for "developing ideas" without specifying the nature of development much beyond a request for detail. The difference between general elaboration and specific evidence appears to be particularly responsible for the kinds of thinking that states endorse and that teachers sponsor in classrooms. My assistants and I have examined assessment materials from nearly all states. Many display all three of these characteristics: Alabama, California, Connecticut, Delaware, Florida, Indiana, Illinois, New Jersey, Ohio, Tennessee, and Texas, for example.

When states provide for writing over more than one session, or when they provide a set of data or a text for analysis, or when criteria call for specific data and the criterion is backed by benchmark papers that use evidence, persuasive writing is not so likely to be formulaic. Only a few states allow for the development of a piece of writing over more than one session: Alaska, Kansas, Nevada, Oregon, Pennsylvania, Washington, for example. Even fewer provide a data set or text about which to write persuasive or expository pieces: Louisiana, Massachusetts, and New York, for example. Most scoring rubrics that we examined, however, do not call for evidence, only support. In most cases, the benchmark papers indicate that support means general elaboration of the sort found in Texas and Illinois rather than specific, warranted evidence. Thus the student writing exemplifying even the highest levels is no more than blether.

Writing assessments control thinking in other ways as well. As I have suggested elsewhere in this book, although the category of expository writing is highly suspect, many states require it. This kind of writing dominated college writing classrooms for over a hundred years in the United States (Connors, 1981; Berlin, 1984). It is based on an objectivist epistemology that proceeds as though knowledge were packageable and transportable through language. It assumes that writing can convey knowledge as a final, finished product.

The problem is that most of our knowledge is not definitive. Toulmin (1958) argues that only mathematics and some parts of the hard sciences can treat knowledge in absolute terms, that is, through syllogistic arguments. Most of what we know, we know in terms of probabilities, not definitively. Such knowledge must be dealt with in those terms. If we teach students that exposition simply deals with the truth, does not have to be argued, and cannot be challenged, we also teach them to accept what is written without question. It is this kind of writing that Socrates feared in the *Phaedrus*, and while he seems to champion the spoken word, he is aware that the spoken word can take on the characteristics of exposition, of providing interpretations as though they were obvious and beyond any question. Many Platonic dialogues show Socrates questioning the expository statements of acquaintances to open them to the light of thoughtful questioning and deliberation.

In an increasingly complex and diverse society, we need more than ever to question our oral and written expositions. Newscasters, fearful of an impatient public, provide stories without explaining the sense in which we know the facts, what the actual observations are, who made them, what the inferences are, thus omitting important bases for questioning them. School history texts tend to tell the story of the United States in a series of sweeping generalizations without providing the grounds or the warrants for them, suggesting no alternative to accepting the generalizations. Until recently, they told the story of U.S. history with little or no reference to African Americans, without, of course, revealing the reasons for such omissions (cf. Loewen, 1996).

Many of our most cherished beliefs are passed on as expository statements with no qualification and no question. We assume that these things are so obvious that they need or ought not be questioned or argued: The world is the center of the universe; the king rules by divine right; life is generated spontaneously, an idea that accounts for the appearance of maggots in rotting flesh. At some point in the past, when people made such statements, they were speaking in expository prose, without considering underlying assumptions or any evidence for the claims. The statements were simply true on the face of it, until someone proved them wrong.

Today, in our increasingly diverse society, we pass on statements about the other, the non-us, in this expository vein as though they were true in some absolute way. How many times have you heard expository statements that begin, "Every time I go to (fill in an ethnic neighborhood), those people behave (choose your adverb or adverbial phrase)." The exposition continues, providing illustrations, not evidence, of the generalizations and additional claims. But there is no doubt or qualification or any framework for questioning the claims. Such claims become part of the tradition of "knowledge" (what everyone "knows" and never questions) within one group about others from different groups. It is for essentially this reason that Martha Nussbaum (1997) argues that we need to teach argument and "Socratic self-examination" to all college students.

Like New York, all states have standards that call for thinking "logically and creatively" and applying "reasoning skills to issues and problems." If we want to teach critical thinking, it seems to me that questioning everything is fair game. As we have seen, many of the prompts that are supposed to elicit expository writing in Illinois, Texas, New York, and Oregon really elicit argument. We need to recognize that and call for thoughtful writing.

If the confusion of exposition and argument harms critical thinking in the curriculum, so does the exclusion of imaginative writing. Recently, at a meeting for the evaluation of a state's language arts learning standards, a member of the committee informed me, in expository prose, that once people were out of school, they didn't "sit around writing stories and poems" and that, therefore, students should devote their time to only exposition and persuasion. Most people do not sit around thinking through problems in algebra or physics either, but that is no reason to diminish them in the curriculum.

Imaginative literature abounds in our culture in the forms of movies, songs, TV shows, as well as print literature. When taught well, the study of imaginative literature enables students to interpret and evaluate not only literature and popular culture, but their own lives and, at the same time, examine the assumptions that underlie our responses (cf. Appleman, 2000). Writing imaginative works is a way into reading such literature.

More important, it is a way into rethinking and imagining what has been and what could be. I know of no evidence that engaging in imaginative writing actually results in more imaginative thinking. But it seems obvious that imagining is basic to understanding others. In order to plan anything successfully, one must imagine the desired outcome. To challenge the doctrine of the divine right of kings, one has to imagine a world without kings. To challenge any set of accepted beliefs, one must imagine alternatives and their consequences.

When states establish writing assessments and determine certain categories of writing to test, they privilege the selected categories in the eyes of the schools and teachers. When school scores are reported to a central authority and compared to the scores of other schools, the procedure of testing and reporting demands attention to what is taught. Teachers teach what is on the test and ignore what is not. When Illinois, New York, Texas, and many other states exclude imaginative literature from the assessment, they send a message that teachers do not have to include such writing in their curricula. They sabotage their own goals for creative thinking.

WHAT'S TO BE DONE?

In my most cynical moments, I wonder if the master plan is to train people not to think. The logic of political speeches has much in common with the logic of the five-paragraph theme. If students learned to think and question, they might detect the nonsense in their representatives' speeches. Is that what the fear is? Is there a plan to keep students from thinking, a kind of subtle *1984*?

Probably not. There is a fear, however, of setting the standards of passing too high. As we have seen, the standards for passing or meeting state standards in most states is fairly low. If we make the standards too high, too many students will fail to meet them, and politicians will be embarrassed, particularly if they see themselves as advocates for education as does President Bush. When the standards are low, it is easier to boast of more and more students reaching the same low standard.

At the center of the K–12 testing fury is the myth that testing alone is able to raise standards and the rates of learning. Certainly, testing assures that what is tested is taught, but tests cannot assure that things are taught well. If states want *teaching* to improve, they will have to intervene at the level of teaching. Teachers need opportunities to learn more effective procedures for teaching writing. Tests of writing cannot teach that. Kentucky is the only state in this study to provide funding for improving the teaching of writing through their eight Writing Project sites. Other states merely offer training for scoring the writing resulting from state prompts. The workshops on scoring indoctrinate teachers into the state's ways of thinking about writing: what counts for good organization, good support, good development, and so forth. They do not deal with teaching. But all states need to make efforts to improve the teaching of writing. Making funds available to qualified universities and colleges to provide in-service training would be a useful start

If states really want student writing to improve, they need to insure that teachers have adequate time to teach writing well. Effective teaching means planning for instruction and responding to student writing. Planning for the effective teaching of writing is very time consuming in itself. Because existing textbooks do not go beyond CTR, teachers must plan and create more effective material on their own. Responding to writing is even more time consuming. Effective response to student writing requires careful reading, analysis of strengths and weaknesses, constructive suggestions, and words of praise where possible.

Normal student loads for middle and high school English is the same as for other teachers, somewhere between 125 and 150 students per day. In one large urban school system in Illinois, teachers reported that they would have 175 students per day because of funding cutbacks. However, assume that 130 is average. If the teacher assigns a personal narrative after appropriate preparation, students will likely write over 500 words. If the teacher spends only 5 minutes on each, responding to the entire set will consume 650 minutes, nearly 11 hours. Every additional minute per paper will add 2 hours and 10 minutes. In my experience, the average on such a set of papers is more likely to be 10 minutes per paper. This is an unconscionable load and could well be responsible, in part, for the growth of formulaic writing. The formula permits quicker and easier responses. If states want better teaching of writing, they need to reduce per pupil teacher loads. Unfortunately, this move costs more tax dollars than testing.

Finally, this study indicates that many writing assessments do not have the intended effects. There is little question that the assessments have made the teaching of writing a more common and extensive activity than Applebee found in 1981. Nearly all administrators interviewed agree that more teachers are teaching writing than was the case prior to the assessments.

However, what they are teaching appears to have a negative effect on the students in states with poorly thought out assessments. The strongest assessment we studied was the portfolio assessment in Kentucky. It provides for a rich array of writing, time for students to develop pieces of writing adequately so that they do not have to revert to the formulaic, a large enough sample to provide a reliable estimate of an individual's writing ability, and strong professional development initiatives that include eight Writing Project sites and enough writing consultants to work with individual teachers in schools.

At the beginning of the research reported here, I believed that the level of stakes in the assessment would likely determine the impact of the assessment on teaching. From the preceding chapters, however, it should be clear, that the stakes do not matter much. In Illinois, students and teachers have far less at stake than those in any other state we examined, but the assessment encourages strict adherence to the writing standards and, therefore, the most five-paragraph themes and the weakest writing. In Texas, the stakes are high, but the writing is about as weak as in Illinois. I have to conclude that it is not the stakes that matter so much, but the nature of the assessment itself. In most states, the assessment must be altered if writing and thinking are to flourish.

MOST WRITING ASSESSMENTS examined for this study share far more characteristics with the Illinois and Texas assessments than with the Kentucky one. Yet most of these are accepted uncritically. The test-makers in these states have settled for test reliability, the fact that two scorers are likely to agree on the assigned score. But this does not serve the purposes of a useful education. Change will depend on public pressure on lawmakers and state officials.

Educators and other citizens should examine carefully a state's writing assessment from learning standards to benchmark papers. Do learning standards include statements about critical thinking or supporting ideas or providing evidence? If they do not, there is a good chance that the testing programs deal only with the simplest academic skills. Even if they do, you will still need to discover what the standard writers really mean by their phrases about supporting ideas and critical thinking. Examine the writing prompts to see if they reflect the language of the standards. Then look at the criteria for judging the compositions. Do the criteria reflect the language of the standards, or do they fudge the issues of critical thinking? Next, examine the benchmark papers that are supposed to illustrate the criteria. Do the pieces of student writing that score the highest exhibit critical thinking, the use of evidence, or other indications of thought? Does the test provide material for the students to write about? Or does it leave students to somehow generate concrete material out of nothing? Could you or another educated adult write a thoughtful response to the prompt in the time allowed? If not, it seems unreasonable to ask students to do so.

Similar analyses can be made with narrative and other kinds of writing tested. If the standards and tests do not reflect good writing, then you will have discovered a serious complaint against the testing program. Remember that countless hours are spent on preparing for these tests, often over several school years. For example, in one Chicago high school, English class meets for 45 minutes—135 hours in a school year of 180 days, which is precious little time to deal with the complex learning of high literacy that our culture now requires. In many schools, at least half that time is ripped away to prepare for tests that do far more harm than good. This is a crucial time in American education. As a society, we cannot afford to spend valuable time on vacuous thinking and writing.

References

Anagnostopoulos, D. (2000). *Setting standards, failing students: A case study of merit promotion in two Chicago high schools.* Unpublished doctoral dissertation, University of Chicago.

Applebee, A. N. (1981). *Writing in the secondary school: English in the content areas* (NCTE Research Report, No. 21). Urbana, IL: National Council of Teachers of English.

Applebee, A. N. (1986). Problems in process approaches: Toward a reconceptualization of process instruction. In A. R. Petrosky & D. Bartholomae (Eds.), *The teaching of writing* (pp. 95–113). 85th Yearbook of the National Society for the Study of Education, pt. 2. Chicago: National Society for the Study of Education.

Appleman, D. (2000). *Critical encounters in high school English: Teaching literary theory to adolescents.* New York: Teachers College Press and National Council of Teachers of English.

Aristotle. (1947). *Nichomachean ethics* (W. Ross, Trans.). In R. McKeon (Ed.), *Introduction to Aristotle* (pp. 308–543). New York: Random House.

Aristotle. (1991). *The art of rhetoric* (H. Lawson-Tancred, Trans.). New York: Penguin.

Attneave, F. (1974). Multistability in perception. In R. Held (Eds.), *Image, object and illusion: Readings from scientific American* (pp. 90–99). San Francisco: W. H. Freeman.

Atwell, N. (1987). *In the middle: Writing, reading, and learning with adolescents.* Portsmouth, NH: Heinemann.

Bazerman, C. (1988). *Shaping written knowledge: The genre and activity of the experimental article in science.* Madison: University of Wisconsin Press.

Bereiter, C., & Scardamalia, M. (1987). *The psychology of written composition.* Hillsdale, NJ: Erlbaum.

Berlin, J. A. (1982, December). Contemporary composition: The major pedagogical theories. *College English 44*(8) 765–777.

Berlin, J. A. (1984). *Writing instruction in nineteenth-century American colleges.* Carbondale: Southern Illinois University Press.

Braddock, R., Lloyd-Jones, R., & Schoer, L. (1963). *Research in written composition.* Champaign, IL: National Council of Teachers of English.

Britton, J. N., Burgess, T., Martin, N., McLeod, A., & Rose, H. (1975). *The development of writing abilities (11–18).* London: Macmillan.

Bridwell, L. S. (1980, October). Revising processes in twelfth grade students' transactional writing. *Research in the Teaching of English, 14* 197–222.

Bush, G. W. (1999, October). The future of educational reform. Paper delivered at the Manhattan Institute Forum. [Available on line at manhattan-institute.org/ htm/Bush_speech.htm]

Bush, G. W. (2001, January 29). *Transforming the federal role in education so that no child is left behind* [On-line]. Available: www.ed.gov/inits/nclb/part2.html

Callahan, S. (1997). Tests worth taking?: Using portfolios for accountability in Kentucky. *Research in the Teaching of English, 31*, 295–336.

Callahan, S. (1999). All done with the best of intentions: One Kentucky high school after six years of state portfolio tests. *Assessing Writing, 6*, 5–40.

Calkins, L. M. (1994). *The art of teaching writing.* Portsmouth, NH: Heinemann.

Chapman, C. W. (1989). Teaching to the writing test is O.K.: Integrating class-room instruction with assessment. *Excellence in Teaching, 6*, 9–11.

Chapman, C. W. (1990). Authentic writing assessment. *Practical Assessment, Research and Evaluation,* [On-line serial] *2*(7). Available: ericae.net/pare/ getvn.asp?v=2&n=7

Coe, P., Leopold, G., Simon, K., Stowers, P., & Williams, J. (1994). *Perception of school change: Interviews with Kentucky students.* A report submitted to the Kentucky Caucus of the AEL Board of Directors. Charleston, WV: Appalachia Educational Laboratory. (ERIC Document Reproduction Service No. ED 376 000)

Connors, R. J. (1981, December). The rise and fall of the modes of discourse. *College Composition and Communication, 32*(4), 444–455.

Crowell, S. C. & Kolba, E. D. (1996) *The IGAP Coach, Grade 10, Writing.* New York: Educational Design.

Darling-Hammond, L. (1995). *Authentic assessment.* New York: Teachers College Press.

Derrida, J. (1981). *Dissemination* (B. Johnson, Trans.). Chicago: University of Chicago Press. (Original work published 1972)

Dewey, J. (1938). *Logic, the theory of inquiry.* New York: H. Holt.

Edelman, M. (1977). *Political language: Words that succeed and policies that fail.* New York: Academic Press.

Emig, J. (1971). *The composing process of twelfth graders.* Urbana, IL: National Council of Teachers of English.

Fuller, G. (1994). *Step up to the TAAS writing for exit level.* Waxahachie, TX: The Teacher's Touch.

Gallarzo, E. (1971). *Barrio boy.* Notre Dame, IN: University of Notre Dame Press.

Goodlad, J. (1984). *A place called school: Prospects for the future.* New York: McGraw-Hill.

Graves, D. (1983). *Writing: Teachers and children at work.* Portsmouth, NH: Heinemann.

Hamilton, S. (1996). *The higher power writer within me.* Chicago: Hamilton Con-sultants.

Hill, W. E. (1915). *My wife and my mother-in-law. Puck,* November 16, 11.

Hillocks, G., Jr. (1979). The effects of observational activities on student writing. *Research in the Teaching of English, 13*, 23–35.

Hillocks, G., Jr. (1986a). *Research on written composition: New directions for teaching.* [New York]: National Conference on Research in English; Urbana, IL: ERIC

Clearinghouse on Reading and Communications Skills, National Institute of Education.

Hillocks, G., Jr. (1986b). The writer's knowledge: Theory, research and implications for practice. In A. Petrosky & D. Bartholomae (Eds.), *The teaching of writing* (pp. 71–94). 85th Yearbook of the National Society for the Study of Education, pt. 2. Chicago: National Society for the Study of Education.

Hillocks, G., Jr. (1995). *Teaching writing as reflective practice.* New York: Teachers College Press.

Hillocks, G., Jr. (1999). *Ways of Thinking, Ways of Teaching.* New York: Teachers College Press.

Illinois Certification Testing System (2000). *Enhanced basic skills test. Elements of the new assessment.* Amherst, MA: National Evaluation Systems.

Illinois State Board of Education [ISBE]. (1994). *Write on, Illinois!* Springfield, IL: Author.

Illinois State Board of Education [ISBE]. (2000a). *Illinois standards achievement test: Sample writing materials.* Springfield, IL: Author.

Illinois State Board of Education [ISBE]. (2000b). *Prairie state achievement examination: Teachers' handbook, 2000–2001.* Springfield, IL: Author.

Jefferson County Public Schools. (n.d.). *The Jefferson county public schools curriculum handbook/content guidelines.* Louisville, KY: Author.

Jefferson County Public Schools. Office of Curriculum and Instruction. (2000). *Teaching students to write a short story.* Louisville, KY: Author.

Kentucky Department of Education [KDE]. (1996). *Writing portfolio scoring training, grade 12* [videotape]. Frankfort, KY: Author.

Kentucky Department of Education [KDE]. (1999a). *Commonwealth accountability testing system, Kentucky core content test: Released questions and final scoring guides, Spring 1999 and 1998–99 CATS assessment open-response item scoring worksheets* [On-line]. Frankfort, KY: Author. Available: www.kde.state.ky.us/oaa/implement/KCCT_99_Annotated/annotated%2099.asp

Kentucky Department of Education [KDE]. (1999b). *Writing portfolio development, teachers' handbook* [*Handbook*]. Frankfort, KY: Author.

Kentucky Department of Education [KDE]. (1999c). *Writing portfolio scoring, teachers' handbook, grade 4.* Frankfort, KY: Author.

Kentucky Department of Education [KDE]. (1999d). *Writing portfolio scoring, teachers' handbook, grade 7.* Frankfort, KY: Author.

Kentucky Department of Education [KDE]. (1999e). *Writing portfolio scoring, teachers' handbook, grade 12* [*Scoring Handbook*]. Frankfort, KY: Author.

Kentucky Department of Education [KDE]. (2000). *2000 district assessment coordinators implementation guide.* Frankfort, KY: Author.

Kentucky Department of Education [KDE]. (2001). *Writing, On-Demand* [On-line]. Available: www.kde.state.ky.us/

Kentucky Department of Education [KDE]. (n.d.). *1999–2000 writing portfolio audit.* Frankfort, KY: Author.

Kentucky Revised Statutes. KRS 158.6451, 158.6453 [On-line]. Available: http://www.lrc.state.ky.us/KRS/158-00/CHAPTER.HTM

Kinneavy, J. L. (1971). *A theory of discourse.* Englewood Cliffs, NJ: Prentice-Hall.

Kinneavy, J. L., & Warriner, J. (1993). *Grammar and composition*. Austin, TX: Holt, Rinehart & Winston.

Langer, J., & Applebee, A. (1987). *How writing shapes thinking: A study of teaching and learning*. Urbana, IL: National Council of Teachers of English.

Legislative Research Commission [LRC]. (1994). *The Kentucky Education Reform Act: A citizen's handbook*. Frankfort, KY: Author.

Leont'ev, A. N. (1981). *Problems of the development of the mind*. Moscow: Progress.

Loewen, J. W. (1996). *Lies my teacher told me : Everything your American history textbook got wrong*. New York: Simon & Schuster.

Luria, A. R. (1976). *Cognitive development: Its cultural and social foundations*. Cambridge, MA: Harvard University Press.

Madaus, G. (1988). The influence of testing on curriculum. In L. N. Tanner (Ed.), *Critical issues in curriculum*. (pp. 83–121). *87th Yearbook of the National Society for the Study of Education*, pt. 1.

Mammen, L. (1990a). *TAAS master; Writing, grades 4/5*. San Antonio, TX: ECS Learning Systems.

Mammen, L. (1990b). *TAAS master; Writing, grade 10/Exit level*. San Antonio, TX: ECS Learning Systems.

Meyers, M. (1996). *Changing our minds: negotiating English and literacy*. Urbana, IL: National Council of Teachers of English.

Miller, G. A. (1956). The magical number seven, plus or minus two: Some limits on our capacity for processing information. *The Psychological Review, 63*, 81–97.

Mincey, K. (1996, March). *The impact of KERA writing portfolios on first-year college writers*. Paper presented at the 47th annual meeting of the Conference on College Composition and Communication, Milwaukee, WI. ED (ERIC Document Reproduction Service No. 403 576)

Murray, L. (1849). *English grammar*. New York: Raynor.

National Commission on Excellence in Education [NCEE]. (1983). *A Nation at Risk* [On-line]. Available: www.ed.gov/pubs/NatAtRisk/risk.html

Neulieb, J. (1999). *Course guide for English 101: Langauge and composition*. Normal, IL: Stipes.

New Jersey Department of Education. (2000). Grade eight proficiency assessment 2000 sample test form. In *2000 GEPA sample forms for language arts literacy and mathematics* [On-line]. Available: www.state.nj.us.njded

New York State Education Department [NYSED]. (1994). *Preliminary draft framework for English language arts: Curriculum, instruction, and assessment* [Framework]. Albany, NY: Author.

New York State Education Department [NYSED]. (1996). *Learning standards for English language arts*. Albany, NY: Author.

New York State Education Department [NYSED]. (1997). *New York state testing program for elementary and intermediate grades; information brochure*. Monterey, CA: McGraw-Hill.

New York State Education Department [NYSED]. (1998). *Revised Regents comprehensive examination in English: Test sampler draft*. Albany, NY: Author.

New York State Education Department [NYSED]. (1999). *The information booklet for administering and scoring the regents comprehensive examination in English.* Albany, NY: Author.

New York State Education Department [NYSED]. (1999, June 18a). *Comprehensive examination in English, session one* [On-line]. Available: www.emsc.nysed.gov/ciai/testing/regents.htm

New York State Education Department [NYSED]. (1999, June 18b). *Comprehensive examination in English, Scoring and rating guide, session one* [On-line]. Available: www.emsc.nysed.gov/ciai/testing/regents.htm

New York State Education Department [NYSED]. (1999, June 23a). *Comprehensive examination in English, session two* [On-line]. Available: www.emsc.nysed.gov/ciai/testing/regents.htm

New York State Education Department [NYSED]. (1999, June 23b). *Comprehensive examination in English, Scoring and rating guide, session two* [On-line]. Available: www.emsc.nyseed.gov/ciai/testing/regents.htm

Nussbaum, M. (1997). *Cultivating humanity.* Cambridge, MA: Harvard University Press.

Nystrand, M. (with Gamoran, A., Kachur, R., & Prendergast, C.) (1997). *Opening dialogue: Understanding the dynamics of language and learning in the English classroom.* New York: Teachers College Press.

O'Donnell, R. C., Griffin, W. J., and Norris, R. C. (1967). *The syntax of kindergarten and elementary school children: A transformational analysis.* Champaign, IL: National Council of Teachers of English.

Oregon Department of Education [ODE]. (1996a). *Writing assessment and instruction: A two-part resource packet for teachers, grades 8 and 10.* Salem. OR: Author.

Oregon Department of Education [ODE]. (1996b). *Writing assessment and instruction: Performance standards, grade 8 benchmark, certificate of initial mastery.* Salem, OR: Author.

Oregon Department of Education [ODE]. (1997a). *Oregon statewide writing assessment: Test specifications, grade 3 (version 2.0).* Salem. OR: Author.

Oregon Department of Education [ODE]. (1997b). *Oregon statewide writing assessment: Test specifications, grade 5 (version 2.0).* Salem. OR: Author.

Oregon Department of Education [ODE]. (1997c). *Oregon statewide writing assessment: Test specifications, grade 8 (version 2.0).* Salem. OR: Author.

Oregon Department of Education [ODE]. (1997d). *Oregon statewide writing assessment: Test specifications, grade 10 (version 2.0).* Salem. OR: Author.

Oregon Department of Education [ODE]. (1998). *Oregon writing assessment, 1993–1997.* Salem, OR: Author.

Oregon Department of Education [ODE]. (2000). *Writing work samples, sample prompts* . [On-line]. Available: www.ode.state.or.us/asmt/resource/writing/

Oregon Educational Act for the Twenty-First Century. (1995). Oregon Revised Statutes, 329.465, 329.025, and 329.035 [On-line]. Available: www.leg.state.or.us/ors/329.html

Plato. (1973). *The Phaedrus and letters VII and VIII* (W. Hamilton, Trans.) (pp. 21–103). London: Penguin.

Ramage, J. D., & Bean, J. C. (1992). *Writing arguments: A rhetoric with readings* (2d ed.). New York: Macmillan.

Rose v. Council for Better Education, Inc., No. 88-SC-804-TG, 1989. Kentucky Supreme Court [On-line]. Available: http://web.lexis-nexis.com/universe/document

Sacks, P. (1999). *Standardized minds: The high price of America's testing culture and what we can do to change it.* Cmabridge, MA: Perseus Books.

Spalding, E., & Cummins, G. (1998). It was the best of times. It was a waste of time: University of Kentucky students' views of writing under KERA. *Assessing Writing, 5,* 167–199.

Spradley, J. P. (1979). *The ethnographic interview.* New York: Holt, Rinehart & Winston.

TAAS preparation booklet. (1992). Evanston, IL: McDougal, Littell.

Texas Education Agency [TEA]. (n.d.). *English language arts framework: Kindergarten–grade 12 [Framework].* Austin, TX: Author.

Texas Education Agency [TEA]. (1991a). *TAAS and the composing process: A composition handbook, grades 1 through 3.* Austin, TX: Author.

Texas Education Agency {TEA]. (1991b). *TAAS and the composing process: A composition handbook, grades 3 through 5.* Austin, TX: Author.

Texas Education Agency [TEA]. (1991c). *TAAS and the composing process: A composition handbook, exit level, grades 9 through 12.* Austin, TX: Author.

Texas Education Agency [TEA]. (1993a). *Exit level 1993–1994 writing collection scoring guide for persuasive writing.* Austin, TX: Author.

Texas Education Agency [TEA]. (1993b). *Exit level writing collection scoring guide for persuasive writing, musical lyrics.* Austin, TX: Author.

Texas Education Agency [TEA]. (1993c). *Grade 4 writing collection scoring guide for classificatory writing.* Austin, TX: Author.

Texas Education Agency [TEA]. (1993d). *Grade 4 writing collection scoring guide for "how-to" writing.* Austin, TX: Author.

Texas Education Agency [TEA]. (1993e). *Grade 4 writing collection scoring guide for narrative writing.* Austin, TX: Author.

Texas Education Agency [TEA]. (1993f). *Grade 4 writing collection scoring guide for persuasive/descriptive writing.* Austin, TX: Author.

Texas Education Agency [TEA]. (1993g). *Grade 8 writing collection scoring guide for classificatory writing.* Austin, TX: Author.

Texas Education Agency [TEA]. (1993h). *Grade 8 writing collection scoring guide for "how-to" writing.* Austin, TX: Author.

Texas Education Agency [TEA]. (1993i). *Grade 8 writing collection scoring guide for narrative writing.* Austin, TX: Author.

Texas Education Agency [TEA]. (1993j). *Grade 8 writing collection scoring guide for persuasive/descriptive writing.* Austin, TX: Author.

Toulmin, S. (1958). *The uses of argument.* London: Cambridge University Press.

Vygotsky, L. S. (1978). *Mind in society: The development of higher psychological processes.* Cambridge, MA: Harvard University Press.

Walton, Douglas N. (1998). *The new dialectic: Conversational contexts of argument.* Toronto: University of Toronto Press.

Warriner, J. (1988). *English composition and grammar: Complete course.* Orlando, FL: Harcourt Brace Jovanovich.

Zancanella, D. (1992). The influence of state-mandated testing on teachers of literature. *Educational Evaluation and Policy Analysis, 14,* 283–295.

Index

About the Author

George Hillocks, Jr., received his B.A. in English from the College of Wooster, a Diploma in English Studies from the University of Edinburgh (Scotland), and his M.A. and Ph.D. from Case Western Reserve University. He taught secondary school English in Euclid, Ohio, where he was Director of the Project English Demonstration Center from 1963 to 1965. He taught English at Bowling Green State University where he served as Director of Freshman English Programs. Since 1971 he has been at the University of Chicago where he is currently professor in the Department of English Language and Literature and continues to serve as Director of the Master of Arts in Teaching. His articles have appeared in the *American Journal of Education* and other journals. He is author or coauthor of several books and monographs, including *Research on Written Composition: New Directions for Teaching*, published by the National Conference on Research in English; *Teaching Writing as Reflective Practice*, published by Teachers College Press in 1995 and which won NCTE's David H. Russell Award for Distinguished Research in the Teaching of English; and *Ways of Thinking, Ways of Teaching*, published in 1999 by Teachers College Press. In 2000, he was the Thomas R. Watson Distinguished Visiting Professor of Rhetoric and Composition at the University of Louisville and was elected to membership in the National Academy of Education. In 2000–2001, he was a Fellow at the Center for Advanced Study in the Behavioral Sciences in Stanford, California. He is currently working on a book on teaching production strategies for writing effective narrative and argument, techniques that have proven equally successful with students in inner city and suburban settings.